THE ILLUSTRATED ENCYCLOPEDIA OF
WORLD RELIGIONS

THE ILLUSTRATED
ENCYCLOPEDIA OF
WORLD
RELIGIONS

EDITOR: *Chris Richards*

BARNES
&NOBLE
BOOKS
NEW YORK

INTRODUCTION

Seek truth and you will find more questions than answers

This encyclopedia brings the world's major faiths vividly to life. You may have bought it to help you answer basic questions about religion, or to extend your knowledge. You will find plenty of information in this book, but you must also be prepared to face further questions as you seek answers. Learning about religion, whether it be your own or that of someone else, involves many more questions than answers. For a start, here are three questions that need to be explored to understand religion: what is a human being; why do people believe in a god; what is a religion?

What is a human being

One characteristic that d————————————— other forms of life is the ability ————————t goes beyond a description of i——————scribe ideas, such as time and ———————pts of meaning and purpose. T—————————char- acteristic. Much of our kn—————————oples comes from burials; o————————— with tools, food, and weapo—————————been intended for use in the ———————— species exhibits behavior remot———————————

So it is clear that, fro————————————d the kind of philosophical que—————————today: who am I; why am I he——————————what happens after I die? It is——————————been formulated which invol———————————being and existence outside an—————————ence.

Why do people believe in a god

Not only did early peop————————————prac- ticed other rituals and c——————————tainly were intended to influe————————————s that they perceived as ruling———————————eople believed in a god.

There are three bas——————————ve in god today. The primitive—————————ver in the universe accounts fo——————————ments in early culture, but mo——————————led to defend the idea of a god—————————

Firstly, some people—————————————have had a direct experienc——————————y has "revealed" himself to the—————————expe- rience cannot be unders——————————at has led great prophets to ch——————————some cases, to change the hist——————————might say that such revelations—————————tation of natural phenomena, bu——————————belief which goes beyond the ——————————

Secondly, some peop——————————y have looked at all the eviden———————————must

The Dome of the Rock in Jerusalem, a significant and holy city for three of the world's major religions: Islam, Judaism, and Christianity

be a god. The evidence may be drawn from natural phenomena, it may be deduced from rational thought processes and logic – theology. The rational argument for the existence of God is often based on what is called the watchmaker argument, which goes like this: if a person from a primitive, non-mechanical society were to come across a watch, that person would know that the watch was created for a specific purpose by a conscious mind – it could not just exist. So, the argument goes, the earth, and the universe in which it moves, cannot be an accident. The more we understand about the complexity of life, the more we must see that it is deliberate and purposeful, with a creator, or god, taking the part of the watchmaker.

The third common reason why people believe in God is simply because they have been told to believe. This may seem a poor foundation for belief. Yet most people are not blessed by a direct revelation; most people lack the time and inclination to enter into the deep theological debates that would lead to belief by rational argument.

*The crucifixion is a Christian symbol for a concept that is central to
religious faith, the meeting of the human and the divine*

A Hindu temple in Udaip—————————————— is communal although the initi————————————————onal

The universal desire to glorify God is exemplified by the richly decorated Cathedral of the Holy Family in Barcelona

Most people accept w———————————————whom they respect as having ha—————————————ence, such as a priest, teacher, c—————————————eople are nurtured into holding—————————————does not make their belief any t—————————————held; it does help to explain wh—————————————n are so closely linked in many————

What is a religio—

The step from personal b—————————————diffi-cult. There have always b—————————————ctices and beliefs through which—————————————essed and shared. Common ex—————————————se to common organizations to——————————

So, at its simplest, ————————————d to describe a group of peop—————————————same basic beliefs about a god—————————————milar way of worshiping that g—————————————s too simple. As this encyclope—————————————some

features common to all religions, there is enormous diversity among religions, and sometimes within what is commonly thought of as one religion.

For example, if belief in a god is considered an essential characteristic of a religion, where does this leave Buddhism? For all its religious character and tradition, Buddhism is not based on belief in a god, or on a set creed, or on a universal authority.

The picture is complicated further by the tendency of religions to fragment and to show a very wide range of different practices. Hinduism and Christianity are good examples of this rich diversity. Sometimes, sects or denominations of an established religion become religions in their own right, as has happened with some forms of Christianity. At what stage will some of today's sects become recognized as religions in their own right?

In the end, it is easy to say that a particular belief system is a religion; yet it is not always easy to say why, because there is no set of common characteristics.

ABOUT THIS BOOK

This encyclopedia has been written to give the reader insights into some of the beliefs and practices of major and influential religions in the world today. Not every religion in the world is listed or mentioned; there are so many laying claim to this title that the book would be little more than a list if it covered them all. Nor do all the religions qualify to be called world religions. In fact, though the religions described here have followers in all parts of the world, only two – Christianity and Islam – have the significant and widespread distribution of followers which entitles them to be called world religions. The other religions have been chosen because they are of particular interest, or because of the influence they have had, and in some cases still have, on the world and its beliefs.

The chapter on each religion does not attempt to tell the full story of the beliefs and traditions of that religion; instead it seeks to give a flavor of the beliefs, and to describe the lives of its adherents. From this initial survey, the interested reader can then follow up their study by reading more detailed texts.

This is not just a reference book, because it goes beyond the merely informational to look at the range of questions and issues facing religions and religious people at the moment. It is written by people who are experts, and, in most cases, believers in their religion. They have illustrated their writing with stories, quotations, and anecdotes to give

Most major religions involve some degree of communal activity which unites the believers, as in this Confucian ceremony at the Royal Shrine at Chong Myo in Korea

some flavor of the ways i▨▨▨▨▨▨▨▨▨▨▨llow
religionists work. This is ▨▨▨▨▨▨▨▨▨▨e of
the religion; it is a vibrant▨▨▨▨▨▨▨▨

The entry on each re▨▨▨▨▨▨▨▨▨ the
religion's founders and hi▨▨▨▨▨▨▨▨vals,
beliefs and practices. U▨▨▨▨▨▨▨▨ are
important questions and ▨▨▨▨▨▨▨▨ions,
and people with religious▨▨▨▨▨▨▨▨story
of humanity, including t▨▨▨▨▨▨▨▨gion,
religion in a shrinking w▨▨▨▨▨▨▨▨ and
fundamentalism, religiou▨▨▨▨▨▨

Science and reli▨▨▨

There is a perception, p▨▨▨▨▨▨▨▨orld,
that rational thought has▨▨▨▨▨▨▨▨d for
belief, and that God is no▨▨▨▨▨▨▨▨s held

*The universal human quest, through meditation and reflection, to find
meaning in life is one of the mainsprings of religious belief*

by those who say that the old "clockmaker" theory is now
discredited because we are able to explain most of the
mysteries of creation through science.

It is true that, in some societies, many people no longer
profess to belong to a religion, or take part in its practices,
except where they give some social cachet. But there is no
correlation between levels of religious belief and industri-
alization or education. For example, one of the most heavily
industrialized countries, the USA, is also one in which there
is a great deal of active religious practice.

Indeed, many eminent scientists say that their belief is
strengthened by their growing knowledge and understanding of the universe. For them, we may have greater
insights into the "how," but are no nearer the "why."

Religion in a shrinking world: the global challenge

Many religions originate from, and are still associated closely with, particular geographical areas. Until the recent past, religions and beliefs tended to spread slowly, except where great crusades, migrations or jihads carried a religion to a new area. The exception was the diaspora (dispersal) of the Jews, which began when the Jews were expelled from Palestine by the Romans. In the past century, many other religions have experienced a diaspora to new areas of the world; Buddhism, Hinduism, Sikhism and The Bahá'í Faith have all spread from their original geographical regions, and adherents can be found in significant, if not large, numbers all over the globe. These diasporas are, in general, closely, though not entirely, related to economic and political factors.

One effect of these diasporas and the ease of international travel is to bring different views of life to areas of the world which are hungry for new spiritual insights. In the West, there is much interest in Buddhism and other Eastern traditions, and many people practice forms of exercise and discipline – yoga, t'ai chi, tai kwon do – with Eastern roots. It is probable that many practitioners of these disciplines have little understanding of the religious systems from which they sprang; but the ground is none the less fertile.

The most recent feature of the shrinking world is the information revolution, which is already having an effect on the pattern of religious beliefs. The ease of direct personal links with other societies is one aspect of this, and, in the next decades, the Internet will almost certainly have a significant effect on religions. Perhaps more important is the use of information systems to aid missionary activity. Radio and television broadcasts have been in common and effective use for evangelization for many years.

This Hare Krishna group in Australia gives eloquent testimony to the fact that religion is not just a matter of piety and abstinence, but also a celebration of the beauties of creation and of human fellowship

Ecumenism, evangelism and fundamentalism

This encyclopedia celebrates the diversity of religious beliefs and practices, but the reader will notice that there are many common threads which unite believers. This has led some religious people to try to bring religions closer, and build on this commonality, for the good of all people. This movement is called ecumenism. Unfortunately, there is no evidence that this is leading to anything more than close and helpful dialog, and, in some cases, to closer personal relations between religious leaders. The history of religion continues to be more about diversity and complexity than unity and similarity.

Another aspect of the drive for commonality is evangelism – spreading one's own belief, and trying to convert people to a religion. Not all religions are evangelical; many of them, and most notably Judaism, make it very hard for a person to convert to the faith. The most missionary religions are Islam and Christianity. Throughout

history the belief that cor⬛⬛⬛⬛⬛⬛⬛⬛⬛⬛⬛⬛⬛ ⬛⬛⬛ ne-
times led to intolerance an⬛⬛⬛⬛⬛⬛⬛⬛⬛⬛⬛⬛⬛ ⬛ers
of other faiths, not just w⬛⬛⬛⬛⬛⬛⬛⬛⬛⬛⬛⬛⬛ are
concerned but in many ot⬛⬛⬛⬛⬛⬛⬛⬛⬛⬛.

A concern with evang⬛⬛⬛⬛⬛⬛⬛⬛⬛⬛⬛⬛⬛ clu-
sively, linked to fundamer⬛⬛⬛⬛⬛⬛⬛⬛⬛⬛⬛⬛⬛ups
within a religion seek to ⬛⬛⬛⬛⬛⬛⬛⬛⬛⬛⬛⬛⬛e to
be the original, basic prac⬛⬛⬛⬛

Religious confli⬛

In the world today, there ⬛⬛⬛⬛⬛⬛⬛⬛⬛⬛⬛⬛⬛ oints
which are linked direct⬛⬛⬛⬛⬛⬛⬛⬛⬛⬛⬛⬛⬛. For
example, the conflicts i⬛⬛⬛⬛⬛⬛⬛⬛⬛⬛⬛⬛thern
Ireland cannot be under⬛⬛⬛⬛⬛⬛⬛⬛⬛⬛⬛lge of
the religious groups tha⬛⬛⬛⬛⬛⬛⬛⬛⬛⬛⬛.

Conflict is a sad and ⬛⬛⬛⬛⬛⬛⬛⬛⬛⬛⬛f religion. There is, in the da⬛⬛⬛⬛⬛⬛⬛⬛⬛⬛⬛adow
that leads people to be ⬛⬛⬛⬛⬛⬛⬛⬛⬛olent,
towards people who th⬛⬛⬛⬛⬛⬛⬛⬛⬛⬛rsecu-

tion has also been a feature of many religions. Because of
the close relationship between national or tribal identity
and religious identity, many conflicts have religious, as well
as economic or territorial, dimensions. Even today, in our
so-called enlightened world, we do not have to go far to
find examples of conflicts where a religious dimension has
overlain other causes.

Equality

The treatment of different people within a religion is an
issue that many religions are having to face. There is a growing
sense in the world that it is not acceptable for people to be
discriminated against on the grounds of gender or race. In
some cases, this conflicts with the traditional ways in which
people, and particularly women, have been treated within
religions, and within societies heavily influenced by those
religions. Reading about the religions in this encyclopedia,
it is interesting to see how many of the religions have a view
that God is, if not "male," at least a deity whose attributes
are distinctly masculine.

Conclusion

Much of this introduction has been concerned with issues
that pose a challenge to religions; it has emphasized the problems and conflicts. The reader should be aware that most
religions, at their heart, are about finding the goodness in
people; they are about seeking positive answers to the questions that face all humanity. For the majority of people,
religion brings peace, happiness and sense to their lives. There
is more good done in the name of religion than evil. This
drive toward goodness should not be forgotten when we
explore the differences in religious belief and practice
described in this encyclopedia.

Religions do not grow up in a vacuum, and often share
stories and traditions although they may use them in
different ways. A good example of this is the tale of the six
blind men and the elephant which appears in the Hinduism
section of this book to illustrate the inclusive nature of that
religion, and also in the Buddhism section, as a story the
Buddha told.

PRIMAL RELIGIONS

"Traditional religions are integral to society

The terms "traditional" and "primal" when used of religions are controversial. They are often wrongly taken to refer to static, unchanging and primitive, or unsophisticated, religions found in underdeveloped societies. But this is not the sense in which the terms are used here.

Rather, they are used to describe those religions that have always been an integral part of the culture of a society and confined their activities to the members of that society; this is different from the newer arrivals with global ambitions such as Christianity and Islam. Traditional religions abound, and include among them Australian Aboriginal, Maori and Melanesian religions, Native American religions such as Navajo and Hopi, countless African religions, and a considerable range of Central and Latin American religions, including Inca and Aztec religions. In this encyclopedia, limitations of space confine the focus to Australian Aboriginal and African traditional religions.

14

Having arrived in Australia some 40,000 years ago, the Aborigines have developed many different religions, each based on its own set of myths and rituals

The sky-being

Aboriginal religion is diverse, and there is no single system of rituals and beliefs that binds together all Aborigines. Even so, within Aboriginal societies, there are a number of common beliefs and rituals that are widely, although not universally, shared. Most Aborigines believe in a personal sky-being and in auxiliary spirits, sometimes understood to be the sons of the sky-being, who provided them with sacred instruments and rituals. These spirits are also depicted by other Aborigines as taking the form of snakes or human-like sisters, and they are seen as separate entities that are unrelated to the sky-being. The sky-being is sometimes depicted as an extremely powerful All-Father with a human form who, although he has departed for the sky, continues to take a keen interest in what is happening on earth. There is also a belief that this sky-being left behind on earth various holy objects that contain his power.

In some Aboriginal communities, this sky-being exists in the form of an All-Mother and is associated more with the earth or with water than with the sky. Rituals are performed under the guidance of a medicine man, or shaman, to dramatize the creative powers and activities of the sky-being. There are several ceremonies, one being for the purpose of transforming the spirits of the dead from a wandering state to a state in which they may enter ancestral waters and from which they may undergo reincarnation. Other ceremonies aim to ensure the perpetuation of species of animals and plants, while in others the focus is on the passage of youth to adulthood and the separation of masculine from feminine social roles and activities.

Aboriginal religion

The ancestors of the Abo⬛⬛⬛⬛⬛⬛⬛⬛⬛⬛ ⬛stralia more than 40,000 years⬛⬛⬛⬛⬛⬛⬛⬛⬛ of their ethnic or linguistic orig⬛⬛⬛⬛⬛⬛⬛⬛⬛ned in numbers since the arriva⬛⬛⬛⬛⬛⬛⬛⬛⬛ve lost much of their land to th⬛⬛⬛⬛⬛⬛⬛⬛dants. Today, they number less⬛⬛⬛⬛⬛⬛⬛⬛ralian population, and some 5⬛⬛⬛⬛⬛⬛⬛⬛st only half Aboriginal. Aborigi⬛⬛⬛⬛⬛⬛⬛ speak one of several Aborigina⬛⬛⬛⬛⬛⬛⬛itional way of life based on hu⬛⬛⬛⬛⬛⬛

There are many Abo⬛⬛⬛⬛⬛⬛⬛⬛⬛riginal group developing its o⬛⬛⬛⬛⬛⬛⬛arliest accounts available to us⬛⬛⬛⬛⬛⬛⬛om the late-18th century. The ⬛⬛⬛⬛⬛⬛⬛myste-rious beings, half-human⬛⬛⬛⬛⬛⬛⬛rdinary powers, made an appear⬛⬛⬛⬛⬛⬛or from the distant horizon, or⬛⬛⬛⬛⬛⬛⬛ow the story has developed ⬛⬛⬛⬛⬛⬛⬛ beings created nature and the⬛⬛⬛⬛⬛⬛⬛ered in Aboriginal myths and ri⬛⬛⬛⬛⬛⬛st today, and all, whether living⬛⬛⬛⬛⬛⬛fluence over everyday affairs. A⬛⬛⬛⬛⬛⬛ to their relevance and include⬛⬛⬛⬛⬛⬛h is the eye of the half-human⬛⬛⬛

ABORIGINAL MYTHS

The telling of myths often accompanies Aboriginal ceremonies, and enables participants and observers to understand what the ceremonies aim to accomplish and why they are necessary. Myths also provide the reason for the social and moral rules of the community and the division of labor and responsibility between the sexes. Some myths recount how the existing rules governing relations between members of the same kinship group came to be, how animals and plants came to be named, and how languages acquired the form they now have. For example,

In the spare and featureless landscape of the Australian bush, any feature of significance becomes the focus for religious belief. In the sky-being myth, shared by many Aboriginal religions, the all-powerful deity took human form and spent time on earth, leaving behind hills, mounds, and boulders that are imbued with holy powers

here is the myth of the Wawilak sisters, as told in the 1920s by the Aboriginal Murngin of northeastern Arnhem Land. Variations of this same myth are to be found in other Aboriginal settlements.

The Wawilak sisters set off from the interior, heading northward toward the sea. As they go, they name the plants they gather, the animals they kill, and the places and countries they pass through as they travel. They even change the languages, so that they sound as they do today. The younger sister feels a child moving and growing within her – the offspring of an incestuous relationship – and tells the older sister. They both hurry to a waterhole near the place of the rock python to make a fire and cook the plants and animals they have gathered. But the animals and plants leap from the fire and take the forms of two men, who run and dive into the water.

The elder sister goes to gather bark to make a bed for her younger sister. She is menstruating and this "pollution" arouses the python. He rises to the surface of the water-hole and the water level rises with him, flooding the surrounding country. At the same time the rains begin to fall heavily, which wakes the sisters. Desperate to see the rain stop, they sing the song of the rock python and the menstrual blood. In return, the python makes magic to send the sisters to sleep. The python swallows and then regurgitates the sisters. This process is repeated for a second time. Later the spirits of the sisters appear in a dream to the two men and teach them a number of ceremonies.

Aboriginal rights

Aboriginal religion has changed greatly, especially with the move from a life on the move to a more sedentary existence. The social order in which the Aborigines now live, and the moral and social rules by which they live, are no longer explained by recourse to such spiritual beings. However, some of the old myths and ceremonies, particularly those relating to land rights, have survived. Indeed, they have taken on new life and meaning as, in recent times, the movement for Aboriginal rights has begun to gain momentum and to win significant reforms.

are the means by which the beliefs of each
from generation to generation. They also
complex inter-relationship between the spirit
for the retelling of stories is one way of paying
gods and ensuring the continuation
f their benign patronage

AFRICAN RELIGIONS

In Africa we find some parallels with Aboriginal religions, and many differences. Here, traditional religions have always been closely bound up with particular linguistic and ethnic groups — and the fact that there are many hundreds of these in the African continent is reflected by the vast range and variety of these religions. While there is not a great deal of information about the earliest forms of African traditional religion, the rock paintings of Southern Africa, some of which date back thousands of years, indicate that the San hunters and their ancestors in Southern Africa engaged in ceremonies resembling shamanistic rites. These are religious activities inspired by shamans — priests or medicine men regarded as able to control cosmic and spiritual forces, and regularly to embody them. Through

Above: *Hunters and priests depicted in the art of the Yoruba people* **Below:** *Traditional religions in Africa are bound up with particular ethnic groups*

dancing, San males exper⸻
presence of a sacred powe⸻
bodies, a power that also ⸻
certain animals, particul⸻
eland, a large antelope⸻
dancing, the San men fal⸻
state of deep trance, or half⸻

Creation myths and hero myths

Although they can vary gr⸻
religions have much in co⸻
ing creation myths that d⸻
the origins of the world an⸻
race, but also with the ca⸻
According to these my⸻
reigned everywhere at ⸻
divine and human beings⸻
freely. Then humans,
and particularly
women, made
mistakes and
were negli-
gent, disobedient,
and even spite-
ful. This led
to the separa-
tion of heaven and ⸻
withdrawal of the Suprem⸻
High God. Death, althou⸻
owes its origins to hu⸻
weakness, is nevertheles⸻
unnatural. It is an esse⸻
part of being human and ⸻ ween
the supernatural and the⸻

The witch, shaman or⸻
between the human and spirit⸻ ly and
control cosmic forces, usu⸻ o
a trance-l⸻

According to the creation myth of the cattle-rearing Dinka people of the Southern Sudan, a woman disobeyed the sky god by planting greater quantities of millet than the amount stipulated. This resulted in her pounding harder with her hoe and, in the process, she pierced the low-hanging sky. Affronted, the sky god withdrew, and sickness, suffering, and death entered the world. Henceforth, human beings had to labor endlessly for the necessities of life.

Another kind of myth is the hero myth, which sometimes relates to important discoveries, such as iron working, or to the foundation of cities and important social institutions, or to the performance of great deeds. For example, Shango, King of Old Oyo, once the capital of the Yoruba kingdom in Western Nigeria, is a deified hero who came to be revered as the god of lightning and thunder.

Trickster myths, which recall the character and behavior of trickster gods — such as Eshu, also a Yoruba god, and Ogo, of the Dogon of Mali — are a blend of psychology, philosophy and humor. The behavior of such gods is unpredictable, and replete with contradictions, expressing the view that it is only through the reconciliation of opposites that wholeness can be achieved.

TRANSITION AND SACRIFICE

African traditional rituals

The two most important kinds of ritual in African traditional religion are animal sacrifice, and rites of passage that mark the transition from one stage of life to another. The blood of an animal is believed to protect a person against evil powers. It is also sustenance for the gods, who give protection and favors in return. Animal sacrifice is also a way of scapegoating, for in this way an illness or some misfortune may be transferred from the person concerned to the animal. Sacrifice is also a social event bringing people together, and it is often the opportunity for the resolution of family and community disputes.

The most important rite of passage is the transition from youth to adulthood. This rite has three parts, and the most

Right: *Animal sacrifice, as depicted in this batik painting, is an important ritual in many African religions.*
Below: *Angolan participants in a circumcision ritual marking the passage from youth to manhood*

*Male initiation ceremonies, li_____ take
many different forms designed _____nts to
take on the respo_____*

important phase is the m_____ransi-
tional, or liminal, phase._____n last
for several years, everyt_____. The
normal becomes abnorm_____ue. It
is the period in which th_____ation
unlearns the ways of you_____alizes
the values of adulthood._____e old
ways and rise again as a n_____orbed
into society to undertak_____oy the
privileges, of adulthood

Healing rituals

In African society, perso_____s individual, and religion con_____more,
it is believed that the ca_____nisfor-

tune can be moral and spiritual. Thus, in order for healing
to take place, relationships must be put right. Moreover,
each person has a destiny, and this is believed to come from
a family ancestor who is, in some sense, reborn in a grand-
child, and who therefore has the role of enabling that person
to fulfill her or his destiny.

Destiny is, perhaps, not the best word because this
implies unalterable fate. An important feature of African
religions is the belief that fate can be modified through ritual.
The people who specialize in performing rituals are the
diviner, the priest, and the prophet. The diviner is usually
the one who diagnoses the causes of illness, misfortune,
and disputes between relatives and neighbors, and then acts
as counselor. The priest is the ritual specialist, and the prophet
is the innovator, the one who warns of impending disasters. You need not use the services of a ritual specialist to
commune with God or the gods. In many African religions,
including the Zulu religion of South Africa, the practice of
private prayer and supplication is common.

GODS AND ANCESTORS

In some African societies, including that in Madagascar, the role of the ancestors is crucial in most aspects of life, and the ultimate reward for a life well lived is to be buried in the ancestral tomb. In every household there will be an ancestral shrine. Only the leaders of communities and extended families can become ancestors, and thus be venerated from generation to generation. Other people become ghosts, and, after being sent with the proper ritual burial to rest in peace, are no longer invoked. Ancestors ensure that traditions are maintained and punish those who violate them.

The deities, thought of as the ministers of the Supreme Being, need their devotees as much as devotees need them. The deities become intimately involved in people's lives, offering them protection on a journey, or advice and guidance. They become almost one with their devotees through possession, and the latter take on the character and attitudes of their particular god when in this state. If deities are not respected and worshiped, punishment will inevitably follow.

On the other hand, if gods fail their clients too often, they may be forgotten and thereby lose all their power over others. Hence the reciprocal nature of the relationship and the paradoxical idea that the devotee is the creator of the god.

With so much attention paid to the gods, and so many temples and shrines dedicated to them compared to the Supreme Being, it is generally concluded that African religions are polytheistic. This is not correct, though the role of the Supreme Being has possibly changed during the past 200 years. Regarded as the principle behind everything, the one in which all things have their being, the ultimate, the unique, it was thought that the Supreme Being was not as approachable as the lesser gods, or was better approached through them. There was probably never a time, however, when prayers were not addressed to the Supreme Being. Archaeological discoveries include altars, for example among the Dogon of Mali, to Amma, the Creator God. Likewise, the name of the Supreme Being, Chukwu, has traditionally been given to the new-born among the Igbo of Nigeria, illustrating that the deity was felt to be very close to people.

Some deities, like this Madagascan goddess (top), protect and guide those who pay them homage while others are mischief makers, counterbalancing the good influence of the benign spirits

Witchcraft

Much of the emphasis in discussion and writing about traditional religion in Africa tends to focus on witchcraft. Various forms of witchcraft exist and their purpose varies.

The medicine man is c   le being to understand and e   r how ambiguou

At times witchcraft is   other-wise be inexplicable in   in such things as chance, or act   f witch-craft are made against   ors. At other times, individuals   se them-selves of witchcraft b   riously wounded their childre   r recog-

nition where their contribution to society is undervalued. They are not considered guilty of a crime, but instead go to the local shrine where, under the care of the priest, they are treated for their illness and given greater respect and attention in the form of gifts from their husbands.

This practice demonstrates that traditional religions, far from being the creation of irrational and superstitious minds, as was once thought, are highly complex systems of belief and ritual whose main purpose is to explain and attempt to deal with the problems — emotional, existential, environmental, medical, and social — of everyday life.

HINDUISM

That which 66 **is One, the wise call by many names**

What is Hinduism? A straightforward answer might be that it is a religion closely linked with the land and people of India. But this would be too simple an answer, for it does not explain the vast range, complexity, and diversity of practices and beliefs covered by the term "Hinduism." Hinduism is better understood as a family of traditions, incorporating a spectrum of philosophical ideas, beliefs, and practices. Unlike Christianity and Islam, Hinduism has no one historical founder, no set of dogmas or creeds, and no single source of authority.

In this sense, Hinduism ⟨...⟩ religion in the commonl ⟨...⟩ ord.
However, there is a wide b ⟨...⟩ crip-
ture and deeply felt persor ⟨...⟩ ndus
would accept as being ⟨...⟩ tion.
Hinduism's rich diversi ⟨...⟩ irent
contradictions and parad ⟨...⟩ d say
that there is an underl ⟨...⟩ rsity.
Indeed, the religion ha ⟨...⟩ aving
unity in diversity, and its ⟨...⟩ nclu-
sive nature.

The origin of th⟨e term "Hindu"⟩

The word "Hindu" orig ⟨...⟩ icient
Sanskrit name for the Ri⟨ver⟩ ⟨...⟩ gh the
northwestern part of th ⟨...⟩ actual
word "Hindu" first appea ⟨...⟩ term
for the people who live ⟨...⟩ By the
end of the 18th century ⟨...⟩ idoo,"
was used by the Britis ⟨...⟩ its of
Hindustan, the geograp ⟨...⟩ India.
During the latter part of ⟨...⟩ e 20th
centuries, the term "Hi ⟨...⟩ isingly
by the Indians themselve ⟨...⟩ ational
identity opposed to col ⟨...⟩

　　Even in contempora ⟨...⟩ dus do
not readily recognize th ⟨...⟩ ription
of their religion. Most ⟨...⟩ ligious

Hinduism is an inclusive faith, with many branches and many spiritual leaders; its strength is the unity which underpins the diversity

tradition as *dharma*. *Dharma* is a complex Sanskrit word which is rich in meaning. It refers to sacred laws, duties, ideas of truth, and ethics. In short, it is the power which upholds or supports society and the cosmos. In simple terms, the word *dharma* is the nearest equivalent to the English word "religion." The 19th-century Hindu reformers spoke of Hinduism as *sanatana dharma* — the eternal religion or law. Many modern Hindus prefer this term to describe their traditions.

A vibrant tradition

Hindus themselves regard their religious traditions as dynamic and vibrant, rooted in one of the world's oldest civilizations. Hindus talk of their religion as a way of life rather than as a set of dogmas. It is through behavior that Hindu values are best expressed, rather than adherence to a specific set of beliefs. To be a Hindu means to be born into a particular group of people related by marriage, and to perform duties in accordance with the *dharma*, as outlined, or revealed, primarily in the earliest of the Hindu scriptures, called the Vedas. A sociological characterization, given by Frits Staal, perhaps best sums it up when he says a Hindu, "may be a theist, pantheist, atheist, communist and believe whatever he likes, but what makes him into a Hindu are the ritual practices he performs and the rules to which he adheres; in short, what he does."

THE OLDEST LIVING RELIGION

The Hindu religion is as old as Indian civilization, and can be traced back for some 5,000 years. Any attempt to discover the origins of ancient belief systems is beset with problems, and this is particularly the case with Hinduism. However, the work of archeologists and historians reveals that Hinduism originates from two ancient centers of culture. These are the Indus Valley civilization, which flourished from 2500 B.C.E. to about 1500 B.C.E., and the Aryan culture, which developed during the second millennium B.C.E.

Traditionally, it is thought that, as the Indus Valley civilization declined, the region was taken over by the Aryans, an Indo-European people originating in the Caucasus, who invaded the Northern plains of the Indian subcontinent around 1500 B.C.E. A contrasting view is that the Aryan culture was an indigenous development from the Indus Valleys civilization, and that it was not introduced by outside invaders. Whichever view is correct, there is little dispute about the eventual predominance of the Aryan culture over the Indus Valley culture.

The earliest times

The Indus Valley civilization was discovered in 1921 when excavations in Mohenjo-Daro and Harappa, two of the civilization's most important cities, resulted in the discovery of a highly developed urban culture. These two cities were vast in scale, each covering several hundred acres, with mud-brick defences, a citadel, streets laid out on a grid plan, sophisticated drainage systems and granaries. The archeological finds from Harappa include seals, stone statues and terracotta figurines. At Mohenjo-Daro a "great bath" was

Indian civilization long ago evolved a rich tradition of community festivals and courtly ceremonies as depicted in this Mogul painting

A page taken from an 18th ▓▓▓▓▓▓▓▓▓▓▓
Markandeya Purana which d▓▓▓▓▓▓▓▓▓*nit*
in a hu▓▓▓▓

discovered that resembl▓▓▓▓▓▓▓▓▓▓▓▓anks
found in later Hindu tem▓▓▓▓▓▓▓▓▓▓▓▓ce of
using water for ritual pu▓▓▓▓▓▓▓▓▓▓▓tant
aspect of the Hindu tradi▓▓▓

Another important fir▓▓▓▓▓▓▓▓▓▓▓wing
a figure seated in a yogic ▓▓▓▓▓▓▓▓▓▓that
this figure is a prototype ▓▓▓▓▓▓▓▓▓yogi
and lord of the animals. T▓▓▓▓▓▓▓▓ts to
practices and beliefs that li▓▓▓▓▓▓▓▓volu-
tion of Hinduism, but thes▓▓▓▓▓▓▓▓ative,
since the language of the ▓▓▓▓▓▓▓▓et to
be deciphered satisfactor▓

The Vedic period

There are hardly any arch▓▓▓▓▓▓▓▓eriod
from 1500 to 500 B.C.E▓▓▓▓▓▓▓▓of the
Aryans is an important s▓▓▓▓▓▓▓▓Vedic
religion and society. One▓▓▓▓▓▓▓▓Veda,
a collection of hymns wri▓▓▓▓▓▓▓▓uage.

The Rig Veda was composed over several centuries, reaching its final form around 900 B.C.E. This is one of the four Vedas that inform the Hindu religion, the others being the collections of ritual and philosophical texts called the Brahmanas and the Aranyakas, and the Upanishads, which many regard as Hinduism's greatest treasure of religious texts.

During this period, the Aryan (meaning "noble") culture spread further east into the plain of the Ganges, eventually reaching the borders of modern Bengal. Important teachings which developed during this time include the belief in the transmigration of souls and the idea of liberation from the cycle of birth, death, and rebirth.

The Puranic period

The period from 500 B.C.E to 500 C.E. saw the rise of early Hinduism. During this time, the rules for the general conduct of life were worked out in great detail, including the concept of the four stages of life, the *ashramas*, and of the duties appropriate to each. This period also saw the emergence of domestic rituals in worship and of personal devotion to the deities Rudra (later known as Shiva) and Vishnu. The great Hindu epic poems, the *Mahabharata* and the *Ramayana*, were composed during this period.

MEDIEVAL AND MODERN TIMES

The early medieval period in north western India saw a further systematic development of theological beliefs and the rise of devotionalism at the popular level. This devotion – *bhakti* – directed towards the major Hindu deities, Vishnu, Shiva, and Shakti, remains a prominent feature of Hinduism.

The modern period, which began around 1800 C.E., has witnessed the rise of reformist movements seeking to strengthen Hinduism in the face of colonialism, and the drive towards Indian independence. Indeed, in the life and times of Mahatma (great soul) Gandhi, Hindu religious ideals provided much of the inspiration for the independence movement. During the latter part of the 20th century, religious ideals, such as the values of *dharma* and the duties associated with a particular class or caste, have been linked with nationalist movements, such as the Bharatiya Janata Party, the BJP, formed in 1980.

Mahatma Gandhi is revered for his example of peaceful reform and religious tolerance, and the continuing development of Hinduism is shown by the establishment of new groups such as the Hare Krishna movement

The Hindu world today

Of all the world's major religions, Hinduism has the third largest number of adherents. The majority of Hindus live in India and Nepal. Of India's population

of approximately 950 mill[...] people, 750 million a[...] Hindus. India is a va[...] country, the world's bigg[...] democracy. The governm[...] officially recognizes sixte[...] main languages and there [...] hundreds of regional diale[...] Given this diversity, it is [...] surprising that Hindu beli[...] and practices vary grea[...] from region to region.

Hinduism beyond India

About 1,000 years a[...] Hinduism spread along [...] trade routes to the Ea[...] Although most of the peo[...] in these lands later beca[...] Buddhists or Muslims, m[...] of the population of B[...] Indonesia remains Hin[...] There are also sizeable Hi[...] communities in South a[...] East Africa. In the W[...] Indies, the island of Trin[...] boasts a large Hindu com[...] nity, comprised of the g[...] grandchildren of 19th-c[...] [...] More recently, Hindus have mig[...] [...] USA, Canada, Europe, Australi[...] [...] USA, the Hindu population is [...] [...] ople and in the United Kingdo[...] [...] ering over 300,000 adherents.

Hinduism does not n[...] many Westerners have become [...] s, or gurus, partly as a result o[...]. For example Bhaktivedanta Sw[...] ideas of a holy teacher called Ch[...] 533)

[...] means that Hindu art, such as this [...] geous in the Sri Mariamman temple in [...] be found in many parts of Asia

to the West in 1965. The movement he established is now popularly known as the Hare Krishna movement (*see Other Sects and Denominations*), a short-hand term for the International Society for Krishna Consciousness.

Other notable examples of more recent movements within the Hindu fold include two rapidly expanding groups: the Swaminarayan Hindu Mission (founded by Shri Swaminarayan (1781-1830) and currently led by Swami Pramukh Swami Maharaj), and the followers of the teachings of the modern guru called Shri Sathya Sai Baba. The majority of the followers in these two movements are Hindu by birth; they see their respective teachers as a means to rediscovering ancient Hindu traditions and truths which have perhaps been lost as a result of migration from the homeland of India.

The Swaminarayan movement first came to public prominence in the United Kingdom in August 1995 when the splendid Swaminarayan Hindu Mandir was officially inaugurated in London. This cultural and religious complex was built over a period of three years from marble quarried in Bulgaria and Italy, transported to India for carving, and then shipped back to London. Most of the construction was undertaken by unpaid Hindu volunteers. The temple is a living example of modern Hindu devotion to God and selfless service to humanity, as well as being a work of great architectural merit.

ULTIMATE REALITY

Hindus believe that the basis for all reality and existence is an entity called Brahman, an all-embracing, infinite, uncreated principle – ultimate reality. It has caused the universe and all beings to emanate from itself and, it is believed, all beings will return to the same source. Brahman is one and it is in all things. It is the true self – *atman* – within all beings. The identification of the human soul, or self, with Brahman is a major strand running through the Upanishads.

Hindus believe that only Brahman is ultimately real and everlasting. It is conceived as impersonal, without attributes or qualities, and referred to as *nirguna* Brahman. When it is thought of as possessing qualities and forms, it is called *saguna* Brahman. In this sense Brahman is worshiped as a god, for example in the form of Vishnu or Shiva. The mystic syllable *om* is the symbolic representation of Brahman. This sacred word encompasses in itself the whole universe, including the past, the present and the future.

The Upanishads contain a mix of reflections on the nature of Brahman. In some passages Brahman is conceived of as impersonal, but, in later passages, it is understood as being theistic and personal. To those Hindus who incline towards mystical and philosophical traditions, the pursuit of divine knowledge and of insight into the nature of Brahman is paramount, as is acquiring an understanding of the relationship between Brahman and atman (the true self) and the consequent implications for how you should live your life.

The identification of the self in humans with the ultimate reality is neatly encapsulated in the following story from the *Chandogya Upanishad*. A boy called Svetaketu went, at the age of 12, to learn from a spiritual teacher, a guru. On returning at the age of 24, the young man's father realized that his son had learned the scriptures without understanding the nature of Brahman. So he asked his son to bring a glass of water and to sprinkle some salt in it. The next day he asked his son to find the salt in the water. As the salt had dissolved, the search proved to be futile. Then the father asked his son to taste the water from the top, middle, and bottom of the glass. "How does it taste?" asked the father. "Salty," replied the son. "Where is the salt?" asked the father. "I cannot see the salt, only water," replied the son. His father responded, "In the same way, my son, you cannot see the spirit, the Brahman, which encompasses the universe. But it is there. That is the Reality. That is the Truth. And you are that Truth."

The god Shiva, represented in this 12th-century bronze statue in the incarnation of Nataraja, King of Dancing

Many gods

Hindu theology conceives of God as being one. But this one can have many manifestations, or forms. Each form represents some aspect of saguna Brahman. Linked with this notion is the belief that God becomes incarnate on earth to restore goodness whenever there is an increase of evil. Traditionally, the god Vishnu is held to have experienced ten incarnations. These are called avataras (literally "one who descends"). Rama, Krishna, and the Buddha are examples of avataras.

The concept of Shakti, Shiva's active energy, is another important aspect of the divine. This active energy is personified through female deities. Mahadevi (Great Goddess) is worshiped as the consort of Shiva, and in her own right. Female manifestations range from the fearsome Kali to the benign Parvati.

Whatever form the ultimate reality takes, most Hindus would accept as part of Hindu theology the underlying notion that God is one, and a part of all existence.

Vishnu are depicted in this 18th-century
...ed manuscript from Jaipur

BIRTH, DEATH AND REBIRTH

Samsara

Among the essential features that typify Hindu beliefs is the concept of *samsara*, the cycle of birth, death, and rebirth. The universe is also subject to cyclical processes of change, from birth to death and re-creation. In this context, the three functions of God are exemplified as Brahma, the Creator, Vishnu, the Preserver, and Shiva, the Destroyer.

All worldly existence is subject to the cycle of samsara. The following Hindu story describes to great effect the state of being caught up in samsara. It also demonstrates the transient nature of existence, and teaches the folly of becoming attached to worldly things.

Samsara is a jungle infested with wild beasts. A man trying to escape falls into a deep pit. Fortunately, he hangs on to some creepers, avoiding an angry elephant at the top of the pit and a serpent at the bottom waiting for him to drop. Even as he realizes that his life cannot last long, the man sees two mice, one black and one white, gnawing away at the creepers. At the edge of the pit is a honeycomb dripping honey, giving him sustenance. Such sweetness makes him forget the perils, but it is short-lived.

In this pessimistic parable, the man is the soul and the jungle is existence. The wild elephant and the serpent represent death, while the mice are symbols of time, the dark and light halves of the lunar month. The honey represents pleasures, which are temporary and trivial in the midst of numerous perils.

Moksha

Liberation from samsara can be found only through the pursuit of the ultimate goal in life, *moksha*. This means liberation, spiritual freedom from the bondage of the cycle of birth, death, and rebirth. In short, Hinduism teaches that human beings should seek to achieve spiritual freedom through non-attachment and spiritual knowledge, by performing good deeds without seeking selfish gains, and being devoted to God. These paths to liberation are traditionally called *jnana yoga* (spiritual knowledge), *karma yoga* (good works or right action), and *bhakti yoga* (devotion and love directed towards a chosen deity).

Karma

The theory underlying *karma* (action) relates to the law of cause and effect. This means that every good thought, word, and deed produces a positive reaction.

Throughout India, holy men serve as spiritual teachers, pursuing knowledge through total devotion to the divine

Likewise, a bad action results in negative reactions either in this life or the next existence. The law of karm[...] all beings residing within it. It [...]ks impersonally, binding inc[...]d. Depending on the cumulat[...]s, present, and future existen[...] it. Hindus believe that karma [...] he suffering and good fortune [...]

The theory is more co[...] It does not mean that existen[...]d. There are three aspects of k[...]ce of parents and the physical c[...]re

[...] shows ascetics under a banyan tree, and [...] aspect of traditional Hindu practice

the result of the sum total of acts performed in a previous life. These, and the time of death, cannot be changed. Another aspect of karma determines your characteristics and aptitudes. Some Hindus use this to explain why two children, born of the same parents and given the same environment, turn out to be very different in their characteristics and capabilities. This aspect of karma is changeable.

So, too, is the third aspect of karma. In the present life, human beings have the opportunity to mold the future. Whatever deeds are performed in the present life, the future existence is determined accordingly. Thus Hindus would say that life is both predetermined and subject to freewill.

LIVING A HINDU LIFE

Hinduism is more about a way of living than it is about having the right beliefs or doctrines. The concept of *varnashramadharma* (the words *varna*, *ashrama* and *dharma* joined together) illustrates how an individual Hindu fits into a family, and into a larger grouping in the wider society, and how the individual should perform duties appropriate to each stage and occupation in life.

Dharma

The word dharma means the performance of righteous duties. A mother, father, teacher, or priest, for example, all have their respective duties to perform, with moral purity as the goal. Hindus believe that it is through the performance of duties that harmony within the family, and, by extension, peace in society can be maintained.

Varna

The original meaning of the word *varna* was an order, or class, of people. There were four classes in this system: the Brahmans, or Brahmins, who were the priests and teachers; the Kshatriyas, or warriors and rulers: the Vaishyas, or traders; and the Shudras, who performed manual labor, as farmers for instance. This categorization is distinct from that of "caste" (from the Portugese word *casta*, meaning "breed"), which is determined by birth.

In time, sects, or *jatis*, came to be more prolific than the four classes. Jatis (meaning "birth") categorize people by occupation. People are ranked according to the degree of ritual purity or pollution associated with traditional occupations, regardless of whether or not the individual members of the sect still practice that occupation today.

The "untouchables", or outcastes, were originally those who had broken caste rules. Today, discrimination against them is unacceptable and banned under Indian law. Many Hindus, most notably Mahatma Gandhi, championed the rights of outcastes. In modern Indian society, outcastes use the term *dalit* (oppressed) to describe themselves.

Holy men and teachers, shown here, form one of the four traditional classes of Hindu society, along with warriors and rulers, merchants, and manual laborers. Each class has duties and responsibilities that, if performed well, lead to moral and social harmony

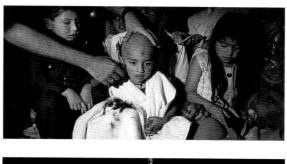

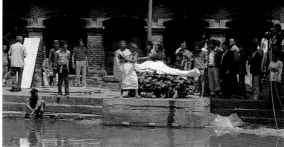

Hindu ceremonies mark the four main stages of life, from birth to young adulthood, through marriage and family responsibility, to old age and death

Ashrama

The word ashrama refer████████████████████ds in a Hindu's lifetime as each ███████████████ stages of being a student, then ████████████████ ge of retirement and, finally, t████████████████m all ties – in preparation for ██████████████ igidly observed, this pattern of █████████████████ndus. Each stage is marked by t███████████████ duties and the fulfillment of air██████████████ desire to achieve righteousnes

Four aims

The first of the four ai████████████████ life is dharma – the carrying██████████████ to the particular stage in life, █████████████ uch as honesty, fidelity, sacrifi████████████ lness, and love. Displaying suc███████████████ erpins the fulfillment of the oth████████████ chieve-ment of material prosp██████████████ bitions

and desires; and, finally, the achievement of moksha — liberation from the cycle of birth and death. A person who carries out their religious and moral duties according to age, caste, and occupation is said to be true to their dharma.

Life cycle sacraments

To achieve moksha, a Hindu has to develop self-discipline without becoming attached to the fruits of success. The scriptures also recommend that 16 sacraments (*samskars*) are performed, especially for those who belong to the first three varnas. This means that certain rituals are enacted during each of the four stages of life. The rituals include ceremonies performed prior to birth and at birth; the shaving of all hair (for males between the ages of one to three); the wearing of a sacred thread (for males usually between the ages of eight and twelve); making vows at the point of marriage; and, lastly, the performance of rituals at the cremation of a body. Most Hindus, circumstances allowing, try to ensure that these sacraments are followed.

DAILY WORSHIP

Although Hindu expressions of belief vary from region to region, certain key elements are evident in the practices of most Hindus, wherever they live. One example is the performance of daily worship.

Puja, or daily worship, is normally carried out in the home and is the main form of Hindu worship. Where homes are located near a *mandir* (Hindu temple), particularly in Indian villages and towns, many Hindus also worship in temples. Daily puja includes offerings to the deities and several recitations of a prayer called the *Gayatri mantra*:

Om bhur bhuvah svahah tatsavitur varenyam
bhargo devasya dhimahi
dhiyo yo nah prachodayat
Om shanti shanti shanti

Many Hindus will combine private devotions with daily public worship at the village temple

Offerings of food, flowers and incense are made daily in Hindu homes at the shrine of the family's chosen deities

This prayer can be translated as:

We meditate on the loving
light of the god, Savitri.
May his brilliance, like that
of the sun, stimulate our thoughts

In Hindu homes, worship is conducted at a shrine where the family's chosen deities are represented in the form of pictures and statues, called *murtis*. Murtis are there to assist the worshiper to concentrate and direct his or her energies and devotion to God.

The expression of reverence to God is ritually symbolized through the daily washing of the murtis with milk. The statues and pictures are then adorned with richly decorated clothes and colorful garlands of flowers, such as marigolds and sweetly scented frangipani blossoms. This is followed

The palatial design of templ███████████████████████n Jodphur reflects their st█████████████████

by the burning of incense███████████████████nps, called *divas*. While this is ████████████████████exts from the scriptures and s██████████████

Temple worship

Hindu temples are usual███████████████████eity. Temples are also under█████████████████ God "resides," though many Hi███████████████████man, the Supreme Being, is pre████████████████s and goddesses of the Hindu pa██████████████of the different aspects of Brahm███████████████many temples and shrines, each ██████████████████urti. Many temples in the Wes████████████████ty of murtis housed under one██████

Temples are normally███████████████ indi-vidual worship. Congrega██████████████████rmed twice a day, and is similar████████████████ome,

the main difference being that the ritual is performed and led by a priest. All worshipers take part in the ceremony of *arti*. This highly ritualized ceremony includes the lighting of five divas by the priest, who repeatedly circles the lamps in front of the central deity while the congregation sings a devotional scriptural verse, called an arti. Worship ends with the sharing of food, which has been blessed and offered to God during worship.

Wholeness in worship

Wherever worship is conducted, it involves the total self and makes use of the natural elements. The lighting of divas and incense, the use of water and milk, the offerings of fruit and flowers, the sounding of bells and singing, all these create a close affinity between the worshiper, natural creation, and the Creator. The five natural elements are linked to the five human senses: hearing to space or ether, touching to air, sight to fire, taste to water, and smell to earth. For a Hindu believer, all these different elements come together in an act of worship.

Most Hindus, particularly the orthodox, will practice four daily duties: to revere the deities (by making an offering of fire); to respect their ancestors (by offering water); to respect all beings (by offering food); and to honor all humans (by offering hospitality).

Temples are also the focal point of community events and festivals, with the sharing of food an important symbolic ritual

THE HINDU YEAR

For Hindus, time is not linear; it is cyclical, like the turning of a wheel. This cycle of repetition is reflected in the lunar basis of the Hindu calendar. The Hindu month is based on the waxing and waning of the moon, and the celebration and timing of festivals varies accordingly, the dates changing every year.

Festivals

Many colorful and important festivals are celebrated during the Hindu religious year. Some festivals mark events in the lives of deities, while others celebrate the seasons. Festivals

Right: *Krishna and his retinue celebrate Holi, the Hindu festival at which participants mark the arrival of spring by spraying each other with colored paints in a boisterous outpouring of high spirits.*
Below: *Pilgrims gather for ritual bathing in the River Ganges at Varanasi, casting garlands of marigolds and hibiscus blossoms on the sacred waters*

provide an opportunity fo ... ces-
sions. They are also a time ... me
together. Festivals are mar ... bra-
tions that involve music, ... vals
are known throughout In ... here
Hindus live, while others ...

Festivals linked ...
gods and goddes...

The birthdays of Krishna ... tant
festivals, but other deities ... rtic-
ular festivals. For example ... onor
of the goddess Durga. Th ... and
is especially celebrated by ... arati
Hindus honor the Moth ... -day
festival of dancing called ... ndia,
the elephant-headed goc ... the
festival of Ganpati Puja.

Diwali is celebrated ... or of
the goddess Lakshmi. Di ... rated
festival in India and is inc ... lus in
the West. In some regior ... a new
year, marked by the heroi ... emon
Ravana, symbolizing the t ... vities
include the dramatizatio ... Rama
and Sita, as recorded in ...

Diwali ... ts are
paid a ... given
a new ... lumi-
nated ... People
exch ... ng. In
Ke ... estival
of ... ali. In
t ... estival
...

... marily
... India.

It marks the arrival of spring, but is also associated with
the god Vishnu who, as told in one story remembered during
the festival, protects and saves a boy worshiper from the
powers of a female demon.

A remarkable religious festival, which takes place
approximately every 12 years, is the Kumbha Mela, held at
four sacred places in Northern India. The city of Allahabad,
where the sacred Ganga and Jamuna Rivers meet, is the location for one of the largest Kumbha Melas, where as many
as ten million pilgrims gather for ritual bathing.

Pilgrimages

The making of pilgrimages is an important practice among
devout Hindus. Some Hindus regard the whole of India as
a sacred land, but certain sites are believed to be especially
auspicious and they become very crowded at festival times.
Pilgrimage sites include the "abodes" or homes of God. These
are believed to be located at the four cardinal compass points
in India, namely the cities of Badrinath in the north, Puri
in the east, Dwarka in the west, and Rameshvaram in the
south. Other holy places are Vrindaban (linked with the life
of Krishna), Hardwar and Varanasi (known as Benares in
English). Kurukshetra, where the great battle recorded in
the *Mahabharata* is believed to have taken place, is also considered to be a holy site.

Pilgrimages are undertaken by individuals, families, and
sometimes even the entire population of a village.
Some places are particularly sacred for
specific groups and sects, and it is said
that every day there is a pilgrimage
taking place somewhere in India.
Pilgrimages are undertaken for a
number of reasons, including the
fulfillment of vows and the seeking
of blessings and merit. They also
provide an opportunity to thank
deities for favors bestowed.

... gh the streets of Allahabad during the Kumbha
... e of the largest Hindu festivals

HINDU PHILOSOPHY

Systems of Hindu philosophy are more than attempts to analyze life and truth. Hindu philosophy is better characterized as aiming to achieve moksha, or liberation from the wheel of birth, death, and rebirth. As such, philosophy cannot be distinguished from religion in Hinduism, so Hindu philosophy is more akin to theology than to theoretical philosophy.

Over a period of time – certainly by the beginning of the Christian era – six distinct philosophical schools emerged, all of them accepting the authority of the Vedas. However, their interpretations of the Vedas vary, giving Hinduism a rich diversity of teachings and practices. The six schools, or *darshanas*" are grouped in pairs: Nyaya and Vaisheshika, Sankhya and Yoga, and Mimamsa and Vedanta.

Vedanta

Vedanta is probably the most significant of all the philosophical schools. It gave a systematic form to the teachings of the Upanishads, concentrating particularly on the attainment of liberation through *jnana* (knowledge) of the unity of Brahman and atman (the true self). Since the 19th century the teachings of Vedanta have become more widely known in the West, through the interpretations of two of India's great teachers, Shankara (who taught in the early 9th century C.E.) and Ramanuja (who taught during the 11th century C.E.). Ramanuja emphasized devotion to Vishnu and his theistic interpretation greatly influenced the development of bhakti (devotion) as a popular means of attaining liberation.

Yoga

The word "yoga" comes from a Sanskrit word *yuj*, which means to unite, or join. The term "yoga" has both a specialized and a more general meaning. It refers to a philosophical school and, more widely, to different methods of self-control and meditation. The yogic school of thought takes as its basic text the *Yoga Sutra* of Patanjali, which dates from the 2nd century B.C.E., although the practices of yoga may be even more ancient.

Patanjali set out eight steps or "limbs" for yoga. Through these eight steps, Raja Yoga teaches techniques for achieving deep concentration and meditation. These steps include embracing truthfulness

and chastity. Later ⬛⬛⬛⬛⬛⬛⬛⬛⬛ of
postures and exercis⬛⬛⬛⬛⬛⬛⬛⬛ys-
ical, mental, and s⬛⬛⬛⬛⬛⬛⬛⬛ ges
of deep c⬛⬛⬛⬛⬛⬛⬛⬛ he
⬛⬛⬛⬛⬛⬛⬛⬛ *hi,*
⬛⬛⬛⬛⬛⬛⬛⬛ ce
⬛⬛⬛⬛⬛⬛⬛⬛ cal

awareness. Sometimes this stage is referred to as the achievement of self-realization.

Yoga has become popular in many parts of the world in one form or another. In the Western world, it is usually practiced as a series of physical exercises, and the spiritual aspects are either ignored or played down. Many would claim that this approach is half-hearted, and that to reap the full benefits from yoga, it is necessary to follow the spiritual precepts as well as the physical ones. In so doing, the practitioner aims to achieve a balance between the physical, mental, and spiritual aspects, remembering that many Hindus use yoga as a means of attaining liberation.

Yogic exercises are aimed at achieving control over physical and mental energies in order to achieve a deep state of concentration and meditation

HINDU CULTURE

Hinduism's contribution to civilization

Hindu writings, from the earliest Vedas to the devotional songs of Mirabai and Kabir, encapsulate the essential flavor of the search for truth, meaning, and purpose in life. The great Hindu epics are formidable in their recording of events over a vast expanse of time. The *Mahabharata*, which includes the popular Hindu scripture, the *Bhagavad Gita*, is thought to be the longest poem in the world. The *Bhagavad Gita* itself is a daily source of inspiration for countless Hindus all over the world, and its power to call humans to reflect on their existence is not confined to Hindus. Tolstoy is only one of many Western writers and thinkers to find much of illumination within its pages.

This 19th-century Indian miniature depicts Vishnu as the source of order and unity in the world, the point from which all things emanate

Language

Sanskrit is believed to be the origin for many of the languages now spoken in the world, particularly in the West. It is thought to be the most systematic language to have survived from earliest times, though nowadays it is used chiefly in the performance of religious rituals. Sanskrit is a versatile and rich language, as illustrated by the fact that it has 65 words for earth and 70 for water.

Contributions to the sciences

The contribution of Indian philosophers and scientists to astronomy, geometry, physics, mathematics and medicine is extensive, and Hindu thinking has sometimes predated discoveries made by other civilizations in other epochs. Today, Ayurvedic medicine, to quote just one example, is re-emerging as an extremely valuable therapy in the context of modern medical practice.

This wall painting, from a Hindu temple in Sri Lanka, is typical of the Hindu artist's love of color and of natural plant forms

him the title "Mahatma" (meaning "great soul") from fellow Hindus. Gandhi's life has also been the inspiration for other human-rights activists, notably Martin Luther King who challenged injustice and discrimination against Afro-Americans in the United States.

Hindus are, by and large, known for their peaceful nature. Part of the Hindu dharma (duty) is to regard the whole of humanity as comprising a "world family." The following Indian story captures the mood of what many Hindus would claim to be Hinduism's particular strength, notably the ability of Hindus to be inclusive.

The story of the six blind men and the elephant

There were once six blind men living in a village somewhere in India. One day they were told that there was an elephant in the next village. Not knowing what an elephant was, they decided to investigate.

When they arrived at the village, the first blind man took hold of the elephant's trunk and exclaimed: "Ah! I know what an elephant is; it's long and rubbery, like a snake." The second blind man took hold of the elephant's tusk. "No!" he said, "An elephant is long and curved with a sharp point." The third blind man felt the elephant's ear. "No! No!" he cried, "An elephant is a big leaf." The fourth man touched the elephant's leg and insisted that an elephant was more akin to a tree. The fifth man bumped into the elephant's side and so claimed that it was like a solid wall. Lastly, the sixth man felt the elephant's tail and said: "I really know what an elephant is; it's thin and long, like an old rope."

After listening to the six men quarreling over who was right, the elephant assured them that, in their own way, each one of them had a partial grasp of the truth!

In the Vedas, it is written: "That which is One the wise call by many names." Perhaps this is one of the reasons why Hinduism continues to be one of the greatest living religions in the world.

The arts

The aesthetic dimensio⸺⸺⸺⸺⸺⸺m the influence of Hindu ar⸺⸺⸺⸺⸺⸺ch has greatly enriched the wo⸺⸺⸺⸺⸺nextricably linked to religious⸺⸺⸺⸺ınd the performing arts gener⸺⸺⸺⸺ries of parable, insight, and w⸺⸺⸺⸺⸺ntinue to have a dynamism, a⸺⸺⸺⸺on, for Hindus living in the m⸺⸺

Ethics

The wealth of Hind⸺⸺⸺⸺⸺s many profound insights. Am⸺⸺⸺⸺found a reverence for all form⸺⸺⸺⸺lified in the concept of *ahimsa*,⸺⸺⸺⸺his idea, coupled with the conc⸺⸺⸺⸺f truth, reached its epitome in⸺⸺⸺⸺, earning

JUDAISM

"How shall we sing the Lord's song in a foreign land?

Judaism is the world's oldest monotheistic religion and it can claim a continuity of tradition covering some 4,000 years. For all this length of history, the 20th century has been one of the most momentous periods, because, in this century, Jewish demography has radically changed as a result of two major events: the Holocaust and the establishment of the state of Israel.

The Holocaust reduced the worldwide Jewish population by more than a third, to some ten million, and decimated Judaism's major centers of learning in Eastern Europe. The modern state of Israel effectively grew out of those ashes. While the force of tradition ensures a central sense of continuity, the integration of these 20th-century events into the collective psyche of the Jewish people presents a major challenge.

Jewish identity has inevit[...]th-century challenges. For [...]rs, the Jews" identity and fate [...]res in which they lived as "ou[...] to pursue professions of their[...] life open to them were heavily[...]ced to live in ghettos (named aft[...]e). At various times, Jews hav[...]tity symbols. Such processes of[...]ute low point in the Nazi perioc[...]heir sense of self-dignity and inc[...]eed not include religious belief[...]rich diversity of aspirations i[...]per connection to Jewish root[...]lual Jew establishing a persona[...]s of tradition associated with r[...]

The Torah

Central to this path is the[...] the Bible), and a sense of pers[...]. The Torah is believed to be Goc[...]ple, and the religious history[...] of a progressive unfolding of th[...]ses, the other Prophets establ[...] the biblical life of Israel. The[...]ntly took over from the Proph[...]aries before the Common Era.[...]tera-ture, the most important l[...]cted the lifestyle based on t[...] (the "dispersal"). At various[...]years different aspects of the pl[...]cepts in the Torah's teaching h[...]ipha-sized by particular Rabbi[...]

The Torah presents[...], the essence of which is capt[...]ents, and an idealized way of l[...]s into the world. Religious and[...]t one with secular laws. With t[...]irder, and sexual immorality, t[...]aw of the land should override[...]

In the modern world, assimilation is a major issue for Judaism. Although there are centers in America and Israel where the religion is practiced with great intensity, large numbers of Jews in sec-ular societies no longer follow a Jewish way of life. With its worldwide population stand-ing at only about 12 million, assimilation and the problems associated with intermarriage erode the

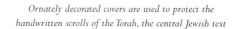

Ornately decorated covers are used to protect the handwritten scrolls of the Torah, the central Jewish text

strength of the religion. Many Jews are searching for ways of integrating key aspects of modernity into a viable Jewish path that maintains its continuity with the past. Such move-ments seek a more flexible attitude to would-be converts, a more prominent role for women than that traditionally allowed, a move away from large-scale, formal worship in synagogues to smaller informal spiritual groups, and a stronger emphasis on the more inward and experiential dimensions of the religion.

CORE BELIEFS

It is recorded that the great teacher, Hillel (who died in 10 C.E.), summarized the essence of Judaism for a would-be convert by saying: "That which is hateful to you, do not do to your fellow humans; this is the whole Torah, all the rest is commentary. Now, go and learn."

Similarly Rabbi Akiva taught that the central premise of the Torah was the command to "Love your neighbor as yourself" (*Leviticus 19:18*). Another sage, Ben Azzai, argued that the statement in Genesis that Adam – the archetypal human, incorporating both male and female – is made in the image of God, constituted the principal teaching.

These rabbinic opinions convey the core beliefs of Judaism, for, considered together, they include the four major areas of belief: the nature of God, the relationship of God to humankind, the centrality of Torah study, and the importance of society.

A central paradox in Judaism is that God is believed to be both unknowable in His infinite essence and yet recognizable as a personal presence in our lives. He may also be known through the events of history, which are believed to reflect a divine plan. The teaching that we are made "in the image of God" is understood to imply that, just as God is ultimately unknowable and infinite, so there is an aspect to ourselves which is similar: our inner essence or soul is unknowable in its totality. The goal of human endeavor becomes one of emulating the divine nature, which is essentially compassionate. Treating one's neighbor with respect and love is a means of manifesting the divine image in society.

Converts to Judaism

While not an actively proselytizing religion, Judaism has always accepted serious converts. Hillel's aphorism indicates the importance of study for one who wishes to convert. It is not sufficient for a convert to feel an affinity for Judaism, or simply to profess its beliefs: only through study of the Torah and its ways will the individual gradually begin to understand from within themselves the real message of Judaism. It is for this reason that would-be converts to Judaism often find the going tough. They will invariably meet with rebuttals by rabbinical authorities, and will be expected to persevere in their intentions despite difficulties. This approach is intended to ensure that converts wish to embrace the religion, not simply through reasons of convenience or the needs of others, but through a deeply felt sense that Judaism is their true path. When Hillel said, "Now go and learn," he was stressing the critical importance of establishing your own connection with the lifeblood of Judaism – the Torah.

An antidote to ritualism

While the reasons for converting to Judaism can involve many individual factors, two seem to predominate. First,

The emphasis Judaism puts on family life, for instance in the sharing of the Friday evening meal, is something which many find attractive

converts often remark th[...]
Judaism, as the olde[...]
monotheistic religion, [...]
somehow close to the sour[...]
of revelation. They express [...]
empathy with its emphasis [...]
the oneness of God witho[...]
any kind of intermedia[...]
figure. The second factor is t[...]
way of life that Judais[...]
promotes. Judaism reach[...]
into all of an individual's li[...]
there is no place for "secul[...]
compartments.

A spiritual attitude idea[...]
permeates all activity [...]
implied by the central [...] [...]rd
before me contin[...]dly
holistic[...] the
world[...]ish
ritua[...] or

A 16th-century woodblock print of a Rabbi studying the Torah. Jewish traditions have always placed great emphasis on rabbinical authority

bodily activity is seen as part of the plan of creation. Many converts are also particularly attracted by the role the Jewish way of life plays in unifying the family and giving it a sense of purpose and value. They seek an antidote to the apparent nihilism in Western society, which seems to be daily breaking down under the unremitting force of materialism and egotistical desire. To them, Judaism offers a more rooted, more hopeful, and ultimately much more fulfilling message.

BIBLICAL HISTORY

The father of Judaism is the biblical Abraham. Although the name "Judaism" derives from the tribe of Judah, which comes later in biblical history, the central characteristics by which Judaism defines itself are found in the life of Abraham and his relationship with God.

The story of Avram, whose name was later changed to Abraham, begins when he hears and responds to the calling of God: "Now the Lord said to Avram, Get thee out of thy country, and from thy kindred, and from thy father's house, to the land that I will show thee. And I will make of thee a great nation, and I will bless thee, and make thy name great, and thou shalt be a blessing. And I will bless them that bless thee, and curse him that curses thee. And in thee shall all the families of the earth be blessed" (*Genesis 12: 1-3*).

Abraham recognizes the One God, rejects the idolatry which had been practiced by his father and country, and follows God's instructions to remove himself from the influence of idolatry. Here we see a central tenet of Judaism:

The Jewish patriarch Jacob's dream of a ladder to Heaven, shown in a woodblock print from a German Bible of 1494

individuals must make the first move in matters spiritual by themselves, but once they have initiated such change then God responds and furthers their endeavors.

The Sea of Galilee, part of the Promised Land to which Moses led the Jewish people according to the Hebrew Bible, now part of modern-day Israel

The Tomb of the Patriarchs of Abraham, Isaac, and Jacob

The theme of the

The overt theme of the Heb— —ng. Here, at the origin of Judai— —en introduced. Abraham will j— —ed by impure spirituality, but t— —or- ical dimension is also conv— —The Hebrew words translated a— —lso have the literal meaning "g— —y is inward as well as outward.— —but that the intention of this c— —uld "know and perfect himself"— —ell as to those who would foll—

Abraham's grandson, — —ose families become the 12 trib— —the name given to Jacob by Go— —to Egypt where, several ge— —me enslaved. Then begins the — —the Children of Israel from Egy— —the journey to the promised lan— —bes attain a level of responsibilit— —on.

Moses as leader and intermediary

Central to such an idea of nationhood is the experience of receiving the revelation from God on Mount Sinai, for the unification of the people is dependent on their role in the divine plan. Moses, God's chosen agent, is both leader for the journey and intermediary between the people and God. The journey to freedom is personal, as well as historical, for it echoes the individual Jew's quest for closeness to God. The journey leads through the desert, symbolizing a turning away from the everyday world with all its distractions in order to find inner strengths.

The kingdom attained

The Hebrew Bible further chronicles the growth of Israel as a kingdom. It celebrates the role of its kings, and more especially its prophets, in maintaining the spiritual way of life instituted through Moses. King David established Jerusalem as the capital of Israel, and his son, Solomon, built the First Temple, completing it around 950 B.C.E. In 586 B.C.E. this temple was destroyed by the Babylonians, who took the Jews into captivity. A second temple was built in 515 B.C.E., but it was not until the time of Ezra and Nehemia, several decades later, that its central role was re-established.

POST-BIBLICAL HISTORY

The defining moment in the development of Judaism, as it is practiced today, came in 70 C.E. when the Second Temple was destroyed by the Romans. The teaching of the Pharisees (Rabbis), stressing the importance of scholarship and religious observance in home and synagogue, had been growing in influence and, following the loss of the Temple, became the dominant expression of Judaism. Rabbi Yohanan ben Zakkai escaped the ruins of Jerusalem and gathered disciples at Yavneh, on the Mediterranean coast of Israel. These Rabbis established the definitive teachings and legal system associated with the Torah. Their tradition culminated in the composition of the Mishna, and the Babylonian and Jerusalem Talmuds.

Although Judaism became a religion exiled from its geographical center, these scholarly works continually connected prayer and other religious observances back to the earlier Temple period. Thus the continuity of the tradition, reaching back to God's revelation at Sinai, was upheld. As the Jews became a people in exile, so their religion survived precisely because it mirrored that exile; the Rabbis foresaw the need not only for portability but also for a sense of continuity with what had gone before.

By the close of the Roman period, Jews had spread along the Mediterranean coast of North Africa and throughout most of Europe. The talmudic period was succeeded by that of the Geonim (singular: Gaon), who exercised leadership

---

The Jewish diaspora is the name given to the dispersal of the Jews from Israel from biblical times onward. Although Jewish communities were established all over Europe, the Jews remained outsiders

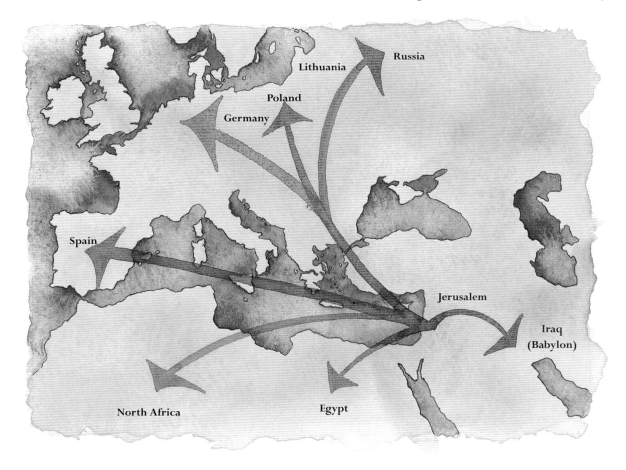

throughout the diaspora (dis███████████████e 6th to the 11th centuries. ████████████████n Babylon (Iraq) but receive████████████████n communities throughout the██████████████er-petuated the rabbinic schola██████████████████e authority of the Talmud throughout the Jewish world. The most important Gaon was Sa'adiah (882–942 C.E.) who wrote works of philosophy, mysticism and grammar, as well as the earliest significant systematic digests of law. Despite the regulating influence of such leaders, the customs of different Jewish communities became diverse, most notably between the Sefardic communities of north Africa and Spain and the Ashkenazic communities in northern Europe.

A golden age

A particularly creative period for Judaism came in Muslim Spain from the 10th century to the end of the 12th. This rare period of inter-religious tolerance ████████████████ing which Jewish poets, physicia████████████████ed. The period of harmony w█████████████████ian rulers, Ferdinand and Isabe████████████████the Jews. This event ranks alor███████████████of Jerusalem and the 20th-cen███████████████and enormity of its impact on J███

Perhaps the greatest J███████████████des (1135–1204), was born in███████████████ced to flee. In addition to his pl██████████████ab-

██████████████ story include the Jews' enslavement in
██████████████ establishment of Jerusalem

binical thought with Aristotelian logic, he wrote a highly influential work, codifying Jewish law, called the Mishneh Torah. In terms of logical organization, clarity of ideas and beauty of language, this work remains one of the pinnacles of Jewish achievement. The other towering achievement of the medieval period came in France from the pen of Rabbi Shlomo ben Yizhak (1040–1105), also known as Rashi. Rashi's lucid commentary on the Babylonian Talmud is unrivaled, and his biblical commentaries remain authoritative.

Even as Rashi was writing, his community was under attack from the Crusaders. Destruction and expulsions from countries of Western Europe led to further movements of the Jews. By the 17th century the centre of Jewish life was in Poland and Lithuania, where great talmudic centres flourished and the popular movement of modern Hasidism was born. Its founder, Baal Shem Tov (1700–1760), brought a potent blend of mysticism and joyous practice to his followers.

As minorities in the lands of Europe, the Jews were inevitably outsiders. The way they were demonized in Christian cultures, however, testifies to a hatred more deep-seated than that reserved for other outsiders. With rare exceptions, the Jews were, at best, treated with contempt; at worst they were subjected to forced conversion, pogroms, expulsions and murder. Complex psychological and religious forces generated a scarred cultural landscape, which climaxed tragically in the events of the 20th century.

THE LAND OF ISRAEL

"By the rivers of Babylon, there we sat down, we also wept, when we remembered Zion ... How shall we sing the Lord's song in a foreign land?" (*Psalm 137*).

The Hebrew Bible emphasizes that the relationship between the people of Israel and the Land of Israel is integral to the divine plan. When, therefore, the Jews found themselves in exile in Babylon (in the 6th century B.C.E.), it was not simple nostalgia which motivated the above lament, but a realization that the intended relationship with God was no longer possible. Although some Jews remained in Israel (as they have done throughout history),

The flag of the state of Israel – created on 14 May 1948 – flies over the pilgrims gathered to celebrate the Passover in Jerusalem

the majority were cut off from their spiritual home, and the yearning for a return to the Land of Israel accompanied the Jews throughout their various dispersions. Israel, Jerusalem in particular, has always played a central role in Jewish prayer and the celebration of festivals. Indeed rabbinical literature continually stresses the relation between religious observance and the holiness of Israel. Zionism is therefore rooted in the religion.

It was a secular Jew, however, who injected a new vitality into Zionism in the 19th century. Theodore Herzl (1860-1904), a journalist, witnessed the rise in anti-Semitism in the German-speaking world in the 1880s. Following the Dreyfus affair in France, in 1895, he realized that a Jewish homeland offered the only secure future for his people. The French army officer Alfred Dreyfus, Jewish by birth, had been prosecuted on trumped-up charges, and, despite his

David Ben-Gurion, the Polish ———————————
first prime minister, he ———————

innocence, he was public———————————— case
for his newspaper, Herzl ———————————— d's
hysterical screams of "Dea—————————

Forging the mod———————
Herzl's book, *The Jewish S*————————— nd,
as support for his ideas be————————— der
of the Zionist movement. F————————— vish
people, lobbying political ————————— to
subsidize immigration to ————————— the
British, then rulers of Pa—————————
Declaration which asserte—————————
the establishment of a ————————
Palestine. Chaim Weizmann————————
to become Israel's first p——————
mental in winning this de————

  Turning the declarat—————————
was extremely problema—————————
tensions and hostility ramp—————

Many hoped that the treaty s—————
and the Palestinians in 1993—————
in the Middle East, but the l———
President Rabin showed that t————

and Jews in Palestine. A plan to partition Palestine was drawn up and passed by the United Nations (UN) in 1947, leading to the establishment of the state of Israel in 1948, with David Ben-Gurion (1886–1973) as its first prime minister. No sooner had the state been declared than it was invaded by the forces of its Arab neighbors. In this, and subsequent wars, the Arabs pursued their avowed intention of removing Israel from the Middle-Eastern map and driving the Jews into the sea. Israel, however, survived and absorbed immigrants from around the world, especially from regions where persecution was strong. Israeli society comprises a rich mixture of diverse Jewish cultures.

  Following the Six Day War of 1967, Israel occupied territories which had been ceded to Arab countries within the UN plan. These Occupied Territories have been the focus of Jewish-Arab tensions ever since, with Israel viewing them as necessary to her security and Arabs struggling to regain hegemony. In 1993, Israeli prime minister Yitzhak Rabin and Yassir Arafat, chairman of the Palestine Liberation Organization (PLO), signed a peace treaty granting limited autonomy for Palestinians in the previously Occupied Territories and timetabling a withdrawal of Israeli troops. Sadly, in 1995 Rabin became the first Israeli prime minister to be assassinated, a sign of the continuing tension over the security implications of the peace accord.

THE TORAH

The Torah, or Pentateuch, comprises the first five books of the Hebrew Bible (the Christian Old Testament). The Hebrew word *torah* derives from a root meaning "direction," or "teaching," reflecting the belief that all of God's teaching is contained within the Torah. More than merely a repository of laws and stories, it is viewed as the inner, or spiritual, dimension to the world itself, the medium through which the individual may gain access to higher realms. Indeed, a statement in the Mishnah (*see below*) counsels, "Turn it around, turn it around, for all is in it." The transcendent status of the Torah is further emphasized by the teaching that the Torah was pre-existent, and was employed by God as a blueprint for creation.

It is one of the beliefs of Orthodox Judaism that the entire Jewish people had a direct experience of God at Mount Sinai when He gave the Torah to Moses. The revelation is said to include not only the five books (the Written Torah) but also the insights and legal details allied to the scriptural text which were passed on orally (the Oral Torah) until they were finally written down by the Rabbis in the Mishnah and the Talmud. In introducing the revelation, the Torah itself records that "God spoke all these words" (*Exodus 20:1*). Since, for Judaism, the Torah is the perfect expression of the perfect divine mind, the Rabbis held that every word and letter was included for a specific purpose. The word "all" in the quotation above was therefore understood as showing the all-inclusive nature of the revelation: "even the answers to questions which wise men would ask their teachers in the future did God reveal to Moses" (Midrash).

Hidden meanings

This attitude of absolute reverence towards the text of the Torah means that every spare or unusual word, or even a strange spelling, becomes a hook for imaginative homilies or expansive details of law. In the story of Adam's creation, for example, the Torah uses the word *vayiizer*, meaning "formed," in which one of the letters is doubled. This dou-

Much Jewish ritual is centered around reverence for the Torah, whose contents provide the basis for religious and social conduct

bled letter has been interpreted as showing things about the inner nature of Adam, including his gender duality, his possession of two inclinations – one for good and one for evil, and his participation in both higher and lower worlds: "Behold, I will create him in My image and likeness; thus he will be of the character of celestial beings but he will pro-

Top: *Study of the Torah and its commentaries
is a central obligation in Judaism*
Above: *The reverence with which the Torah is regarded
is reflected in the ornaments which decorate the scroll covers*

best translated as "The Way," for it derives from the word meaning "to walk." Details of Halakhah were established by the Rabbis in their intense oral debates over the nuances of meaning in the written Torah. Halakhah covers all paths of life, comprising civil and legal law as well as religious and social conduct.

Weekly portions of the Torah are read aloud in the synagogue. The Torah scrolls used in the synagogue are "dressed" in covers and ornaments. The scrolls are stored in an ark at the front of the synagogue, and ceremonially brought to the centre of the congregation for the reading, symbolizing the need to keep the Torah and its teachings in the heart of the community. Indeed, the final letter of the Torah combined with the first forms the word *lev* (heart), showing that the continuity of the Torah maintains the heart of Israel and Judaism.

create as is the nature of t_____ This interpretative literature, _____ ethical teachings and include_____ the stories contained in the T____

The Law

The Torah includes God_____ct of humankind, and is, acc_____ "the Law." Judaism refers to su_____rhaps

THE MIDRASH

In the biblical story, Abraham's faith is tested when God requires him to sacrifice his beloved son, Isaac. At the last moment Isaac is reprieved and a ram takes his place. The biblical text simply states that Abraham took Isaac, wood for the sacrificial fire, and "rose up and went." But what conflicts must have afflicted him! In the Midrash the source of the test becomes Satan. The following text, compiled from the Midrash, shows how the Rabbis grappled with this difficult story.

"'And it happened after these things that God tested Abraham' (*Genesis 22:1*). The word *achar* (after) also means 'behind,' and implies the involvement of Satan.

Satan said to God, 'Master of the Universe, You gave this man a son when he was one hundred. Has he acknowledged Your role in the miraculous birth with a gift of sacrifice?' God replied, 'Even were I to require him to sacrifice his son, he would immediately do it!'

During the journey Satan appeared to Abraham as an old man. 'Where are you going?' Satan inquired. 'To pray,' replied Abraham. 'Nonsense,' Satan continued, 'otherwise why would you carry fire, a knife and wood?' 'Perhaps we shall stay a few days and need to kill animals and cook them,' came Abraham's answer. Satan, however, persisted: 'Old man, I was there when The Holy One, blessed be He, requested you to take your son. You're completely insane to proceed with this.' 'Nevertheless, I must do it,' Abraham asserted.

Later Satan appeared again. 'You say that God told you to do this dastardly deed. How do you know it was really God speaking; it may have been a false prophecy?' 'I know what I know,' said Abraham. 'But how do you know?

Abraham's willingness to sacrifice his only son is a key example in Judaism of the power of faith to overcome doubt

You may have misinterpreted God's intent. After all, should you go ahead, God Himself will call you a murderer, and you will be guilty.' 'Nevertheless, I must do it,' Abraham insisted.

'And what next? Will there be a further test, more terrible than this? When will you say no? And think of the effect on other people. You will break your wife's heart. Moreover, what of your work as a spiritual teacher? You have brought many to recognition of the One true God, but when they hear what you have done they will deny you and your teaching.' 'Nevertheless, I must do it.'

Unable to dissuade Abraham with words, Satan returned again, this time in the form of a mighty river. Abraham immediately stepped into the water. When the water reached his neck, he turned his eyes heavenwards, 'Master of the Universe, you chose me and said: "I am One and you are One, and through you shall My Name be known in my world, so now offer up your son!" I did not hold back and behold, I am now engaged in Your command. But look, the waters endanger our lives. Should we drown, who will fulfill Your word and who will unify Your Name?' The Holy One, blessed be He, answered him then: 'By your life, through you My Name will indeed be unified in the world!' Immediately He rebuked Satan. The river dried up and he stood on dry land."

In this passage, the Rabbis externalize in Satan the kinds of thought processes which might accompany spiritual challenges; and if the thoughts are silenced, the doubts can confront people in concrete physical terms, here depicted as the river. The gushing waters symbolize unconscious doubts rooted so deeply they cannot even be articulated. The Midrash thus asserts the role of faith and integrity in the face of doubt.

...urtle decorating this 13th-century Hebrew
...the potential for symbolic readings of the text

JEWISH MYSTICISM

The Torah is held to comprise four levels of meaning: the literal (*peshat*), the allegorical (*remez*), the homiletical (*derash*), and the secret or mystical. The central command of Judaism, to be immersed in the study and implications of Torah, therefore leads ultimately to mysticism. Mystical interpretations view the Torah as depicting God and his attributes in all their many manifestations and inter-relationships. It is in this sense that the great writer Nachmanides (1190–1270) writes that the whole Torah, as understood in conjunction with the oral tradition, is a composite of the Names of God. By penetrating to this level of understanding, the mystic gains knowledge of the true nature of God.

The long hard road to becoming a rabbinical scholar begins at a tender age with mastery of ancient Hebrew

The most influential strand of Jewish mysticism, the Kabbalah, conceives of God's attributes as a series of ten *sefirot*, or spheres, through which the supernatural influence from the most concealed divine source reaches our world. Jewish mystics gain knowledge of this system both through study of mystical meanings in the Torah and by meditating on individual sefirot.

Additionally, the commandments and prayers are seen as expressing the inner dynamics of this sefirotic system. All aspects of outer reality and human subjectivity are ultimately mere expressions of the sefirot which constitute the deepest reality, our contact with the divine.

The central text of the Kabbalah is the *Zohar*, which was first circulated in Spain in the 13th century. It portrays the tenth *sefirah* as being the feminine dimension of God, known as Shekhinah, which has become dissociated from the King (the male aspect of God). In this imagery the role of the Jewish people, and most especially the mystics, is to encourage a restoration of the union between these two aspects of the Godhead.

The shofar, a musical instrument mentioned in the Bible and made from a ram's horn, is sounded to announce Rosh Hashanah, the New Year

Forms of meditat[illegible]

Meditations known as *yich*[illegible] as taught by the 16th-century [illegible] key role in this aim. Such yich[illegible] cti-tioner to seek withdrawa[illegible] ss, with its emphasis on the se[illegible] ely on mental images associate[illegible]

In many cases such ima[illegible] ons of the Hebrew letters in [illegible] sm involving the Hebrew lett[illegible] est branches of the Jewish tra[illegible] ich has existed in written for[illegible] ury C.E., attempts to plumb t[illegible] ese letters. It proposes that G[illegible] the letters as His agents: "He e[illegible] ut, weighed and transforme[illegible] and formed through them … a[illegible]

The mystic's path beco[illegible] ork of God. The letters are "en[illegible] the inner screen of the med[illegible] ous thoughts are kept at bay as the work of permuting them begins. Because the mystic believes the letters to be the agents of God's work, a special kind of closeness to God may be achieved. Abulafia (1240–*c*1291), one of the foremost advocates of this kind of mystical technique, writes that it "aids the soul to actualize its potential with much greater ease than any other means."

The visionary Ba'al Shem Tov (1700–1760) became the leader of a popular mystical movement, Hasidism, which flowered in the late 18th century and continues to command a large following, both in Israel and abroad, to this day. Hasidism grafted ecstatic song, dance, and story-telling onto the older meditative and scholarly aspects of the Kabbalah. In recent years a renewed interest in mysticism has paralleled the widespread interest in meditation and psychological processes, as part of the change from a scientific world view towards more holistic perspectives.

Rabbinic scholars immerse themselves in studying the interpretations of leading rabbinical authorities

THE ZOHAR

This extract is from the *Zohar*, the central text of the Kabbalah, which is believed to be the mystical teachings of Rabbi Simeon bar Yochai and his followers, who lived in the Land of Israel in the 2nd–3rd centuries C.E.

"How confused are the people of the world in their understanding, failing to see the path of truth in the Torah! The Torah calls to them each day with love, but they do not even turn their heads towards her. When the Torah uncovers a matter, it is revealed for a moment but is immediately concealed again. Such revelation is granted only to those who know her and are capable of recognizing her value.

To what may this be compared? It is like a woman, beautiful, gracious, and much loved, who is kept confined in her palace. She has a special lover whom nobody knows, for he is hidden. Out of his love for her, he constantly passes by the entrance to her house, searching on all sides. She knows that it is her lover who is always roaming at the entrance to her house. What does she do? She opens a secret opening in the palace where she dwells and reveals her face to her lover, only to withdraw immediately and become concealed again. No-one in her lover's vicinity sees or understands. Only her lover knows, and he yearns for her with his whole being, heart and soul, for he knows that it was out of her love for him that she revealed herself to him for one moment in order to awaken his love.

So it is with the Torah. She reveals herself only to her lover. The Torah knows that a wise man walks at the entrance to her house every day. What does she do? She reveals her face to him from her palace and shows him a hint. Immediately she withdraws to her palace and hides. Nobody there knows or understands. He alone knows and his whole being yearns for her. In this way does the Torah reveal and conceal herself, bringing love to her lover in order to awaken his love.

Come and see! This is the way of the Torah. At first, when she begins to reveal herself to someone she gives him a hint. If he understands, it is well, but if he does not understand she sends to him and calls him a fool. The Torah says to her messenger, 'Tell that fool to come here that I may speak to him.' Thus is it written (*Proverbs 9:4,5*) 'Whoever is foolish, let him turn here;' he that lacks understanding, she says to him: 'Come, eat of my bread, drink of the wine which I have prepared.' He comes to her and she begins to speak with him through the curtain she has drawn before him. She speaks words commensurate with his understanding so that he might progress one step at a time. This is derash (homiletical interpretation).

Then she talks with him through a very fine veil, discussing enigmatic subjects. This is *haggadah* (archetypal narrative). And then, when he has become more familiar with her, she reveals herself to him face to face, and speaks of all her concealed mysteries and hidden paths which she had kept hidden in her heart from ancient times. Then he becomes a whole man, a true master of Torah, the lord of the house, for she has revealed to him all her secrets, nothing remains covered or withheld.

She says to him: 'You saw the hint I gave you at the beginning. Now you see how many mysteries it contains.' He realizes then that nothing may be added to, nor subtracted from, these words [of the Torah]. The real meaning (peshat) of the scriptural text is then apparent, that one should not add or subtract even a single letter.

Thus, a person must be ever alert and pursue Torah in order to become her lover, as I have explained."

When praying in the synagogue, men wear prayer shawls and cover their heads as a mark of respect

THE POWER OF PRAYER

Prayer and contemplation

The Hebrew for "to pray" – *lehit-palel* – is a reflexive form of the verb "to judge." Prayer is thus a form of self-judgement or analysis. But, in Jewish thought, this is only possible through the agency of God, so prayer is the medium of connection to the higher spheres. The rabbis viewed prayer as a continuation of the process of sacrifice as practiced in the Jerusalem Temple which was believed to have effected communion between this earthly realm and the heavenly one. The talmudic sage, Rabbi Eleazer, taught, however, that prayer is greater than either good deeds or sacrifices. It was accepted that prayer had biblical origins. The morning, afternoon, and evening prayers were said to have been initiated by Abraham, Isaac, and Jacob respectively.

The Talmud defines prayer as "the service of the heart," which is taken to mean that concentration on inner intent

The Western Wall is all that now remains of the Second Temple in Jerusalem

For daily prayer, Jewish men p...
tefillin (two leather boxes...

is essential. Bahya ibn Pek... ...)
explains: "Words are a matt... ...g
is a matter of the heart. The ... ...e
prayer, but the meaning is li... ...

Meditation

Bahya suggests that the mean... ...d
to words alone. Ideally, a p... ...se
distracting thoughts from th... ...r
itself. Maimonides writes that... ...d
of all other thoughts and rega... ...g
before the Divine Presence." ... ...d
not be a fixed, mechanical p... ...d
and direct appeal to God.

In prayer, particular atte... ...g
verse of the Shema and the ... ...h.
The former is a declaration ... ...n
of love between ourselves a... ...of
the Shema affirms that God... ...d
immanent aspects is eternal... ...t
prayer, offering the closest ... ...n
humankind and God. The firs... ...d
and God of our Fathers," stat... ...e

that your own spiritual experience must be aligned with
the tradition established by Abraham, Isaac and Jacob.

Private devotion

All prayer services close with the hope that the messianic
age will arrive soon, when all humanity will be united and
"On that day the Lord shall be One and His name One."

Throughout daily life a sense of the spiritual is engen-
dered through *berakhot*, blessings. The Orthodox Jew is
expected to recite at least one hundred blessings each day.
For example, whether eating an item of food, washing hands,
or witnessing a beautiful natural scene, you utter an appropriate blessing. Blessings are in the present tense, affirming
the belief that God continually creates the world anew. The
blessing functions both to focus consciousness on the target
action and to draw holiness into this world. The Hebrew
word *berekh* means "knee" and the *berakhah* expresses both
human humility and the bountiful act of God in bending
His influence down into the world.

After putting on the tallit *and* tefillin, *worshippers follow the service
using the* siddur *(prayer book) and* humash *(Torah text)*

SHABBAT AND FESTIVALS

The emulation of God is an exalted goal in Judaism. The 2nd-century C.E. disciple, Ben Azzai, declared that the greatest principle of the Torah was the statement that Adam was made in the likeness of God (*Genesis 5:1*). This likeness becomes actualized through emulation of God's ways. Jews therefore cease from creative work on Shabbat, the seventh day, "for in six days the Lord made heaven and earth and on the seventh day he rested, and was refreshed" (*Exodus 31:17*). The Hebrew for "refreshed" – *vayinafash* – implies "soul" (*nefesh*), conveying the idea that Shabbat is a day set aside for spiritual work. In a deeper sense, Shabbat, as a day of recollection of the work of Creation, reminds Jews that the work of Creation is ongoing. By observing Shabbat, Jews align themselves with this purpose, cementing their sense of partnership with God.

Observing Shabbat

The Halakhah expands on the Torah's instructions for Shabbat, describing all the practical ways in which it is observed. The Orthodox tradition tends to interpret these ways more rigorously than those adopted by non-Orthodox approaches. Jews of differing persuasions may therefore have different practices. For Orthodox Judaism, the definition

Hanukkah, the festival of light, commemorates the purification and rededication of the Temple in 165 B.C.E.

of creative work includes all activity resulting in any tangible change of state, including, for example, turning on electrical appliances. Shabbat is associated with a joyous atmosphere generated through songs and festive meals, and generally offers time for study of the Torah and other religious works.

During Shabbat, and all Jewish festivals, the role of the family is paramount. Rabbis compare the family meal table to the altar in the Temple, thereby emphasizing its importance as a spiritual focus. During the spring festival of Pesach (Passover) a symbolic re-enactment of the slavery of the Children of Israel in Egypt, and their redemption by God, takes place at the family table. This *seder* meal conveys the importance of education: the participation of children is encouraged during the retelling of the Exodus story. Throughout Pesach no leavened bread or other food is eaten. Instead, Jews eat *matzah*, the unleavened "bread of affliction."

Purim, usually falling in March, celebrates the success of Queen Esther and her uncle, Mordechai, in averting the first recorded attempt to destroy the Jewish people. This occurred in Persia, as described in the biblical Book of Esther. A joyous festival, it is marked by giving gifts and dressing up to create a carnival atmosphere. Hanukkah, in December, records the victory of the Jewish spirit in fighting off the inroads of paganism in the 2nd century B.C.E.

Jews believe that these festivals are not merely celebrations of events long past; they are opportunities to relive those events in the present and to reflect on their continuing significance. They are gateways into a dimension of time in which the sacred history of Judaism is eternally present.

As illustrated in this 15th-century manuscript, for hundreds of years Jews have commemorated Pesach (Passover) by sharing a meal of unleavened bread and retelling the story of the Exodus

Remembering the

The events of the Exodus _____ the festivals of Shavuot, the ann_____ of Torah at Mount Sinai, and_____ n given by God during the C_____ in the desert is recalled. Thr_____ festivals, the Exodus fro_____ mentioned as a reminder o_____ Jewish people, and also to_____ treating all people with the_____

Rosh Hashanah, the New_____ is a time for reflection, w_____ emphasized. Teshuvah, fror_____ implies returning to ways o_____ self of harmful character tr_____ culminates in Yom Kippur, _____ a fast that lasts for 25 hour

THE SEEKER OF TRUTH

The following story is a Jewish folktale which is variously thought to have originated in Afghanistan or Eastern Europe. It forms part of the rich story-telling tradition of Hasidism.

A man once set out on a journey seeking truth. In a dream he was told that a special ability would help him – he would be able to see a glow surrounding any place or person where truth might be found.

His journey took him through countless villages and cities, and he encountered many who claimed to have truth to impart. But the more they spoke with him, the more any glow faded. His strength was sapped, and he became despondent. One day he saw a glowing forest in the distance. As he drew closer, it seemed to him that the trees were alight, so bright was the glow. At last, he felt, his quest would be successful. He wandered in the forest for many days until, finally, he saw a hut which glowed so intensely that he realized it must be the source of the whole light of the forest. Speedily he approached the door and knocked. There was no answer, but the door was not locked, so he entered.

The lamp tender

A sight greeted him the like of which he had never seen. Everywhere he looked – on the floors, in cupboards, on shelves – burned a myriad of oil lights. The flames flickered and danced. He was so mesmerized by the glow and the plethora of different lights that he failed to notice an old man in a white robe approach him. "May I help you?" asked the old man; "What is it you seek?"

"I am searching for truth," the other replied, hurriedly trying to regain his composure.

The old man drew close, and looked into his eyes. "Truth?" He paused. It seemed that the glow was emanating

not only from the flames, ▢▢▢▢▢▢▢▢▢▢▢ this old man. "Are you sure?"

"Yes," he replied, and h▢▢▢▢▢▢▢▢▢▢en searching for what seemed ▢▢▢▢▢▢▢▢▢ had never seen anything like th▢▢▢▢▢▢▢▢ts. What were they for?

The old man gestured ▢▢▢▢▢▢▢▢▢ly. "These are soul lamps. Each ▢▢▢▢▢▢▢▢ile it keeps burning, the person▢▢▢▢▢▢▢▢es out, he departs this life."

The lamp of the soul

Then the man who sought ▢▢▢▢▢▢▢▢ild see the lamp of his own so▢▢▢▢▢▢▢ a corner and pointed to a rust▢▢▢▢▢▢▢tle oil left. As the flame flickere▢▢▢▢▢▢n. Was he about to die, or wa▢▢▢▢▢▢n- tion wandered to the neighb▢▢▢▢▢ng and its tin full with oil. "An▢▢▢▢▢g. "To whom does it belong?"

"I cannot answer" said the old man. "I can reveal a lamp's owner to the owner alone." With that he disappeared from the room, and the man was left on his own.

The man's eyes were transfixed by his lamp. There seemed to be only a few drops of oil remaining. The light of the neighboring lamp forced itself again into his attention, the flame so bright, the oil so full. An idea flashed like quicksilver into his mind. Glancing around to ensure that he was definitely alone, he reached out and grasped the full tin. As he held it ready to pour oil into his own lamp, he suddenly felt himself held by the iron grip of powerful hands.

"Truth?" The old man's questioning eyes pierced him through. "Are you sure? Is it indeed truth you seek . . . or is it merely your own self?"

When the seeker of truth turned around, all had gone. He was alone in the forest, with only the wind's lament to disturb his solitude.

The dramatic beauty of the Israeli landscape looking south toward the Red Sea

CONFUCIANISM

Do not impose "" on others what you do not desire

Confucian teachings and values have had a crucial influence on the moral, social and religious life of traditional societies in China, Korea, Japan, and Taiwan, and they have influenced the beliefs and values of Chinese settlers all over the world. Confucian teachings stress loyalty, humanity, integrity, filial piety, ritual correctness, respect for tradition, personal self-restraint, harmonious family and social relationships, and respect for teachers. In Imperial China, Confucian officials regulated the traditional rites of passage, and all aspects of public behavior. For the educated few, Confucianism offered the way to ethical sagehood.

The term "Confucian" ▓▓▓▓▓▓▓▓ the name of the Chinese ▓▓▓▓▓▓ 479 B.C.E.). The common ▓▓▓▓ of traditional values and hum▓▓▓▓▓ ar;" educated followers of the ▓▓▓▓▓ *ju chia*. In the West, a range o▓▓▓▓▓ ena and traditions are, confu▓▓▓▓▓ The word is used to describe th▓▓▓▓▓ ung Fu Tzu, any Chinese cor▓▓▓▓▓ ues, scholars trained in the Co▓▓▓▓▓ to the official examination p▓▓▓▓▓ and those who, in imperial tin▓▓▓▓▓ the effectiveness of the state c▓▓▓▓▓ in annual sacrifices.

The term "Neo-Confu▓▓▓▓▓ ners who refined and develope▓▓▓▓▓ 1th century C.E. onward. Teac▓▓▓▓▓ 200 C.E.) and Wang Yang-min▓▓▓▓▓ ined

Dating from the Qing dynasty (1644–1912), this scene from the life of Confucius (551–479 B.C.E.) emphasizes the courtly origins of the Confucian school of ethics

Confucian teachings with elements of traditional Chinese cosmology and elements of Taoist and Buddhist theory. These syntheses became the dominant intellectual and ethical influences in China, Korea, and Japan from late medieval times until the mid-19th century.

With the collapse of imperial China in 1911, the Confucian state cult and official examination system based on the Confucian Classics were no longer sustainable. However, the values contained in the Classics continue to be respected by Confucian traditionalists, and Confucian teaching has so deeply permeated the fabric of Chinese society that, even under Communism, the great majority of Chinese people hold values that were first articulated by Confucius and his followers.

ETHICS, SOCIETY, AND RELIGION

Confucius was not the founder of a religion but a would-be social and ethical reformer. He turned to teaching in the hope that his students would implement his ideas once they gained office in the feudal states of Chou-dynasty China. While he was skeptical of, or indifferent to, many of the traditional religious ideas of his day, he was a firm advocate of filial piety and ancestor rites.

Confucius felt a sense of mission, which he derived from T'ien (Heaven), a power which he regarded as a positive moral force (*te*), and on which he relied at times of personal threat or political failure. It is clear that he was not a total sceptic, but though he had a developed sense of a sacred power, he understood this in specifically moral terms. Not all later Confucian scholars have subscribed to such an interpretation of T'ien, but it is unquestionably present in both the Analects (the writings of Confucius) and in the teachings of his disciple Mencius (Meng Tzu 371–289 B.C.E.).

Confucius saw himself primarily as an educator and transmitter of knowledge, rather than as a creative thinker. Unfortunately, his rather modest self-assessment has led later interpreters to treat him, sometimes dismissively, as a rather prosaic and straight-laced moralist, or even as an apologist for unreformed values and institutions.

Moral insights

From the 19th century, and particularly during the anti-Confucian campaigns of Mao Tse Tung's "Cultural Revolution" (1966–1972), a strongly negative image of Confucius and his teaching was current among many Chinese. Confucius was seen as the symbol of unreconstructed conservatism, and of submissiveness to outdated authority. Even recent Confucians, and scholars sympathetic to Confucian traditions, have not sufficiently acknowledged the challenge and originality of his moral insights, bearing in mind the context of the society in which they were developed.

Confucius appears to have been prepared to teach students for a minimal fee without regard to their social and economic status. The Confucian formulation of the "Golden Rule" is a good example.

Tzu kung asked: 'Is there a single word which can be a guide to conduct throughout one's life?' The master said: 'It is perhaps the word shu (reciprocity). Do not impose on others what you do not desire.'

Such teaching is commonplace in later Confucian moralizing; but in the context of a China divided into warring states, when many rulers exercised power with ruthless

brutality, and when the noti███████████████ct, extending across social and███████████████ vas unknown, then its radical i███████████████

Many of the key term███████████████ of Confucius, and in later Cor███████████████ to have been redefined by the m███████████████us, for example, the term *jen* ███████████████vo-lence) was applied to relati███████████████hin specific social groups, usua███████████████For Confucius it becomes a ke███████████████ to describe an attitude reflect███████████████ any social or class boundaries.

Similarly, the term te (force) had described the exercise of power, often in a political context, with no connotation of a moral dimension to such a function. In the Analects, te refers specifically to morally authenticating power or moral character. The term *li*, for ritual action, used to refer to formal rites and sacrifices correctly performed, was extended by Confucius to refer to the appropriate formalities which all interactions should embody.

The annual ceremony at Chang Myo in Korea, during which Confucian priests pay homage to the shrine of the rulers of the Yi Dynasty

CONFUCIAN WAY TO HARMONY

Confucius, and early Confucians such as Mencius (371–289 B.C.E.), believed that the moral force of humanity was ultimately derived from Heaven (T'ien). For ordinary people, who did not have direct access to Heaven, morality was pursued by careful attention to the rites and proprieties governing family and social relationships. The model and starting point was always the relationship with your parents and, by extension, your ancestors. Filial piety, respect for elders and for legitimate authority, as well as self-restraint, respect for classical Confucian learning, ritual and protocol, became characteristics of Confucianism in traditional Chinese societies.

In the Analects of Confucius the role of respect for parents, or filial piety, is emphasized as a virtue in its own right, and as the practical basis for maintaining an ordered and harmonious society.

"It is rare for a man whose character is such that he is good as a son and obedient as a young man to have the incli-

Almanacs and wall paintings reinforced the moral messages contained in exemplary tales of filial piety popular in the Tang dynasty (590–618 C.E.)

nation to transgress against [...]
of for one who is obedient [...]
rebellion. The gentleman v [...]
efforts to the roots; once t [...]
established, the Way will de [...]
a good son and an obedient [...]
root of a man's character."

Such ideas were syste [...]
developed by Confucian sc [...]
recorded in the Classic of [...]
which discusses the role o [...]
all levels of society and arg [...]
is the foundation of virt [...]
harmony, and good govern [...]

Exemplary tales

For the general education of [...]
lation as a whole, 24 exer [...] ere
published and widely distrib [...] ent
of mass printing in the T'an [...] ese
tales were frequently told t [...] acs
and found on the walls of C [...] les.
The tone and content of th [...] om
the following examples:

> *A dutiful boy, worried the [...]*
> *by mosquitoes, slept nake [...] e*
> *mosquitoes to feed on him [...]*

> *Another eight-year-old b [...]*
> *bed for them in winter, a [...] er*
> *to cool them.*

Charmingly naive tales s [...] ious
concept, touching on the [...] st in
this life, but in the spirit v [...] uals
that follow the death of a [...] d to
ensure the safe passage of [...] alm.
To make a safe transfer, [...] nale
descendants present at the [...] ffer-

*Respectful relationships between parents and children are
fundamental to Confucian notions of morality and the basis
of an orderly society*

ings. Before transfer, the soul has to be freed from the body
and must descend to the underworld to answer for its
conduct in life. Safe passage through the halls of the underworld requires worthy and meritorious conduct in life,
combined with assistance from the living mourners and
specialists in rituals – usually Buddhist monks and Taoist
priests. The living descendants make offerings of paper "spirit
money" as bribes to underworld officials, along with wine,
incens, and food to nourish the soul.

If someone is without descendants to attend to these
procedures, or if they die far from home or in tragic circumstances, then that person's soul may not make the transfer.
In such cases, rather than becoming a peaceful ancestor at
rest or enjoying heaven, the soul takes on increasingly *yin*
characteristics and becomes a lonely, hungry, potentially
troublesome ghost, causing illness and misfortune, especially to living relatives. Correctly observed funeral rites,
as well as regular offerings to the ancestors, are vital to the
success and safety of living family members.

MENCIUS ON MORALITY

Mencius is honored as the second greatest teacher after Confucius. He proposed a positive and optimistic ethic resting on the assumption that, in the right environment, human nature will tend towards goodness, and that humans are fully human when they co-operate and treat each other with respect. He maintained this belief despite the widespread violence, oppression, and injustice of his day. He remonstrated with rulers for causing suffering to their subjects, urging them to lead by setting the best possible example.

Mencius' basic argument for the innate moral capacity of all humans is set out very clearly in the following passage:

No man is devoid of a heart sensitive to the suffering of others. Such a sensitive heart was possessed by the Former Kings and this manifested itself in compassionate government. With such a sensitive heart behind compassionate government, it was as easy to rule the Empire as rolling it on your palm.

Mencius (371-289 B.C.E.) is honored as the second greatest teacher, after Confucius himself

Mencius cites a hypothetical case: anyone who sees a child about to fall into a well, would immediately react with alarm, concern and sympathy. He does not have to prove that everyone would leap to the rescue, merely that their initial reaction is concern. This, he argues, is the basis for human compassion and sympathy, and all humans have it. It is up to them to train and develop it through moral reflection and discipline. Mencius used such arguments to show the rulers of China how they had the moral capacity to institute just and compassionate government.

Nurturing compassion

In some passages Mencius provides clues as to how compassion, once it has been discovered, can be nurtured and developed into true benevolence (jen) through moral reflection (or meditation). Mencius develops the notion of *ch'i* (life force) as a fundamental factor in moral cultivation. For Mencius, the purpose of learning is to recover the lost mind/heart (*hsin*). Once the hsin is discovered, it becomes the means of moral reflection – a process of quietening and steadying the mind and focusing the will. This in turn controls the functioning of ch'i. According to Mencius, ch'i can actually be nurtured and accumulated by the sustained performance of moral acts in accordance with propriety (li).

What Mencius seems to be saying, is that stilling the mind and accumulating ch'i facilitates, and results in, the performance of correct behavior and moral acts. The efforts of the Confucianist are therefore to be devoted to the development of moral wisdom and sincere intentions which are at one with universal morality. This fusing of cosmo-logical, psychological, ethical, and political themes represents a tendency which became typical of much later Neo-Confucian thought.

...ng, home of the Chinese emperors, for whom
...eloped complex systems of divination

Confucianism taught that, while the emperor ruled justly and ensured his officials were upright and fair, then the cosmic, natural, and human order was maintained and Heaven's approval assured. However, if the emperor persistently failed in his duties, then cosmic and social disorder would follow, indicating Heaven's disapproval. Ultimately, this could lead to the withdrawal of the Heavenly Mandate and a change of dynasty. If order was restored, this was taken as an indication that Heaven approved of the new ruler, and the new dynasty could claim the Mandate of Heaven.

Since Heavenly forces do not communicate directly with people, the indicators of approval or disapproval were sought in the regularity of the seasons, the fertility of the land, and the security and orderliness of the people. So the

A late Chhing illustration of the legendary emperor Shun, the epitome of the good ruler who, according to Confucian teaching, is one who rises early and attends diligently to affairs of state

emperor and his Confucian-trained officials had a vested interest in the detailed monitoring of the climate, in celestial changes, in the condition of the land, and in the mood of the people.

The Theory of Portents

From the 2nd century B.C.E., the Han imperial bureaucracy established a sophisticated surveillance system for monitoring and recording all these processes. The Confucian scholar Tung Chung-shu devised the "Theory of Portents," a coding system for interpreting events and predicting changes. In a manner that is typically Confucian, Tung's system also reminded the emperor of his considerable moral and cosmic responsibilities.

"The ruler of men uses his love and hate, his joy and anger, to change and reform the customs of men, as Heaven employs warm and cool, cold and hot weather to transform the grass and trees. If joy and anger are seasonally applied, then the year will be prosperous, but if they are used wrongly and out of season then the year will fail.

Heaven, earth, and man are one, and therefore the passions of man are one with the seasons of Heaven. So the time and place for each must be considered. If Heaven produces heat in the time for cold, or cold in the time for heat, then the year must be bad, while if the ruler manifests anger when joy would be appropriate, or joy where anger is needed, then the age must fall into chaos.

Therefore the great concern of the ruler lies in diligently watching over and guarding his heart, that his loves and hates, his angers and joys may be displayed in accordance with right, as mild and cool, the cold and hot weather come forth in the proper season. If the ruler constantly practices this without, then his emotions will never be at fault, as spring and autumn, winter and summer are never out of order. Then may he form a trinity with Heaven and earth. If he holds these four passions deep within him, and does not allow them recklessly to come forth, then may he be called the equal of Heaven."

Emperor Yang Ti on his boat on the Grand Canal, China, from an 18th-century Chinese painting on silk

DIVINATION

Divination, the art of predicting the future and the will of Heaven, is an activity found in many societies and religions. The natural human desire to see into the future was strong in ancient China, and, by the Shang period (1500–1027 B.C.E.), was closely linked with the desire of royalty to communicate with their ancestors. This led to the use of tortoise shells and animal bones in divination. A question would be asked, heated bronze rods were applied to the bone, and the resulting cracks were read as answers by the divination expert. Later in the Shang period the questions and answers were engraved into the bones. Thousands of such engraved oracle bones have survived, providing modern scholars with important information in the interpretation of ancient Chinese religion, royalty, and the development of written Chinese.

Divination procedures relate directly to the Confucian notion of Heaven and the Heavenly Mandate. Since Heaven does not speak directly to humanity, indirect means of establishing Heaven's approval had to be found. Emperors and Confucian officials had an interest in anticipating any disruption in the human and natural order, as a way of determining Heaven's opinion, and as a way of averting natural disasters, political unrest, or military threat.

Observing and documenting geographical, climatic and political and social changes became an integral part of

---

Chinese books of divination taught practitioners how to understand the will of the gods and avert natural or man-made disasters

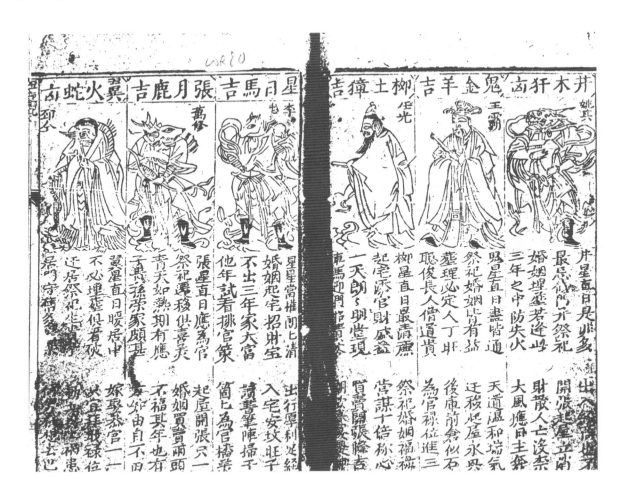

Confucian statecraft, as dic███████████████████on procedures. Divination was███████████████████ial who had to advocate a possib████████████████se it shifted responsibility onto███████████████so use divination procedures to█████████████████cy.

During the early Chou p█████████████████the drawing of lots developed as████████████████ed stalks of the yarrow plant we████████████████ualized random selection pro███████████████m of the I Ching (one of the f███████████████he fully developed form which██████████████is procedure. I Ching consultat████████████████of the state divination system██████████████████d by elaborate ceremonial.

Fortune tellers can still be found plying their trade on the streets of Chinese communities around the world

Such procedures were too complex and time-consuming for ordinary people to follow, so simpler systems were adopted for divination in local temples and by fortune tellers. These systems were widespread during Imperial times and are still used today.

One popular method is the shaking of a container of wooden sticks, until one falls out. Each stick has a number which gives the hexagram number of the I Ching, so the prediction can be looked up in the text. A simplified set of predictions based on the 64 hexagrams of the I Ching is usually consulted. Another method is casting moonblocks, which are two blocks of wood each with a flat side (for yin or "no") and a rounded side (for *yang* or "yes"). These are ritually thrown on the floor of the temple to obtain a yes or no answer from the god or ancestor addressed. Normally the blocks are thrown three times. These and many other divinations continue to be widely practiced in Chinese communities.

Wooden sticks are now used for divination in place of the dried yarrow stalks of ancient China, but the essential procedures remain unchanged

CONFUCIAN RESPECT FOR LEARING

Love of learning, respect for traditional values, and a fondness for ceremonial protocol are fundamental to Confucianism. Confucian teachers, as repositories of these moral values and of traditional learning, were greatly respected. Even in modern times, Chinese children and students are expected to show respect and deference to their teachers. In Taiwan, Teachers' Day is still celebrated in September in honor of Confucius and all teachers.

The story of the mother of Mencius is often told as an example of Confucian propriety and respect for learning. Mencius' father died when he was a baby, so his mother assumed responsibility for his education. The family lived near a cemetery, and young Mencius learned to imitate the behavior of mourners. His mother decided this was inappropriate behavior for a child, so she moved to live near a market. The young Mencius played at being a trader, and his mother, thinking it improper for her son, moved to a house near a Confucian academy. When she saw her son imitating the formal bearing and etiquette of the scholars, she was satisfied with the location.

One day, young Mencius asked his mother why the butchers were slaughtering pigs. She answered, "To feed you." Then she reflected that she was not being quite honest, since she had not bought pork for him. She further reflected that she had always observed honesty and propriety, even when she carried him in her womb. She would only sit on a mat that was correctly aligned, and would only eat meat that was correctly cut, but now she was misleading him.

Confucian love of learning and respect for tradition and propriety are summed up in the story of the mother of Mencius, who moved house twice in order to be near a Confucian school where her son could grow up displaying good manners and courteous behavior

Education remains an im⬛⬛⬛⬛⬛⬛⬛⬛⬛⬛
and schoolchildren are requir⬛⬛⬛⬛⬛⬛⬛⬛⬛⬛

Rather than even slightly ⬛⬛⬛⬛⬛⬛⬛⬛⬛⬛ and bought some pork for him

Some years later, Menc⬛⬛⬛⬛⬛⬛⬛⬛⬛⬛ one day and his mother asked hi⬛⬛⬛⬛⬛⬛⬛⬛⬛ well at school. He casually repl⬛⬛⬛⬛⬛⬛⬛⬛⬛ She immediately took a knife ⬛⬛⬛⬛⬛⬛⬛⬛⬛ her weaving. Shocked, Mencius⬛⬛⬛⬛⬛⬛⬛⬛⬛ told him that her wastefulness i⬛⬛⬛⬛⬛⬛⬛⬛⬛ ike his wasteful neglect of his ⬛⬛⬛⬛⬛⬛⬛⬛⬛ was never indifferent to his s⬛⬛⬛⬛⬛⬛⬛⬛⬛ the greatest teacher in China ⬛⬛⬛⬛⬛⬛

Scholars and offi⬛⬛⬛

Education in the Confucian⬛⬛⬛⬛⬛⬛⬛⬛⬛⬛ for its own sake. From the Ha⬛⬛⬛⬛⬛⬛⬛⬛⬛⬛ the basis for admission to the i⬛⬛⬛⬛⬛⬛⬛⬛⬛ year

across China, public examinations in the Classics were held, when about 30,000 candidates would present themselves in each province. There were three levels of examination in all. Preparation for the lowest level of examination took at least six years, and to graduate at the highest level and qualify as a *jin shi*, or presented scholar, could take 18 years or more. Success at this level meant that the scholar was qualified for the higher levels of the civil service, as a judge or provincial governor or an adviser at court. Those who qualified at the lower levels could apply for posts as clerks, tax collectors or any of the lesser bureaucratic positions.

The relatively small elite group of scholar officials was vital to the running of the empire. Knowledge of the Classics was not enough, however, to succeed in the examinations. They had to be interpreted according to Confucian orthodoxy and precedent. One weakness of the examination system, and the way it was run, was that it tended to encourage conservatism and a narrow, theoretical orthodoxy along with indifference to technical and financial skills.

SELFLESS PUBLIC SERVICE

The great advantage of the official examination system was its encouragement of the virtue of selfless public service and the development of a Chinese work ethic. These qualities are exemplified in the legend of Yu the Great as told in the Confucian Classic of History. Yu was an engineer, and spent 13 years working on a massive flood control project without ever visiting his home. After the work was complete, the emperor Shun, guided by Heaven, abdicated to allow Yu to become emperor and subsequent founder of the Hsia dynasty.

Many Confucian officials modeled their conduct in office upon Yu's example. One such official was Li Bing, the governor of Sichuan in 250 B.C.E., who developed a large-scale flood prevention and irrigation system on the Chengdu plain. One of his sons was killed during the work, and Li Bing's selfless example is still honored at the temple dedicated to him that stands by the Mingchien river.

Confucianism in the 20th century

When imperial China collapsed in 1911, the Confucian state cult and the official examination system based on the Confucian Classics could no longer be upheld. However, the values of filial piety, family loyalty, a generalized respect

This peasant painting of Confucius being condemned is typical of the propaganda used by the Maoist government to discredit Confucianism

Confucian values of hard wo▚▚▚▚▚▚▚▚▚▚▚▚
superiors continue to exercise an▚▚▚▚▚▚▚▚▚▚▚▚
southeast Asia as well as ▚▚▚▚▚▚▚▚▚▚

for tradition, personal sel▚▚▚▚▚▚ ▚▚▚ ▚▚▚ for
harmonious and rather form▚▚▚▚▚▚▚▚▚▚▚▚ ial
relationships continued to b▚▚▚▚▚▚▚▚▚▚▚▚ di-
tionalists and by most ordin▚▚▚▚▚▚▚▚

Confucianism and economic enterpr▚

With the emergence of Japar▚▚▚▚▚▚▚▚▚▚▚▚ re
as major economic forces in▚▚▚▚▚▚▚▚▚▚▚ nd
of the Second World War,▚▚▚▚▚▚▚▚▚▚▚ to
attribute their economic ▚▚▚▚▚▚▚▚▚▚ of
Confucian values and traditio▚▚▚▚▚▚▚▚▚▚)),
a resident of Taiwan and a d▚▚▚▚▚▚▚▚▚▚ s,
has often made such claims ▚▚▚▚▚▚▚▚▚▚ or
Confucian values in the mo▚▚▚▚▚▚

In general terms, it is a▚▚▚▚▚▚▚▚▚▚ ic
growth in these countries ▚▚▚▚▚▚▚▚▚▚ an
respect for hard work, and ▚▚▚▚▚▚▚▚▚▚ fit
of the family, regardless of ▚▚▚▚▚▚▚▚▚▚ it.

Another factor is the success of the small and medium-scale family businesses that underpin rapid economic growth in southeast Asia. This success can be attributed in part to the Confucian preference for non-contractual, informal business relationships based on networks of mutual trust and reciprocity, known as the *guanxi* system.

Some scholars are critical of the claim that Confucianism has facilitated the southeast Asian economic boom. They point out that rapid economic growth in these regions has always followed the introduction of Western forms of economic and business organization. These scholars argue that, in reality, the merchant classes of traditional China were, in many ways, the least Confucian members of that society. Furthermore, the Confucian emphasis on classical learning, and the scholar's contempt for trade and technical skills, was, in fact, a hindrance to the development of business and enterprise, rather than a help.

A different response to the modern world is expressed by the contemporary Japanese Confucian teacher, Okada Takehiko (born 1908), who advocates Confucian meditation (*seiza*), or "quiet sitting." This is seen as a method cultivating a moral sense, and as an antidote to the dehumanizing effects of modern technology.

BUDDHISM

Always think ❝ compassion. That is all you need to know

Buddhism is one of the world's major religious traditions. It originated in India, and has a history going back 2,500 years. Consciously missionary from the start, Buddhism soon spread to other lands, and countries where Buddhism has been significant include Sri Lanka, Burma, Thailand, Cambodia, Laos, China, Japan, Korea, Mongolia, Tibet, Nepal, Sikkim, Bhutan, and Vietnam. In the 20th century, Buddhism has spread to the Western world, and the number of adherents in Europe, America, and Australasia is increasing. It has been estimated that, in the 19th century, Buddhism touched the lives of 40 per cent of the world's population, and, even after the disruptions of the 20th century, there are probably about 500 million Buddhists in the world today.

Some people have ques■■■ ■■■■ ■■■ ■■■■ory "religion" really suits Bu■■■■ ■■■■■■■ ■■■■ays it differs from the way religi■■■ ■■ ■■■ ■■■■rn world. Buddhism is not bas■■■ ■■■ ■■■ ■■■■ ■■es it have a set creed, nor a un■■■■■ ■■■■■■ ■■■ ■■■■p- ture, nor a central authori■■ ■■■■■■■■ ■■■ ■■ ■■es put forward a goal for huma■■■■ ■■■■■■■■■■■ ■■■ ■■■■rld perceived by the senses, esp■■■■■■ ■■■■■■ ■■■■■■fe, and advocates ways of beha■■■■ ■■■■■■.

Buddhism is a rich and v■■■■ ■■■■■■■■■ ■■■■ ■■■■■■ed to many different social anc■■■■■■■■ ■■■■■■■■ ■■■ ■■ver demanded sole allegiance fr■■■■■■■ ■■■■■■■■■ ■■■■ ith local religious traditions, fo■■■■■■ ■■■■ ■■■■■■■■■ut seeking actively to replace ■■■■ ■■■■■■■■ ■■■■■■sm can appear to be quite differ■■■■■■■ ■■■■■ ■■■■es. This makes it difficult to su■■■■■■■■■■ ■■■■ ■■■ven more the practices, of Bud■■■■.

Contemporary ch■■■■■■■■

As the 20th century gives ■■■■ ■■ ■■■ ■■■ ■■■■■■■■ are exploring how their traditi■■■■ ■■■ ■■■ ■■■■■ ■■■■■ral, and political circumstances■■■■ ■■■■■■■■■■■ ■■■ ■■■■. The establishment of Buddhism ■■■ ■■■■ ■■■■■■■ ■■■■ ■■pid changes in the East, challen■■■■ ■■■■ ■■■■■ ■■■■■■tly to question what in the trad■■■■■ ■■■ ■■■■■■■ ■■■ ■■ere- fore disposable, and what is ■■■■■■ ■■■■■■■ ■■■■■■me, Buddhists face the related ■■■■■■■ ■■■■ ■■■■ ■■■■em- porary culture is positive c■■■■■■■■■ ■■■■■■■■■■ ■■■be adopted, and what is ha■■■■ ■■■■ ■■■■■■■ ■■ be opposed. The issue of gene■■■■ ■■■■■ ■■■ ■■■■■■ing, as traditional roles for me■■■ ■■■■ ■■■■ ■■■■■■■ed.

As more Buddhists o■■■■■ ■■■■ ■■■ ■■■■■■ome better educated, the role c■■■■■■ ■■■■■■■■■■■■■■ One of the most pressing issue■■■■■ ■■■■■■■ ■■■■■ ■■■■e of the natural environment, ■■■■■ ■■■■■■■■■ ■■■ ■■een

examining the implications of Buddhism for this and other social issues. The concept of the "socially engaged" Buddhist has been developed to counteract the stereotype of the Buddhist as meditator, concerned only with his or her own spiritual development. Like other faiths, Buddhism is coming to terms with the existence of a plurality of beliefs and values in the world, and engaging in interfaith dialog. At the same time, Buddhists are exploring the implication of the variations within their own tradition, previously separated by geography, now meeting together.

Developments in the political world have had a great impact on Buddhism throughout its history. In the 20th century the violent introduction of Communism into traditionally Buddhist countries, such as China, Tibet, Vietnam, Cambodia, and Laos, dealt a great blow to the Buddhist tradition. The human rights issues raised by the Tibetan government in exile, against the Chinese rulers of Tibet, is an important moral, as well as political issue, for Buddhists today.

Not all Buddha images represe■■■ ■■■ ■■■■■■■ ■■■■■■■ha; they may represent past or futu■■■ ■■■■■■■■■ ■■■■■■■■lha, who represents the next Buddh■■ ■■■■■■■■ ■■■■■■■ ■■■ld- systems, or may symb■■■■■■■■■■■■■■■■■■■■■■■■■.

**THE BASIC
TEACHINGS
OF
BUDDHISM**

Buddhism is so rich and varied that any attempt to identify a single basic belief or essence is doomed to failure. However, the quest for true happiness and peace for all beings is a common feature of all Buddhist traditions. The Buddha pointed out that life, as most people experience it, is unsatisfactory and characterized by suffering and impermanence. Much of this we bring upon ourselves, through our own greed and selfishness, and our ignorance of the true nature of reality.

Buddhists believe that individual people do not possess any unchanging inner essence, soul, or self, but, like everything else, we change from moment to moment. While we remain ignorant and selfish, the process of change continues, even from one life to the next, through a cycle of rebirth. If we can discover the truth about life, and learn to act appropriately, we can find peace, and no longer have to be reborn into this unsatisfactory life. Buddhism is thus a religion of wisdom and compassion. Religious practices, and even beliefs, are only a means to this end, and nothing special in themselves. The Buddha compared such practices to a raft used to get across a river – once it has served its purpose, it can be discarded. Thus it is not surprising to find that Buddhist practice differs in different places, because the crucial question is always: does it work?

Five moral precepts

When talking to busy lay people, the Buddha stressed the need for unselfish kindness and compassion to all, living a moral and responsible life, and the importance of not looking for happiness in material possessions. Relationships with family and friends, between pupils and teachers, and between employers and employees, work, domestic life and leisure activities should reflect these values. Most Buddhists are familiar with a list of five basic moral precepts that are undertaken on becoming a Buddhist. They are: to abstain from killing, taking what has not been given, sexual misconduct, false speech, and intoxicants that cloud the mind.

Buddhists believe that undertaking a moral, compassionate, and non-materialistic lifestyle will bring contentment in this life and a better rebirth next time.

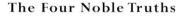

*Buddhist religious practices, such as the giving and
receiving of alms, are the means by which Buddhists
pursue wisdom, truth, and compassion*

The Four Noble Truths

For those who want to go further, the Buddha taught an analysis of life known as the Four Noble Truths, summaries of which are given below.

ONE: All life involves suffering (*dukkha*). There are many evils in the world; no pleasant thing lasts forever (*anicca* – impermanence); our lives are limited and uncertain.

TWO: This suffering is caused by selfish craving and clinging to things that do not last. The same applies in this life, and from life to life (*samsara* — the cycle of rebirt... force that keeps the proces... is called *karma* (literally "ac... our actions have consequen... ourselves, as well as for oth...

THREE: Having identifi... cause, the problem is sol... eliminating the cause rathe... the symptoms. If ignoran... selfishness can be totally el... ed, and replaced by wisdo... compassion, an alternative s... being can be reached. This... monly known as *nirvana*, a... scribable state of peace, wh... forces of karma no longer o... Mahayana Buddhists cal... "reaching Buddhahood."

FOUR: The way to elimina... ishness and ignorance, and... wisdom and compassion, is t... tice the Buddhist way o... referred to as the "Noble Ei... Path" and consisting of righ... right intention, right speec... conduct, right livelihood... effort, right mindfulness... contemplation. The first two... ht into the truth about life and... on compassion. The following... ral way of living, acknowledgi... we say, as well as what we do, a... lic world of work and business... he final three relate to trainin... ed meditation. Thus the Buddh... ath of wisdom, morality, and m...

Anatta — selflessn...

Many religions propose th... oul within a material body. Bud... oul

...uddha give alms to the poor;
...painting by Choud Chi Chang

or self. Buddhist analysis of a human being proposes five categories or elements: physical form, feelings or sensations, sense-perceptions, impulses or volitions and consciousness. All of these are constantly changing, are impermanent and subject to external conditions, and there is nothing else. Thus, although we use the word "self," there is no real entity to which this word refers. Understanding this core concept is pivotal to the process of shaking off our normal state of ignorance and selfishness.

Shunyata — emptiness

One major Buddhist philosophy, Madhyamaka, developed this idea into the concept of *shunyata*, or emptiness, where this lack of essence applies not just to human beings, but also to the five elements identified above, and, indeed, to everything there is that exists. Nothing in the universe has separate, essential being, independent of other things, but all things exist only relatively and interdependently. To achieve a full understanding of shunyata is to realize the Buddhist goal.

Among the great thinkers from the history of Buddhism who have helped to formulate these basic teachings, mention must be made of Nagarjuna (2nd century C.E.) who is credited with the discovery of the Mahayana scriptures known as the Prajnaparamita Sutras and also with developing the Madhyamaka philosophy of emptiness. From the Theravada tradition there is Buddhaghosa (5th century C.E.), whose work, the Path of Purification, is an influential summary of Buddhist belief.

THE BUDDHA

When people refer to "the Buddha" they usually mean an historical person who lived in northern India, on the borders of Nepal, some 2,500 years ago (recent scholarship favors 448–368 B.C.E. over the earlier dates of 563–483). However "Buddha" (which means "the enlightened one") is a generic term, and there have been, and are, other Buddhas. Unlike the Western view of a cosmos proceeding in a straight line from beginning to end, the Buddhist cosmology is cyclical. Just as individual beings die to be born again, so world systems come into being and pass away, to be succeeded by new world systems.

Thus there have been other Buddhas in previous world systems, and there will be others in the future. Some Buddhists also believe that there are countless world systems in existence simultaneously, and that each has its own Buddha, some of whom have names and can be interacted with. Thus a "Buddha" image or statue may not necessarily represent Shakyamuni Buddha himself, the historical Buddha, to whose life we now turn.

Siddhartha Gautama

The life story of Siddhartha Gautama, the man who became the Buddha, is of fundamental importance to the Buddhist tradition, since it illustrates many of the basic teachings of Buddhism, including the need for great effort, the importance of complete detachment, of discovering the truth about life and of limitless compassion.

Siddhartha Gautama was born to a people known as the Shakyas, who lived in the foothills of the Himalayas, on the borders of India and Nepal. He belonged to the Kshatriya, or ruling class. The story of his birth is surrounded by portents of his greatness and his childhood was exemplary.

The death of the Buddha is a subject frequently portrayed in oriental art, as in this 10th-century stone stuppa, now in the British Museum

He is said to have lived a life of great luxury, never having to face the realities of suffering and impermanence, until the age of 29, when four "sights" of age, sickness, death, and renunciation caused him to reject his trivial lifestyle and venture out into the world to seek the truth about life and the answer to suffering. He gave up his riches and became an ascetic, experimenting with practices such as meditation and fasting, as advocated by the religious teachers of the time. After six years he came to the conclusion that both indulgence and extreme austerity were inappropriate ways of life, and that a moderate lifestyle was preferable.

Seeking truth

So, one night, he sat down under a tree and entered a deep meditative state, vowing not to leave the spot until he had come to a realization of the truth. This "enlightenment experience" is said to have involved recall of all his previous lives, the ability to see the workings of karma (action) in the lives of all beings, the complete destruction of ignorance and selfishness, and the attainment of nirvana — perfect peace, perfect knowledge, ultimate truth. This was not the sort of truth that could easily be put into words, but, out of compassion for others, the new Buddha decided to spend the rest of his life teaching, so that others might be led to realize the truth.

The Buddha taught for 45 years, matching his teaching to the needs and aptitudes of his audience. He gained many followers, some of whom also gained enlightenment. He established a *sangha*, an order of monks, and later of nuns, to preserve and spread his teaching, and he gradually evolved the rules that should guide their life. He debated with other religious teachers, gained the patronage of local rulers, told many stories, and helped many individuals. He is said to have passed away peacefully at the age of 80.

...uddha here depicted in a 19th-century
...erfect peace, perfect knowledge, and ultimate
...of his life to helping others do the same

TYPES OF BUDDHISM

Buddhism is a tradition rich in diversity, with several different scriptures and schools of thought. The tradition has been very flexible, and has adapted to the different countries and cultures to which it has spread. For convenience, it is possible to see within the complexities of Buddhism two main branches: Theravada and Mahayana. Theravada ("the way of the elders") is the tradition found in the more southerly countries of Sri Lanka, Thailand, Burma, Cambodia, and Laos. Mahayana ('the great vehicle") is a blanket term for the varieties of Buddhism found in the more northern and far-eastern countries of Asia. Tibetan Buddhism, a variation on Mahayana, is followed in Tibet, Mongolia, Sikkim, Bhutan, and northwestern China, whereas a variety of traditions are followed in China, Japan, Korea, and Vietnam.

The two branches are distinguished not only by geography: there are also differences in accepted scriptures and their conception of the Buddhist goal. Their cosmologies, concepts of Buddha, concepts of divine beings, and schools of philosophy are also different.

Thai Buddhists tend to follow the Theravada tradition, known as the way of the elders, with its emphasis on monasticism

Theravada principles

In Theravada teaching, the Buddha was a man; a very special person, but nevertheless human. Buddhas are those who discover the truth about life for themselves. Such beings are very rare as most people need a teacher to show them the way. The Buddha has now passed beyond reach, but has left his teachings to enable others to reach enlightenment. This is something each person must achieve for him or herself. One who has achieved enlightenment is known as an *arhat*.

Theravada teaches that there is no reality corresponding to the concept of God that we can rely on for salvation. There may be gods, who may even interact with humans, and help or hinder in minor matters, but these are merely other life forms, subject to the cycle of rebirth.

The monastic sangha (the word means order, or assembly) is at the heart of the practice of Theravada Buddhism. As well as working towards realization and enlightenment for themselves, the role of Theravada monks is to preserve

A Tibetan lama *or priest. Buddhists in Tibet follow a variation of the Mahayana tradition*

individuals: it is used to refer to the underlying nature that all Buddhas share which is potentially within all beings. Mahayana Buddhists sometimes refer to the Trikaya, or three forms of Buddha: the underlying Buddha nature, glorious celestial manifestations, and earthly manifestations.

Mahayana philosophy is drawn from various scriptures and includes many schools of thought, but there are two that are especially influential: the Madhyamaka, which teaches the emptiness of all things (that nothing is anything in or by itself but only in relation to others) and the Yogachara, which teaches that all things are "consciousness only."

and spread the *dharma*, the ████████████ and example. Lay Theravada B████████████ and attempt to live a life of n████████████████ achment, turning to Buddhisn████████████

Mahayana princi████

Mahayana Buddhists accep████████████████res, some of which are not fou████████████████ tion. They have a somewha████████████████ of the Buddhist goal, w████████████████ Buddhahood itself. The pa████████████████ referred to as the path of t████████████████ being of enlightenment." T████████████████ defined as one who puts t████████████████ before their own, so they████████████████ sacrificing individuals wh████████████████ *samsara* (the cycle of rebi████████████████ others, instead of resting in████████████████

The Mahayana Buddhi████████████████ are many Buddhas in differ████████████████ able to aid those who call████████████████ the bodhisattvas who have████████████████ spiritual paths. The word████████████████ refer to one person, o████████████████

VARIANTS OF MAHAYANA BUDDHISM

Tibetan Buddhism

Tibetan Buddhism has a vast collection of scriptures, including esoteric scriptures, or *tantras*, which describe powerful rituals, and are sometimes said to constitute a third branch of Buddhism, referred to as the Vajrayana (diamond, or thunderbolt) vehicle. There are several schools of Tibetan Buddhism, all of which stress the importance of tradition and of living teachers as repositories of tradition. Some of the more important teachers, or *lamas*, are said to be reincarnations of holy teachers who lived in earlier times, living on earth as bodhisattvas to help others (*tulkus*).

Tibetan Buddhism is characterized by a pantheon of Buddhas and bodhisattvas, and many colorful rituals, artefacts, and works of art. Tibetan Buddhists believe in an

The "disciplined casualness" of Zen Buddhism has influenced calligraphy, painting, and the poetic haiku

intermediate state, between one life and the next, called the Bardo. Ritual practices involve chanting *mantras* (powerful words or syllables), the construction of *mandalas* (special patterns), *mudras* (symbolic movements of the hands), and meditational practices involving visualization. Monastic organization is very strong.

Zen Buddhism

Zen (or Ch'an, meaning meditation) Buddhism developed in China, Korea and Japan. Its iconography is the opposite of Tibetan Buddhism, with space and simplicity characterizing its works of art and meditational forms. However, like Tibetan Buddhism, it stresses the importance of direct transmission of the central teachings from master to pupil. Methods of realizing Buddhahood include *zazen*, or sitting quietly in meditation, and reflection on a *koan*, a riddle or puzzling story that seeks to cut through the mental constructs

Tibetan Buddhism is characteri... as shown at this monastery...

Pure Land Buddhism

Pure Land Buddhism is focused on one particular Mahayana scripture, which tells of a living Buddha who inhabits another world system, a far-off place known as the Pure Land. The Buddha is called Amitabha or Amida. It is believed that faith in Amida Buddha, and repetition of his name, will lead to eventual rebirth in his world, where life is far more conducive to the attainment of nirvana. Different schools of thought within Pure Land Buddhism differ over how much your own efforts are effective in achieving spiritual progress, and how far you are totally reliant on the grace of Amida Buddha.

Nichiren Buddhism

Nichiren was a 13th-century Japanese monk who felt the need to reform Buddhism and Japanese society. His teaching was based on one Mahayana sutra (scripture) known as the Lotus Sutra. This teaches that, although Shakyamuni Buddha appeared to be born on earth and pass away, in reality he has been enlightened since time immemorial and is still actively working for the salvation of all beings. In addition, it reveals the Mahayana secret that "all of you shall become Buddhas." The central practice of Nichiren Buddhism is reciting the mantra of the Lotus Sutra: *namo myoho rengye kyo* (meaning "homage to the Lotus of the Wonderful Law").

impeding the realization of t... ...ne is strictly organized, and it ... ...tic practice by including manu... ...o-nent of the daily routine.

Zen teaches the possibil... ...ere and now, unlike the tender... ...er forms of Buddhism, which ... ...ar-off goal. The "disciplined ca... ...ed Sino-Japanese art forms, s... ...he poetic haiku, the arrangem... ...he tea ceremony, and even mart... ...ols of Zen Buddhism, the best ... ...ich stresses gradual realization ... ...zai Zen, which employs n... ...es.

Zen Buddhists practice meditation and reflection as a means of realizing the Buddhahood within themselves

SCRIPTURES AND MYTHOLOGY

There is no single book of sacred scripture for all Buddhists. The teachings of the Buddha were memorized and recited, but they were not written down for several centuries. The scriptures that are used to guide followers of Theravada Buddhism are known as the Pali Canon, Pali being the language in which they were written around the first century B.C.E. The Pali Canon is divided into three sections, and is often known as the Tripitaka, meaning "three baskets." The three sections are the *vinaya*, or monastic discipline, the sutra or teachings of the Buddha (and others), and the *abhidhamma*, or systematic philosophy.

In book form the volumes of the Pali Canon take up several shelves of a bookcase.

Mahayana scriptures are even more numerous, existing as separate documents in a variety of languages and in two large collections: the Chinese Canon and the Tibetan Canon. The Mahayana scriptures contain material similar to the Pali Canon, plus scriptures that teach distinctively Mahayana ideas, such as the bodhisattva path. Among the more well-known Mahayana scriptures are the Lotus Sutra, the Pure Land Sutras and the Perfection of Wisdom Sutras.

To many Buddhists, the scriptures, or sutras, are more precious even than images of the Buddha

Monks know the vinaya section well, and lay people often rely on monks and teachers to relay the most relevant passages in a suitable form. Some Buddhists focus on one particular scripture as summing up the heart of Buddhism, such as the Lotus Sutra. Scriptures are considered very precious, and the Tibetans keep them wrapped up on the shrine, above even the Buddha images. By contrast, Zen Buddhists point out that the scriptures are only collections of words, and that the truth is found in direct experience.

Teaching through stories

Within the Buddhist scriptures there are hundreds of well-known stories. There are stories of events in the life of the Buddha, stories that the Buddha told as par⬚ ⬚of previous Buddhas, and storie⬚ ⬚to come. There are over 500 sto⬚ ⬚e Buddha's previous lives, illu⬚ ⬚e Buddha needed to develop to⬚ ⬚enment was possible.

Stories include those of th⬚ ⬚d his life to save his people, the⬚ ⬚o feed a starving man, the tree⬚ ⬚n pieces so as not to fall on oth⬚ ⬚d

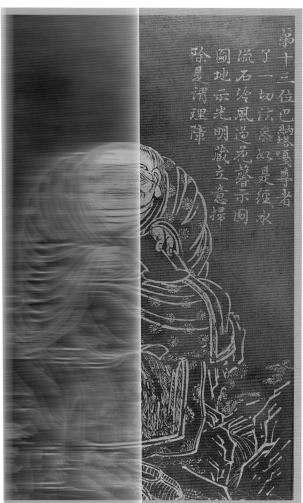

⬚tic rules and philosophical systems;
⬚lives of the Buddha and his followers

the ascetic who did not feel hatred even as he was tortured to death. One story tells how, in his previous life but one, the Buddha was Prince Vessantara, who gave away his wealth, including the country's sacred elephant, his children, and even his wife, demonstrating the generosity and complete detachment required to become a Buddha.

The blind men and the elephant

One of the stories told by the Buddha, to illustrate why there is so much conflict between different religions and ideologies, is the classic tale of the blind men and the elephant, whose universal message has made it one of the world's best-known parables.

"Once upon a time there was a king in the town of Savatthi. In need of amusement, he asked his servant to assemble all the blind men in the town. He then presented the men with a large elephant, allowing each man only to touch a part of it. One felt the ear, another the tusk, another the trunk and so on. He then asked each of the blind men to say what he thought he was touching. The one feeling the tusk said it must be a plough. The one feeling the tail said it was a brush. The one feeling the leg said it was a pillar. They began to argue, each putting forward their own view, and in the end became so angry that they started hitting each other. The king was highly amused."

MONASTIC LIFE

The monastic sangha (assembly) has formed the backbone of the Buddhist community since it was inaugurated by the Buddha to preserve and spread his teaching. The life of the *bhikkhu* (monk) is intended to be as simple as possible in order to avoid distractions from spiritual tasks. Thus monks do not marry or have children, are celibate, have the bare minimum of possessions, shave their heads, and wear a simple robe.

Discipline is very strict. There are several versions of the vinaya (rules for monastic discipline) in the various scriptures followed by different traditions of Buddhism, but all involve keeping around 250 rules. One of the most serious offences, after murder and major theft, is causing quarrels and schisms in the community. There are various interpretations of the vinaya. Theravada monks are not allowed to work but must rely on donations from the lay community for food and robes, whereas Zen monks are allowed to grow and cook their own food. Some monks have to be allowed to handle money to survive in the modern world.

The monastic life involves meditation, scriptural study, and participation in communal ceremonies. Traditionally, monks will go out on a daily alms round seeking food donations which people put in their alms bowls for taking back to the monastery. People may also invite monks to their

Taksang monastery, built on a mountainside in Bhutan, is one of the oldest Buddhist monasteries

Therevada monks own nothing and are not allowed to work, so they depend on the laity for gifts of food and other essentials

homes for a meal, or make donations to the monastery. Some monks (especially those of the "Forest Dwelling" tradition) spend the majority of their time in meditation, whereas others are closely involved with the laity, teaching, counseling and performing ceremonies.

Ordination

In the following passage, Bhikkhu Anandabodhi (previously Steve), tells of his ordination in Thailand.

'After a couple of years as a novice, it was decided that I was ready to take full ordination (*upasampada*) as a bhikkhu (monk) in the Thai forest tradition. It involved lots of preparation, practical as well as spiritual. I had to learn the whole ceremony in Pali, sew and dye my own robes, and make 15

Some monastic communities a_____y contact with the world, su_____

toothbrushes as a gift for th_____ling over the ceremony. The c_____ the *sima* or monastic boundar_____nks. Before the ceremony pr_____vice precepts (no killing, no ta_____ing, no sexual activity, no into_____day,

sleeping on a mat or simple bed, no jewelry, no amusements like dancing and shows, and no money).

I had to have someone to supervise me for the first five years, offer robes and bowl to the officiant and receive them back, answer a series of questions to make sure I was qualified (e.g. free from disease and debt, definitely a human being), and then had to be accepted by all ten monks. I was then instructed in the main vinaya rules. It is customary to be sponsored by a lay person, who provides the robe, bowl, and other requisites. An elderly Thai lady offered to sponsor me, as her own son had been killed in a motorcycle accident – I was very touched. I was quite nervous during the ceremony, especially when three other candidates were added at the last minute, and I had to try and remember the plural forms of all the Pali words, but I have no regrets. It felt like coming home – strange as it might seem, I feel much freer as a monk."

Novices spend several years learning the spiritual and practical side of monastic life before they are accepted for ordination

THE BUDDHIST LAITY

The majority of Buddhists are not monks or nuns, but practice their Buddhism while living ordinary family lives and going to work. Shakuntala comes from Sri Lanka, but now lives with her family in England. This is her description of life as a Buddhist.

"I was born into a Buddhist family in a country where Buddhism is the main tradition. As a child I remember people being content with their few possessions, and always willing to share what they had. On a recent visit back home I felt that things are changing. Many people have television now, and desire the Western consumer goods they see advertised. If the Buddha was around today, I think he would be very critical of advertising to increase people's desires.

We express our commitment to Buddhism by reciting the three refuges: 'I take refuge in the Buddha, I take refuge in the dharma, I take refuge in the sangha.' The dharma is the teaching left us by the Buddha, the sangha is the order of monks. We support monks by taking food to the monastery. We also take the five moral precepts. I am a vegetarian, but my family in Sri Lanka ate meat. This is considered OK if you do not kill the animal yourself; the local

Above: *Monasteries were _____ ___e
and spread his teac_____ ___*
Opposite: *Although p_____ ___
of Buddhism, people visit t_____ ___
Buddha, like this temp_____*

be the footprint of the Buddha, who is believed to have visited Sri Lanka. I don't know if this is really true, but it does not matter; it's the intention that counts.

Most lay Buddhists do not expect to attain nirvana in this lifetime. Instead, by being generous, kind and moral, and participating in religious ceremonies, we hope to attain enough good karma or merit (*punya*) to do better next time. This is not undertaken in a selfish way; you can share your merit with others.

My children learn about a variety of religions at school. They enjoy Religious Education, and I think it is important that they learn about other faiths. We take them to dharma school at the temple every other Sunday, so that they can learn about the practice of their own religion and Sri Lankan culture."

*This 18th-century hanging scroll from Nepal celebrates
the Buddha's inauguration of the practice of giving alms*

butcher was a Muslim! I _____ hus-band will occasionally.

We have a small shri_____ge of the Buddha. We offer flo_____ show respect and thanks for hi_____ a god that can answer prayers._____s, lay people may dress simply_____in the temple, taking some of t_____to eat after midday, no luxuriou_____amuse-ments. Traditionally, pe_____sm by listening to stories and_____s, but nowadays people are b_____d the Buddhist scriptures for_____e also becoming more intereste_____much time for formal medita_____ndful-ness, the cultivation of_____ion on whatever you are doing_____on.

Pilgrimage is not as_____m as it is, for example, of Islar_____places in Sri Lanka. In Anurac_____from a cutting of the tree unc_____enlight-ened, and his tooth is k_____Temple at Kandy. At the top o_____said to

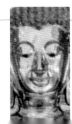

MEDITATION AND SPIRITUALITY

Meditation, in the sense of training the mind to realize the truth and think compassionately, is central to Buddhist practice. Buddhism is sometimes described as a way of spiritual and psychological development rather than a religion. The hindrances to enlightenment lie within the person, and although teachers and bodhisattvas may lend their aid, in the end it is the individual's responsibility. The ideal of the monastic life is intended to free the mind from distractions to meditation, but meditation is widely undertaken by lay people.

There are many different techniques of meditation, and a teacher is required to identify the forms of meditation suitable for the individual. "Mindfulness" develops greater awareness of the body, feelings and thoughts. A simple form of mindfulness is concentrating on breathing, letting all distracting thoughts fade away to calm the mind. Deeper forms of *samatha*, or "calming" meditation, lead to detachment from the world of the senses, and states of pure consciousness and great peace. *Vipassana*, or "insight" meditation, is more analytical and involves contemplation of the fundamentals of Buddhism – for example, the idea of no-self – until they are experienced as true.

Buddhist meditation, whether communal or individual, can be undertaken anywhere. Most forms of meditation begin with simple exercises to achieve a state of calmness and detachment

Simplicity and complexity

Tibetan forms of meditation can be quite complex, involving visualizations, mantras and mandalas, and need initiation and guidance from a teacher. By contrast, Soto Zen advises zazen, or "sitting" meditation: simply sitting in serene reflection, observing the thoughts that arise, without getting caught up in them. Meditation in Rinzai Zen may involve struggling with the meaning of a saying, or koan, which is given by the teacher.

One simple form of meditation, suitable for all, including children, is the generation of feelings of loving kindness to all, starting with yourself and passing through your close friends and family to less congenial people and those you dislike or do not understand, finally embracing the whole universe and all the beings within it.

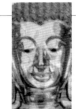

... and observe their own transient thoughts,
... meaning of an ambiguous saying

COMPASSION

Buddhism is not just about cultivating personal spiritual development but also about concern for others. In fact the two are inextricable, as selfishness is the main obstacle to spiritual development.

Quoting from His Holiness the Dalai Lama, a Buddhist friend declared that "Buddhism can be summed up in three words: Always Think Compassion. That's all you need to know." Compassionate concern for others is shown in many different ways. It means living a morally responsible life, looking after the family, being loving and faithful to one's partner, helping friends, choosing an ethical way of earning a living and giving the best in work. Some of the Buddha's moral advice was very down-to-earth, and is still relevant 2,500 years later, including his admonition of the young man, Sigala, for wasting time and money by drinking, hanging around town late at night, spending time on amusements, gambling, mixing with bad company, and being lazy.

Although there are precepts and rules in Buddhism, the most important moral guideline is to do the most compassionate thing. Thus the normal rules may have to be broken from time to time in the interests of helping people; for example, one might have to lie in order to save someone's life. Knowing what is the right thing to do in such circumstances is called "skillful means" and choosing the correct course becomes clearer as enlightenment approaches. It is the motivation behind an act that matters most. Giving large amounts of money to charity will not help spiritual progress if it is done to gain fame and admiration.

Moral and social issues

Because of the need to apply compassion to individual circumstances, and to deal with causes rather than symptoms, it is hard to give "the Buddhist view" on controversial moral and social issues, but the following examples are typical of Buddhist standpoints.

Many Buddhists, but by no means all, are vegetarian out of compassion towards animals. Monks will accept whatever they are given.

Respect for life leads most Buddhists to be against capital punishment, euthanasia, and abortion. Others believe that banning the latter could lead to more suffering.

The majority of Buddhists believe that sexuality, although natural, needs to be controlled, as it can be very distracting. Monks and nuns are expected to be celibate. There are passages in the commentaries which state that homosexual relationships are wrong. Other Buddhists believe that gay relationships are just as acceptable as heterosexual ones.

The Buddhist tendency ⸻ st,
but there are Buddhist sold⸻
The need for clarity of ⸻ to
reject alcohol and drugs, bu⸻ Sri
Lankans drink palm toddy. T⸻ n.

Some Buddhists are vegetar⸻
causing unnecessary suffering to⸻
monks to accept wh⸻

Engaged Buddhists

Some Buddhists feel that compassion demands not just morality and kindness in everyday life, but active campaigning to improve the world. Those who think like this are called "engaged Buddhists." They may be involved with campaigns against the arms trade, against nuclear weapons, or against the destruction of the environment to build more roads. They may choose to work with the poor, the homeless, alcoholics, and drug addicts. There is a Buddhist chaplaincy that helps those in prison and there are Buddhist hospices for the dying. Buddhists may enter politics and economics to develop a fairer and more just world, with regard to human rights or fair trade. Poor treatment of the natural environment is a current issue of much concern to Buddhists, who believe that compassion should extend to all beings, animals, plants, and to the planet itself, as well as to all humans. On the other hand, there is the need to accept that all things are impermanent.

Almost all Buddhist monks shave their heads, wear a simple robe, and have the bare minimum of possessions

FESTIVALS AND CEREMONIES

The calendar of festivities differs among Buddhist countries, which demonstrates that such ceremonies are of cultural, rather than doctrinal or spiritual, importance.

Sri Lanka, Burma, and Thailand start the year in April. In Thailand and Burma, New Year is greeted with a water-throwing festival with elements of fun and fertility. Wesak, the feast celebrating the Buddha's birth, enlightenment, and death takes place at the full moon in late April or early May, and the Buddha's first sermon is celebrated in July.

Kathina Day, marking the end of the traditional monastic retreat for the rainy season, is celebrated in October, when lay people donate a special robe and other gifts to the monastic sangha. In Sri Lanka, the festival called Poson, held in June, celebrates the arrival of Buddhism in the country. In Kandy, a replica of the Buddha's tooth is honored by a procession of deco-

The Buddha's tooth, preserved in Sri Lanka

rated elephants, drummers, and dancers at the feast of Asala Perahera, held in late July or early August.

In Thailand, a festival called Loy Krathong is celebrated in November, with thousands of candles floating on rivers, recalling the story of Vessantara. In February there is the festival of Magha Puja, celebrating the giving of the vinaya (monastic rule). In Burma and Thailand, the festival at the end of the rains celebrates the time the Buddha preached to his departed mother in a heaven world, and is a time for remembering elderly relatives.

China and Tibet

China and Tibet start the year in late January or early February. The Chinese New Year has little Buddhist significance, but in Tibet it marks the period when the country is rededicated to Buddhism. Religious dramas are performed and spectacular butter sculptures made. Other Tibetan Buddhist festivals include the commemoration of the Buddha's enlightenment and death,

In Sri Lanka, a replica of the Buddha's tooth is the focal point of a carnival parade of elephants, dancers, and drummers

in May, and his first sermon⬛⬛⬛⬛⬛⬛⬛⬛⬛'s visit to his mother in the ⬛⬛⬛⬛⬛⬛⬛⬛⬛ in October. In November, the⬛⬛⬛⬛⬛⬛⬛⬛ the founder of the Gelugpa trad⬛⬛⬛⬛⬛⬛⬛⬛ is remembered.

Chinese Buddhist festiv⬛⬛⬛⬛⬛⬛⬛⬛ the "hungry ghosts" in August, wh⬛⬛⬛⬛⬛⬛⬛lf of the less fortunate departe⬛⬛⬛⬛⬛⬛⬛e of the Buddha's chief disciple⬛⬛⬛⬛⬛⬛h rebirth and was able to set he⬛⬛⬛⬛⬛⬛⬛y is celebrated in April or May

Japan

In the 19th century, Japan⬛⬛⬛⬛⬛⬛⬛⬛ "Western," or Gregorian, ca⬛⬛⬛⬛⬛⬛⬛, Buddhist temple bells ring ou⬛⬛⬛⬛⬛⬛⬛ evils of the old year. At the s⬛⬛⬛⬛⬛⬛s (called Higan) Buddhists rem⬛⬛⬛⬛⬛⬛t family graves. The Buddha's⬛⬛⬛⬛⬛⬛⬛ April 8 with a flower festival (⬛⬛⬛⬛⬛⬛⬛ of the baby Buddha are bathed i⬛⬛⬛⬛⬛⬛ of

O-bon, that is celebrated in mid-July, recalls the departed and is a time to visit ancestral homes.

Lifecycle rites, such as births, coming of age and marriages, are not considered of spiritual significance by Buddhists, although monks may bless a new baby, a marriage, or a new house, while in some countries (for example, Thailand), temporary ordination and a short period in the monastery may serve as an entry to adulthood.

Funerals are a different matter, as they illustrate the central Buddhist teaching of the impermanence of all things, and may serve as an occasion for spiritual reflection. In Japan, Buddhist monks perform funerals where the dead are laid out as if for ordination. Memorial tablets for the dead are kept in Buddhist temples. In Sri Lanka, a paper *stupa* (Buddhist monument) may be placed on the cremation pyre, and, at intervals after the funeral, meals are offered to monks for the merit of the departed.

Key events in the life and death of the Buddha are commemorated in Tibet with music and religious dramas

SOME FAMOUS BUDDHISTS

The emperor Ashoka ruled most of India in the 3rd century B.C.E. Sickened by winning a particularly brutal war, he became a Buddhist and turned to a more peaceful way of life, providing hospitals and clean water for his people. He proclaimed Buddhist moral values to his subjects by means of inscriptions carved on rock faces and stone pillars. He gave up hunting and animal sacrifices, and set up *stupas*, or monuments, in places associated with the Buddha. Ashoka sent out missions to other countries, the most successful of which was that to Sri Lanka led by his son and daughter. He is looked upon by Buddhists as India's greatest ruler, and his symbol has been adopted as the national symbol of modern India.

Dr. Bhimrao Ambedkar (1891–1956) was born into an "untouchable" Hindu caste, and experienced at first hand the discrimination which such groups suffer. In spite of his underprivileged origins, he pursued a university education in India and the USA, and qualified as a barrister in England. Back in India, he worked for the removal of prejudice and discrimination by both constitutional means and direct action. He chaired the committee that drew up the constitution of the newly independent India in 1949. In 1956, just before his death, he decided to renounce Hinduism and, along with thousands of his followers, became a Buddhist. Millions of his fellow *dalits* (oppressed people) have since followed suit.

His Holiness the Fourteenth Dalai Lama, born in 1936, is believed to be a tulku, the 14th incarnation of a 15th-century holy man, and a manifestation of Chenrezi, the bodhisattva of compassion. From the 17th century, the Dalai Lamas were rulers of Tibet. In 1951 the Chinese communists invaded Tibet; in 1959 the Dalai Lama escaped to India, where he leads the government in exile. He has become a much respected international figure, awarded the Nobel Peace Prize in 1989 for his non-violent campaigning for freedom and human rights in Tibet, and for the preservation of Tibetan culture and ecology, as well as religion. He stresses that the world's problems can only be solved by looking to the underlying cause – the lack of universal compassion in our hearts.

His Holiness the Dalai Lama, spiritual leader of the Tibetan Buddhist community

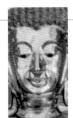

The Birth of the Buddha mur... Buddhapadipa temple, in...

The Peace Pagoda, in London's Battersea Park, was donated to the people of Britain by the Myohoji Buddhists of Japan

Buddhism in the Wes...

Although knowledge of Buddh... possibility in the West for 2,30... Ashoka and Alexander, becomin... a viable option since the end of ... forms of Buddhism are now rep... increasing. The "beat generation... trail" to the East of the 1960s a... spirituality from the 1980s and 1... larize Buddhism beyond the wor...

Buddhism is adapting to th... world. One organization that stres...

opment of a Buddhism suited to the West is the (Friends of the) Western Buddhist Order, which was founded in England in 1967. Drawing on a variety of Buddhist traditions, its members seek to understand and live by the principles at the heart of Buddhism, rather than adopting its cultural trappings. One adaptation is the ordination, in place of the traditional monk, of the *dharmachari*, a serious practitioner of Buddhism who can function effectively in Western society. Other issues for Western Buddhists are the role of women, "engaged" ecological and political action, dialog between the different traditions of Buddhism, and dialog with people of other faiths and ideologies.

JAINISM

Non-violence " is the supreme principle

Jainism is one of the oldest religions of the Indian subcontinent. Although relatively few in number, Jains have made a notable and distinctive contribution to the religious, cultural, and political life of India and Jainism remains a living religion. Today, there are about four million Jains worldwide. Most of them live in the western and southern parts of India, where Jainism is reacting to the problems of maintaining its identity as a minority religion. There are also flourishing communities of Jains in Europe and in the United States. In these places, Jainism is responding actively to the challenges posed by an alien environment.

There is a growing emph_____ religion, one that is ac_____ modern concerns, such as ca_____ ment. These social concerns _____ with the primary teaching o_____ should reject society complete_____ salvation, but they are firmly b_____ Jain ethic of non-violence.

The problems Jainism face_____ minority religion are made _____ difficult by the fact that there _____ several sects or traditions with_____ In India, there is little social cor_____ between the members of th_____ groups, and at times there is host_____ between them, particularly over s_____ issues as ownership of, and access_____ holy places.

In the United Kingdom, whe_____ there are about 20,000 Jain_____ sectarian differences have come _____ have less relevance. A sense of Jai_____ identity is developing at the expens_____ of sect identities. All the main sects within Jainism have their own shrines in the beautiful Jain temple in Leicester, which provides a vibrant example of the continuing vitality of Jainism as a living religion.

Non-violence and self-control

"*Ahimsa* is the supreme principle:" this saying summarizes the central ethic of Jainism. Ahimsa means non-violence, or not-harming. The Jain religion is notable for its wide application of the principle of non-violence. Jains are not only expected to refrain from harming human life, they also take great care to prevent unnecessary harm to animals and plants. This concern for non-violence has characterized Jainism from its beginnings — in the Ganges valley in the 5th century B.C.E. — to the present time, because Jains believe that its practice is necessary for any kind of spiritual progress to be made and for the soul to achieve ultimate salvation.

The cycle of death and rebirth

Jainism is a salvation religion. Like almost all religions originating in the Indian subcontinent, Jainism presupposes that there is a continuous cycle of death and rebirth from which it is the ultimate goal of each being to escape. The teachings of Jainism provide a path which leads to the final release of the soul from further rebirth. The two key elements in the path which leads to salvation are non-violence and self-control; indeed, the word "Jain" itself is derived from the Sanskrit word *jina*, which can be translated as "one who has conquered himself."

It is traditional Jain belief that the truths of the Jain religion are, like the universe, eternal and uncreated. These truths are periodically reactivated by a series of omniscient teachers called "Fordmakers" (*tirthankaras*). They are given this name because their teaching provides the ford by which souls can cross to salvation. Fordmakers are human, but they are endowed with superhuman qualities.

_____ elations of
_____ heir teachings
_____ ing souls may

MAHAVIRA, FOUNDER OF JAINISM

Jains believe that the universe inhabited by human beings is subject to a continuous cycle of time represented by the upward and downward turning of a wheel. As the wheel turns up, conditions become progressively better; as it turns down, conditions get worse. Fordmakers only live and preach when conditions are balanced between good and bad; at other times, human beings are either too blissful or too wretched to benefit from their teaching.

The 24th and final Fordmaker of the present turning of the wheel was Mahavira, the founder of the religion now known as Jainism. Jains believe that 70 years after Mahavira's death, the wheel of time entered the present era, one in which conditions are too bad for Fordmakers to preach. It will be hundreds of thousands of years before conditions will be suitable for another Fordmaker to be born.

Mahavira lived and preached in the Ganges valley area in the 5th century B.C.E. (although traditional dating places him about a century earlier). All the other Fordmakers, with the possible exception of Parsva, the 23rd, are mythical. Jainism originated and developed in response to specific social conditions at a time when the region was becoming urbanized, new kingdoms were being formed, and people were questioning the established norms of religious and social conduct. It is interesting that one of Mahavira's contemporaries was the Buddha (*see page 90*).

This manuscript illustration depicts the birth of Mahavira, the founder of the Jain religion, who lived and preached in the Ganges valley region in the 5th century B.C.E.

The beautifully decorated interior of the Pareshnath temple in Calcutta

Mahavira, in common with the Buddha, opposed the traditional belief of the Brahminical (later the Hindu) religion that spiritual progress depended on the correct performance of the duties of the social class into which one was born. According to this belief there were four ranked social classes: at the top were the priests or Brahmins, followed by the warrior or kingly class, then the farmers and merchants, and at the bottom were the slaves and servants. Outside this hierarchical social system were the untouchables, whose mere approach was thought to pollute the higher classes.

The function of the Brahmins was to ensure the correct performance of elaborate ritual sacrifices, which ensured the continuance of the universe and provided the means by which embodied souls could gain liberation from further

rebirth. Mahavira preached th[...]el-
evant for salvation; he taug[...]in
salvation was to perform se[...].

The meaning of ka[...]

At the time Mahavira was pre[...]d
that after death you were reb[...]f
your future life depended on[...]
your present life. The basic n[...]"
for the Brahmins this mean[...]
performance of sacrifices. Ot[...]

Jains believe salvation to be depe[...]
acts, but on a life of asce[...]

ethical, so that good actions lead to a good rebirth, bad
actions lead to a bad rebirth.

Mahavira's interpretation of karma was more radical.
He taught that all karma was bad since it was the reason
for the soul's bondage in the material world. The Jains
believed that karma was a material substance which somehow
stuck to the soul, defiling it and leading to its bondage in
matter. Since all actions led to the soul's bondage, the only
way to ensure the soul's liberation was for a person to cease
from action, thus making sure that no fresh karma stuck to
the soul; it was also necessary to burn away the soul's existing
karma by leading a life of extreme asceticism. For Jains,
the life of renunciation led by Mahavira provides the best
illustration of this process.

MAHAVIRA AND HIS FOLLOWERS

Mahavira was born into a princely family and was given the name Vardhamana, meaning "increasing," because, after his birth, the wealth of his family kept increasing. At the age of 30, he plucked out his hair, as a symbol of his renunciation of his home and worldly goods, and began to seek enlightenment as a wandering ascetic. For 12 years he wandered through the kingdoms of the Ganges valley, enduring terrible hardships, often fasting for days on end. Even when attacked by men or wild animals, he remained calm and continued to meditate. Because of his endurance, he was given the name Mahavira, meaning "great hero." Finally, he gained omniscience. For the remainder of his life he preached on the true nature of reality. He died at the age of 72, gaining final release from further rebirth, his soul having become free from karma.

According to Jain traditions, Mahavira is said to have established a following of 36,000 nuns and 14,000 monks, who were supported by a lay community of nearly 500,000

The making of offerings to stone images of the Ford-makers is an important part of Jain observance

men and women. After Mahavira's death, Jainism received patronage from rulers and wealthy lay-people, and by 50 B.C.E. had spread into the western and southern parts of India.

Sky clad and white clad

By that time a major division in Jainism had arisen between those who believed that monks should go naked and those who believed that it was permissible for monks to wear simple white garments. The former are known as Digambaras, meaning "sky clad," the latter as Shvetambaras, meaning "white clad." The Digambaras are concentrated in the south of India, the Shvetambaras in the west. This remains the major sectarian division within Jainism.

Jain scriptures

The original teachings of Mahavira and his disciples were transmitted orally from teacher to pupil for generations

before being put into writing. [...] spoken language of the day ch[...] the teachings gradually becam[...] few learned monks. Many of th[...]

5th century C.E., a council of Shvetambara monks in Gujarat prepared an edition of the surviving texts and committed them to writing. However, the Digambaras do not recognize the authenticity of the Shvetambara scriptures and have their own texts. The oldest Digambara texts are the *Scripture of Six Parts* and the *Treatise on the Passions*, which date from the 2nd or 3rd centuries C.E.

The sacred literatures of both the Shvetambaras and the Digambaras are written in highly specialized language and fully understood only by learned monks. As a result, manuscripts of the sacred texts became objects to be venerated, rather than texts to be read. This situation began to change in the 19th century, when editions of the sacred texts were published, making them available to lay scholarship.

Alongside the sacred literature there developed a popular literature, the purpose of which was to teach the truths of Jainism to lay people in a lively and amusing way. This story literature is often based on folk tales which were given a Jain moral, though in the case of some of the racier stories, this is rather tenuous.

The teachings of Mahavira were not written down until the 5th century C.E. Today the language of the Jain scriptures, shown in this 15th-century manuscript, can only be understood by learned monks and scholars

JAIN MONKS AND NUNS

Here is a contemporary description of the initiation and lifestyle of a Jain monk.

"Today, Satish Mehta is going to become a Jain monk. He is 23 years old and he lives in Rajkot in Gujarat. He is escorted by his very proud friends and family with great festivity to the temple for the initiation ceremony. There, in the presence of Jain ascetics, he takes the five great vows of a Jain monk: not to harm any forms of life; not to lie; not to steal; to renounce sexual activity; to renounce all worldly possessions and mental attachments. Then, in imitation of Mahavira, he plucks out his hair. Most of his head has previously been shaved so only a few tufts of hair remain. Satish is given a white robe, a small broom (to gently remove any living creatures before he sits or lies down), a staff, and a begging bowl.

To symbolize his rebirth into a new way of life, Satish takes a new name; henceforth he will be known as Vijayasagara. He has taken this name from his monastic teacher. Vijayasagara fasts until the next day, when in the company of two other monks, he goes for the first time to seek alms. Great religious merit will accrue to the lucky householder from whom Vijayasagara takes alms. Vijayasagara will travel in company with two or three other monks, leading a life of rigorous discipline and begging for all his

The Udayagiri Caves, near Orissa in India, were once the home of a group of Jain monks who lived a life of great hardship, renouncing all possessions and fasting for days on end

food. When walking he wil⬛⬛⬛⬛⬛⬛⬛⬛⬛⬛ he
trample on insects or cause⬛⬛⬛⬛⬛⬛⬛⬛⬛⬛a-
tion sprouting underfoot. I⬛⬛⬛⬛⬛⬛⬛⬛⬛⬛gs
he will visit temples, holy ⬛⬛⬛⬛⬛⬛⬛⬛⬛He
will give instruction to lay pe⬛⬛⬛⬛⬛⬛⬛⬛ws
old, he may decide to unde⬛⬛⬛⬛⬛⬛⬛⬛h,
under the supervision of his⬛⬛⬛⬛⬛⬛⬛⬛ed
death will ensure the eventua⬛⬛⬛⬛⬛⬛⬛⬛er
rebirth within a very few lif⬛⬛⬛⬛

The ascetic life

Satish Mehta became a Shve⬛⬛⬛⬛⬛⬛⬛⬛k
dressed in a white robe. Or⬛⬛⬛⬛⬛⬛⬛⬛ks
renounce all clothing and g⬛⬛⬛⬛⬛⬛⬛⬛e
there have been relatively fe⬛⬛⬛⬛⬛⬛⬛⬛s-
tain the intense asceticism o⬛⬛⬛⬛⬛⬛⬛⬛e
Digambaras have evolved low⬛⬛⬛⬛⬛⬛⬛⬛y
wear clothes and are not sub⬛⬛⬛⬛⬛⬛⬛⬛of
the fully initiated monk. Tod⬛⬛⬛⬛⬛⬛⬛⬛0
fully initiated Digambara mo⬛⬛⬛

The ascetic life has alwa⬛⬛⬛⬛⬛⬛⬛⬛,
and today there are about thr⬛⬛⬛⬛⬛⬛⬛⬛a
nuns as there are monks. The⬛⬛⬛⬛⬛⬛⬛⬛
were noted for their learnin⬛⬛⬛⬛⬛⬛⬛⬛of
Jain nuns is not as high as tha⬛⬛⬛⬛⬛⬛⬛⬛e
general attitude to women in⬛⬛⬛⬛⬛⬛⬛⬛
the most senior nun is held to⬛⬛⬛⬛⬛⬛⬛⬛-
ly initiated monk, and among⬛⬛⬛⬛⬛⬛⬛⬛l
belief that interaction with n⬛⬛⬛⬛⬛⬛⬛⬛s
interaction with monks.

Jain ascetics are not suppo⬛⬛⬛⬛⬛⬛⬛⬛s
rule prevents monks and nun⬛⬛⬛⬛⬛⬛⬛⬛
interacting with the Jain com⬛⬛⬛⬛⬛⬛⬛⬛
persal). Some modernizing sec⬛⬛⬛⬛⬛⬛⬛⬛
tiating lower order ascetics t⬛⬛⬛⬛⬛⬛⬛⬛
apply, and these ascetics have tr⬛⬛⬛⬛⬛⬛⬛⬛
are not always accepted as true⬛⬛⬛⬛⬛⬛⬛⬛
the lay communities whom the⬛⬛⬛⬛⬛⬛⬛⬛
ties of the diaspora, lay peopl⬛⬛⬛⬛⬛⬛⬛⬛
traditional function of giving r⬛⬛⬛⬛⬛⬛⬛⬛

*The statue of Lord Bahubali towers over the Jain holy site of
Sravanabelagola in Karnataka state in India*

THE JAIN LAITY

Mahavira's message was one of asceticism; he preached that it is necessary to abandon home and family to gain salvation. However, Jain monks and nuns depend on the wider community for sustenance, so the life of a householder is seen as having its own value, with rules of conduct that are modified versions of the vows taken by Jain monks and nuns.

Though Jain monks lead lives of extreme austerity, Jain temples, funded by the laity, can be lavishly decorated

The ideal life of the laity is described in an early Jain text called The Ten Chapters on Lay Followers, containing the story of an extremely rich Jain layman called Ananda, who owned over 40,000 cows and a vast amount of gold. After living the life of a Jain layman for 14 years, he decided to spend the rest of his life practicing asceticism. He gave away all his wealth, fasted continuously, gained super-human knowledge and, after his death, was reborn as a god in heaven. That was his penultimate rebirth; at the end of his next life he gained final liberation.

Religion and wealth

Asceticism and wealth are the key themes of the story of Ananda. Many people have been struck by the contrast between the ascetic ethic of the Jain religion, which stresses the necessity of the abandonment of worldly goods as a means to salvation, and the wealth of the Jain lay community. From a very early period, the mercantile professions have been the favored occupations of Jain lay people. One of the reasons for this is that the Jain ethic of non-violence discourages occupations which cause direct harm to life. Eventually, the mercantile ethic of probity in business dealing, sound credit and respectability became inseparable from the religious ethic. Outward prosperity came to be seen as a measure of inner piety. The giving of lavish donations to finance the building or decoration of Jain temples allows the Jain laity to demonstrate both their financial probity and their religious piety.

There is a Jain tradition of didactic stories concerning the virtues of giving, the moral being that giving for religious purposes is the cause of worldly prosperity. One of these stories, dating back to the 6th century C.E., is about a man who lived in great poverty. Despite his poverty, he gave food to a Jain monk. As a result of his generosity to the monk, he was reborn as the merchant Shalibhadra, a man of immeasurable wealth, who remains the proverbial name and type for any wealthy Jain.

Lay people have played an important role in the renewal of the religion. Lonka Shah, who lived in Gujarat in the 15th century, was the originator of a movement which was

The prosperity of the Jain community [...]
success in mercantile professions, and [...]
temples such as this at Mour [...]

opposed to the worship of imag[...]
was a scribe and claimed scriptur[...]
tion of image worship. He was pr[...]
Islam. Out of his teaching grew [...]
the Sthanakavasis, a name that mea[...]
Halls," because its followers reject t[...]
which centre on temples.

A Jain layman, Rajchandra Mehta (1867–1901), was a
formative influence on the young Gandhi. He claimed, at
the age of seven, to have remembered his former lives as a
result of seeing the funeral cremation of a friend. This recov-
ered memory convinced him of the truths of Jainism. He
became very learned in Jain philosophy and, in 1897, wrote
a short verse summary of his beliefs called the *Atmasiddhi*
("The Perfection of the Soul"). Today he is revered as a
teacher, and temples have been dedicated to him in India
and elsewhere.

WORSHIP AND FESTIVALS

Ceremonies and rituals in Jain temples are based on the daily worship of stone images of the Fordmakers. Jain lay people are expected to worship each morning after bathing but before breakfast. An offering of "eight substances" is made: perfume, flowers, rice, incense, light, candy, fruit, and water. A temple attendant, known as a *pujari*, looks after the images and clears away after worship. He keeps the food offerings as his fee. The pujari is not a priest, and does not mediate between the worshiper and the Fordmakers. In many temples the pujari is not even a Jain. Temple worship is primarily a lay activity; ascetics do not participate in it because, having abandoned worldly possessions, they have nothing to give the Fordmakers.

Fordmakers are unlike Hindu gods in that they are not considered to be physically present to the worshiper. Devotion to Fordmakers generates a positive mental state, and generates religious merit in the worshiper, which leads eventually to a good rebirth. Laymen often bid for the right to perform ritual actions in the temple; this enhances the prestige of the successful bidder and raises money for the temple. Bidding is a male activity. Fasting is the main religious activity of

Above: *Jain holy sites such as Sravanabelagola in India are the focus of regular pilgrimages, combining social activity with religious devotion*
Below: *The temple at Ranakpor in Rajasthan. Jain laymen bid for the right to perform temple duties, thus raising money for the temple.*

*Daily temple worship is central ...
tributes to a po...*

Jain laywomen. Women oft... ...al
halls. The completion of a su... ...o
a woman's family, and photog... ...t
to record the occasion.

The Paryushana fe...

The main annual festival of th... ...,
meaning "Abiding," which is... ...
At that time of the year Jain as... ...,
since the ground teems with... ...
be destroyed by their trampl... ...a
retreat, lasting for eight days... ...
the preaching of the monks, ...
is read and ritually re-enacte...

On the final day of the fe... ...
sion and forgiveness takes pla... ...
any offences which may have... ...
year are solicited from one's... ...
tances, with letters requestin... ...
and family who are not preser...

The Digambara fest...

The equivalent Digambara fes... ...
time of year, and is known... ...
Religious Qualities. The ten... ...
gentleness, uprightness, purity... ...
renunciation, abandonment of ... ...
festival revolves around the rea... ...
ities on ten successive days.

Throughout India there are... ...
holy by the Jains, usually becau... ...
tion with the life stories of the ... ...
these holy places is an important... ...
sion of Jains, and is particularly ... ...
the gaining of religious merit w... ...

Every Jain layman hopes to... ...
one visit to a pilgrimage site. Th... ...

sites are Satrunjaya and Mount Girnar in Gujarat, and Mount
Abu in Rajasthan. At both places there are large complexes
of beautiful Jain temples. Sometimes, mass pilgrimages are
sponsored by wealthy members of the lay community, with
coaches or trains being specially hired for the occasion. Great
prestige and religious merit accrue to the person who enables
a large number of people to visit holy places.

CHRISTIANITY

Love God and love your neighbor as yourself

Christianity is practiced in every continent of the world and is, with Islam, the most widespread of the world's religions. It is estimated that there will be two billion Christians in the world by the year 2000, about 32 per cent of the world population. This figure includes Christians of many different theological views and persuasions, for — though they all draw their inspiration from the example and teachings of Jesus — there are many different forms of Christianity in the world today, from rationalists, who accept Christian ethical teaching but not Christ's miracles, to fundamentalists, who insist on the literal truth of the Gospels.

Despite the size and _____ y,
and its long history, _____ c;
it has to be in order to fa_____ ld
issues that arise with each _____ y
Christians recognize that the_____ a
destination. Some of the _____ t
Christianity are attitudes tow_____ ,
and questions about abortion, _____ .
There is also theological deba_____
Bible, and the challenge of fu_____
of continued scientific devel_____
concerned about their relatio_____
particularly where there is a hi_____
as is the case with Islam. In s_____
United Kingdom and the US_____
church and state is also an _____
Christian lobby exerts an incr_____
on government at a local and n_____

Central beliefs

Despite these challenges, and_____
theology and religious practices _____
traditions, there are essential ar_____
and teachings that underpin the _____
belief that sets Christianity apa_____
belief that Jesus was, and is, the_____

Christians follow the example_____
to know how to live their lives. Je_____
others, particularly those who w_____
be beneath consideration, such a_____
tors, and Samaritans. Consequent_____
is devoting time to caring. Proje_____
the international. One of the m_____
nizations providing care is the_____
charities include Christian Aid, th_____
World Vision. Their aim is to pro_____
spiritually, for those they seek to _____

Christianity is predominant_____
converting religion. It is import_____
throughout the world that all peop_____

Jesus Christ, depicted here in a mosaic in the Church of St Sophia in Istanbul, is the central figure for all Christians

to hear about Jesus. In the United States the Christian message has been brought within the reach of millions through the medium of television, with even some small (mostly fundamentalist) sects having their own broadcasting stations.

Missionary work has always been, and continues to be, an important feature of Christianity. The assertiveness of some Christians has led to conflict, particularly where the urge to convert has been seen as indicative of a sense of superiority, and where it has dismissed the claims of other world religions to meaningful spiritual and religious insights.

Despite the energy and volatility of Christianity, it should not be forgotten that, for most practicing Christians, the issues and conflicts which press at the edge of the religion are often somewhat remote. For the majority of ordinary Christians, religion is not about politics, missionary work, or even about theology – it is about their daily life, and how their beliefs about God inform their spirituality and the choices they make.

JESUS, THE MESSIAH

Jesus is the central figure of Christianity. According to tradition, he was born about 2,000 years ago, in Bethlehem in Judea, a client kingdom of the Roman Empire. The ministry of Jesus — that is the time when he was an active preacher, teacher and healer with a band of followers — lasted for about three years and ended with his death by crucifixion in Jerusalem. Details about the life of Jesus can be found in the first four books of the New Testament, and evidence of his existence can also be found in the historical writings of several authors who lived during, or just after, his lifetime.

For example, the Jewish historian Josephus (around 37 – 100 C.E.) wrote about Jesus as a teacher, "a doer of wonderful deeds," a man who "drew to himself many," who died on a cross and whose followers saw him alive three days later. The Jewish Talmud records his existence and speaks of his execution as a criminal. Other evidence comes in the form of burial caskets from the time which show there were followers who looked to the eternal life he promised. It should not be overlooked that Jesus was a Jew, who was brought up, lived, and died in that tradition. It was the followers of Jesus who went on to establish the distinctive religion which is Christianity.

Human and divine

The fact that Jesus existed is accepted by almost all historians, and he is revered as a prophet by several religions other than Christianity, including Islam. For Christians, however, Jesus is more than a prophet: he is the Messiah (or Christ), the Son of God, whose coming was foretold in the Old Testament. Christians believe that, through his death on the cross, Jesus was the ultimate sacrifice to God, enabling all those who believe to enter a new relationship with Him, which culminates in salvation and the enjoyment of eternal life. This central belief is one of the key features which distinguish Christianity from the other major world religions. A passage from the New Testament of the Bible summarizes the belief thus:

> "For God so loved the world that he gave his one and
> only Son, that whoever believes in him shall not perish
> but have eternal life." (John 3:16)

In order for the death of Jesus to atone for the sins of humanity, Christians believe that Jesus had to be both human and divine. Christians would ask, if Jesus was not human how could he atone for humanity? And if he was not God how could anyone believe that God cared and knew what it was like to live as a human and face suffering, temptation,

and death? Christians also b████████████████████n-
tion of God could change h████████████████████he
opportunity to get back into████████████
fying relationship with Him.

Although theologians h████████████
struggled to explain how one ████████████
fully incorporate both the di████████████
the human, Christians point to████████████
in the Bible to show that the tw████████████
existed in Jesus. For example, t████████████
ment of his birth by the angel████████████,
his baptism (*Matt. 3:13-17*), h████████████
to forgive sin (*Matt. 9:1-8*), an████████████
(*John 11*) are amongst events ci████████████
of Jesus.

On the other hand, Christ████████████
Jesus is evident in the story of████████████
(*Matt. 4*), his mourning at the d████████████
and his thirst on the cross (*Joh████████████
interesting biblical passage that████████████
purpose of Jesus' life is the pro████████████

Jesus taught profound truth████████████
parables and metaphors, often be████████████
the shepherd, the careful and d████████████

Parables

One of Jesus' favorite ways of teaching was to
use short stories, called parables, like the story of
the lost sheep:

"There was once a farmer who had one hundred sheep.
He knew every single one of them. One day he was
counting them into the fold and he noticed that one was
missing. He went to look for the one that was missing, leaving
the others. Eventually he found it. He flung the sheep over
his shoulders and carried it back to join the others. That
night he invited his neighbors to a feast, as he was so happy.
Jesus said, I tell you there is more rejoicing in heaven over
one sinner who repents than over ninety-nine righteous
persons who do not need to repent" (*Luke 15:1-7*). The image
of a shepherd is used by Jesus on more than one occasion
and, in the Gospel of John, he refers to himself as the Good
Shepherd, whose task it is to lead the people who have gone
astray back to a proper relationship with God.

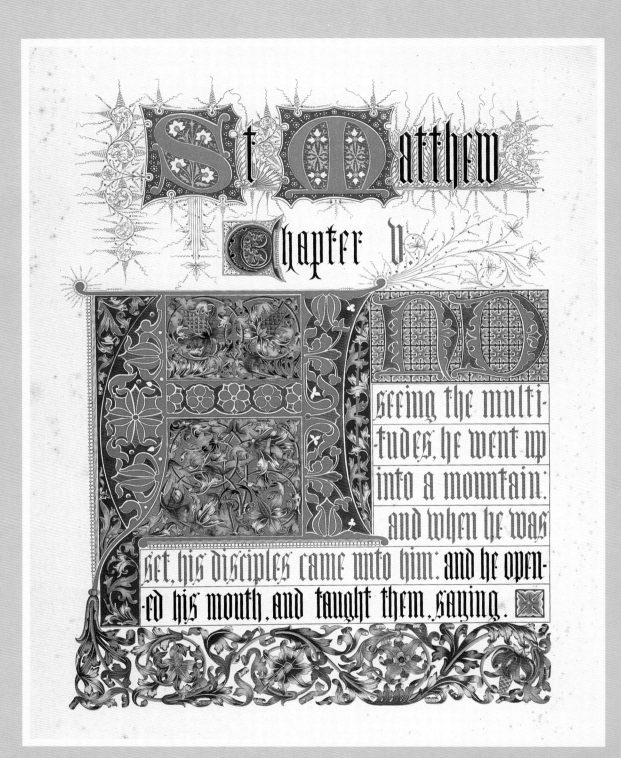

Part of the Gospel of St. Matthew, written around 70-80 C.E., from
a 19th-century illuminated edition of the Bible

THE BIBLE

The _____ a, m_____ _____ ok of Chri_____ s, divided _____ d New Tes_____ is the scrip_____ tant to Christians because it _____ the coming of Jesus – himself _____ Testament reveals much a_____, and His relationship with humanity. Christianity is the only major religion that includes another faith's scriptures in its own holy book.

The New Testament deals with the life of Jesus and the Early Church, and marks the beginnings of a new relationship between God and humanity. For the writers of the New Testament, the Old Testament, alongside the teachings of Jesus, acted as a me_____ theological implications of the arr_____ Testament contains 27 books. Th_____ news") tell the story of Jesus' li_____ The Acts of the Apostles gives insi_____ Church, alongside 21 letters, mar_____ Paul. They deal with the many issu_____ in the early days of the religion. (_____ Testament for advice on living the r_____ and spiritual, for guidance on the_____ and for help in matters of doctrin_____

The Bible was not written as _____ edited and translated compilatic_____ authors, who came from differ_____ different times. Consequently, t_____ renderings and translations of the E_____

_____ y edition of the Gospels from _____ Putna in Romania

most sacred writings are considered to be the exact words of God as revealed to one person. Though these words are often translated into other languages, their real authority is only found in the original language and in one version.

Authority and interpretation

The original languages of the Bible were Hebrew, Greek and Aramaic, and the first translated version of the New Testament was in Latin. Because of the way in which the Bible has been compiled and translated, its authority and interpretation has been an issue for centuries. For example, some Christians believe that the creation narratives in Genesis give an accurate picture of what happened in history. Others see these as symbolic, with the most important point being that God created the world. Different interpretations of scripture and beliefs about the nature of its inspiration give rise to debate within the Church over many issues, from baptism to women priests.

Whatever they believe about the authority of the Bible, it has high status for all Christians. The Bible is the basis for private study and plays an important part in congregational worship. In many services, passages from the Bible are read to the congregation, and the leader of the service will deliver a sermon based on the reading. The sermon will interpret the reading for the congregation, commenting on its meaning and relevance.

For most Christians reading the Bible is more than just an intellectual exercise: the words have power and meaning for them that goes beyond mere literature. People have been converted to Christianity through reading the Bible; it is not simply an activity that follows on from being a Christian.

CHRISTIAN BELIEFS ABOUT GOD

Because Christianity grew out of Judaism, much of what Christians believe about the nature of God is based on teachings found in the Old Testament of the Bible. The teachings of Jesus and his followers, as found in the New Testament, serve to develop further and supplement these ancient ideas about God.

God has traditionally been personalized by Christians as male, and so is referred to as "He" and "Him." God is portrayed as a father in both the Bible and in Christian liturgy. The discipline of God is seen as being akin to the corrective role of a parent, who is acting in love.

"My son, do not despise the Lord's discipline, and do not resent his rebuke, because the Lord disciplines those he loves, as a father the son he delights in." (*Proverbs 3:11,12*)

However, the Bible also describes God using feminine imagery, for example as a mother suckling her young. Feminist interpretation of the Bible often explores these images in an attempt to redress what is sometimes called the "androcentric fallacy." In some branches of Christianity, particularly Catholicism, the female attributes of God are explored and emphasized through the particular veneration of Mary, the mother of Jesus.

God the creator

Christians believe in an eternal God, who was not born and will not die. They believe that God existed prior to the creation of the world and will continue to live after the end of the world. Though Christians may disagree on how the world was created, they all profess that God initiated it.

> "In the beginning God created the heavens and the earth." (Genesis 1:1)

For Christians, God is a God of love. and He created the world and humanity as an act of this love. The traditional

---

In Michelangelo's heroic vision of the Creation of Man, painted from 1508 onward for Pope Julius II on the ceiling of the Sistine Chapel in Rome, the artist conveys the powerful sense of humanity as essentially noble and made in the image of a loving God

Earlier Christian commentators believ[...]
eternal punishment in the fires of He[...]
from a 14th-century manuscript o[...]

A 15th-century painting showing St Michael weighing souls on
Judgement Day when, according to traditional Christian belief, all
people will rise from the dead to be judged for their deeds

Christian belief is that when the w[...]
thing was perfect and the relati[...]
and God was without fault. But [...]
will," and therefore the choice w[...]
disobey and commit sin. The my[...]
book of Genesis attempt to expl[...]
tionship is broken when people [...]
exercise their free will by choosi[...]

God the judge

In some biblical stories, God is s[...]
break his laws, but ultimately He[...]
welcomes those who repent bac[...]
with Him. For example, in the Bo[...]

> *"If you repent I will restore you th[...]*
> *(Jeremiah 16:19b)*

Christians believe that, through the sacrifice of Jesus, God has offered forgiveness of sin and a new way to relate to Him. For Christians the death of Jesus on the cross means that they can have a personal and intimate relationship with God, as Jesus himself did.

Christians believe that God not only created and sustains the world, but that He will also bring it to an end. The New Testament is often read as pointing to a time when Jesus will return, and early Christians fully expected to witness the Second Coming in their lifetime. When Christ returns, there will be a day of judgement for all, with God as the judge. The traditional Christian belief was that those who were judged and found wanting would go to Hell, a place of eternal suffering, while the rest would go to Heaven where they would enjoy eternal bliss. Today, some Christians conceptualize heaven as a full union with God after death, and hell as complete alienation from Him.

THE HOLY SPIRIT

The Christian doctrine of the Trinity says that God has three natures: Father, Son, and Holy Spirit. In the New Testament, the Acts of the Apostles describes how Jesus promised his disciples that he would leave a "helper." This helper was to be the Holy Spirit (*Acts 1:8*).

At its simplest, the Spirit is that which moves or inspires people. It is a human characteristic to experience the spiritual, and to be moved by emotional or demanding experiences. However, it is difficult to describe the spiritual, and attempts can only be made through the use of images. In the Bible, the Holy Spirit is described variously as a fire, as water, and as the breath of life, but the two most common and striking images are violent wind and the dove.

The dove is a recurrent symbol for the Holy Spirit in Christian art

One believer describes the influence of the Holy Spirit on her life in this way: "The Holy Spirit helps me to know the presence of God in my daily life. I believe it encourages me to share what I believe with others through the gifts, or 'fruits,' of the Holy Spirit, such as love, joy, peace, and goodness.

The Holy Spirit is important to me when I pray. It is common to hear people praying that the Holy Spirit will bring about a more personal experience of God, and in occurrences such as healing, the 'Toronto Blessing,' and the baptism of the Holy Spirit, this is certainly the case.

The 'Toronto Blessing' is a particularly recent phenomenon experienced in many churches. It is called this because it was first experienced in Toronto, Canada. It has been described as a huge outpouring of God's Holy Spirit upon Christians, creating a feeling of refreshment and renewal. In this respect it is a type of baptism. What is really important about this is its long-term effect on people, but its immediate power is also very striking.

Christian imagery

The wind, which is powerful, cannot be seen; only the consequences are visible. Similarly, the Holy Spirit cannot be seen, though Christians believe that its work in and for people is evident. A dove often symbolizes the peace and reconciliation that the Holy Spirit can bring. The Bible describes the Holy Spirit descending at Jesus' baptism in the form of a dove. This symbol is greatly used in the visual arts to represent the Holy Spirit, and is a favorite and traditional image in Christian iconography.

Direct experience of the Holy Spirit is considered very important by most Pentecostal and Charismatic churches.

Spiritual healing

Some people claim to have been physically healed through the experience, while others faint or are overcome by a tingling sensation or an overwhelming sense of joy. When I was baptized I sensed the presence of the Holy Spirit as if it was a mild electric shock. On another occasion I opened my eyes after praying and felt the physical sensation of being washed.

Jesus described the Holy Spirit as a 'power from on high' and in this respect I believe it to be God's spiritual power in our daily lives. If God had not sent it after Jesus returned to heaven, Christians would have felt deserted."

...oly Spirit at Pentecost, depicted in this ...ing, is believed to have inspired the Apostles ...uasive advocates for Christianity

THE TRINITY

Christianity is a monotheistic religion – it believes in just one God (*1 Timothy 2:5*). However, Christians also believe that, in the course of history, God has shown Himself in three different and distinct ways: as Father, Son, and Holy Spirit. This doctrine of the threefold nature of God is known as the doctrine of the Trinity.

Christians believe that each of the three "beings" in the Trinity has unique characteristics and has revealed something distinct to humanity about the nature of God. Each of the three is whole, but equally each is God and part of the one Godhead. This is difficult to comprehend, but there are two relatively simple comparisons which have been offered to illuminate the complex idea. In the 5th century C.E., Saint Patrick compared the Trinity to a shamrock, a plant with one stem and three leaves. Each leaf is obviously distinct, but each is still an integral part of the plant. Water can exist in three forms: as ice, a solid, as liquid and as steam. Each form has different properties, but each is also still water.

These images help to give us some insights, but they are not solutions or explanations. Over the centuries many people have offered greater or lesser insights, but the idea that God is one substance, existing as three persons or aspects, will continue to keep theologians busy for the foreseeable future. But for many Christians it is part of the mystery of God which does not have to be understood, only believed. The Trinity is a vital part of the Christian faith, enshrined in the creeds, and appearing in the liturgy of the services of baptism, confirmation, and communion.

Three persons in one

At times the belief in the threefold nature of God has laid Christianity open to the charge that it is not a monotheistic faith. Christians have often refuted this by looking back to the Bible. In the Old Testament, references are made to the personification of God's Word and Spirit, and the plural is used for describing God. For example, in the creation narrative in Genesis it says: "Then God said, "Let us make man in our image, in our likeness.""

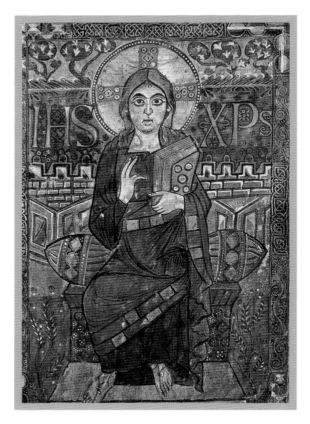

The concept of the Trinity is one of the most difficult to comprehend, and was the cause of division and sectarianism in the early Church. Most Christians accept that this is just one of the many aspects of God that are not susceptible to rational explanation

In the earliest of Christian writings that came to be included in the New Testament, Jesus is referred to by the very same Greek word for God as is used in the Old Testament for God Himself. Jesus is also given the functions previously associated with God, such as forgiveness, creation and judgement. In the famous beginning to the Gospel of John, Jesus is described as coming from the Father thus:

'In the beginning was the Word, and the Word was with God, and the Word was God. He was with God in the beginning."(John 1:1,2)

The "Word" John refers to is Jesus, and this is a clear statement of the belief that Jesus is part of the Godhead.

Elsewhere in the New ▓▓▓▓▓▓▓▓▓▓▓ and Holy Spirit are mentioned ▓▓▓▓▓▓▓▓▓▓▓ s of the baptism of Jesus by his ▓▓▓▓▓▓▓▓▓▓▓ ree are present: the Son is in th▓▓▓▓▓▓▓▓▓▓ords

of approval from the heavens, and the Holy Spirit descends in the form of a dove. Also in reference to baptism, Jesus commands his disciples to baptize in the name of the Father, Son, and Holy Spirit.

▓▓▓▓▓▓▓▓ *he doctrine of the Trinity is found in the* ▓▓▓▓▓▓▓▓ *ism of Jesus, when the voice of God spoke from* ▓▓▓▓▓▓▓▓ *Giotto's Scrovegni Chapel fresco in Padua*

CHRISTIAN WORSHIP

Christian worship takes a huge variety of forms. There is no such thing as "typical" Christian worship, and this section describes only some examples of the different practices that are followed.

Many Christians engage in public congregational worship on a Sunday, but the Sunday service is not the only time for worship – rather it is a high point in a week of devotion. As well as attending services, many Christians pray and read the Bible at different times during the week. Indeed, many Christians would consider their daily life a form of worship, because they dedicate to God those things that they believe God has given to them. Helping others, proclaiming or spreading their faith, giving up time and money for church activities, or even carrying out any task to the best of their ability may also be thought of as worship by Christians, if these things are inspired by the love of God.

This window in the German Church in Stockholm shows the Christian ideal of daily life as a form of worship

Music is a core component of Christian ritual; many of the greatest works of the Western musical canon were composed for liturgical use

Christian congregational worship most often takes place in a dedicated place, such as a church or chapel, but some groups prefer to meet in a hall or in the home of one of their members. There is no typical church service, for the form of worship depends on tradition, geographical region, the branch or denomination, and sometimes even personal preference within a denomination.

However, there are some threads running through Christian worship. Services will, in general, include singing, reading from the Bible, preaching, praying, and, on certain occasions, a ceremony involving bread and wine. It is not unusual for there to be drama, dancing, as well as the recitation of communal prayers, confessions, and creeds. Ritual objects such as crosses, crucifixes, candles, and censers may also play a role.

Music and prayer

Music has always been an important part of Christian worship. Traditional music includes choral singing and hymns. In many churches singing is accompanied by an organ, but in others, for example the Greek Orthodox, singing is unaccompanied. The Quakers have no singing at all, and the Pentecostals are renowned for their gospel choirs.

In churches with an e⬛⬛⬛⬛⬛⬛⬛⬛⬛⬛⬛⬛nal hymns are supplemented ⬛⬛⬛⬛⬛⬛⬛⬛⬛⬛ses accompanied by small ban⬛⬛⬛⬛⬛⬛⬛⬛⬛ms and wind instruments. Man⬛⬛⬛⬛⬛⬛⬛⬛⬛rds updated. Some say this ma⬛⬛⬛⬛⬛⬛⬛⬛y's society; others believe tha⬛⬛⬛⬛⬛⬛⬛⬛can become over-simplified or d⬛⬛⬛⬛⬛⬛⬛st.

Prayer is an important ⬛⬛⬛⬛⬛⬛⬛ian worship as a way of comm⬛⬛⬛⬛⬛⬛ns often direct their prayers to⬛⬛⬛⬛⬛⬛⬛ey believe it was Jesus who br⬛⬛⬛⬛⬛⬛⬛en God and humanity. A prayer⬛⬛⬛⬛⬛⬛ds:

"in the name of our Lord Jesus," or "through Jesus Christ our Lord." Roman Catholics also believe that Mary, the mother of Jesus, can intercede with God.

Prayers may take the form of a set recitation, such as the Lord's Prayer, the Hail Mary, or a prayer from a prayer book. Other prayers may be inspired by the concerns of the moment. Prayers often take distinct forms, with themes such as confession, praise, intercession, or thanksgiving. Prayer can also take the form of meditation and listening, so that the worshiper can discover God's will. This is a vital aspect of prayer, because the desire to do God's will lies at the heart of a Christian's faith.

⬛⬛⬛⬛⬛⬛rship usually takes place in a church, ⬛⬛⬛⬛⬛⬛l contemplation are also encouraged

CHRISTIAN RITES OF PASSAGE

Baptism is the most widely recognized form of initiation into the Christian faith. The word "baptism" comes from the Greek, meaning "to immerse," and baptism has its roots in two ancient practices: naming ceremonies and purification ceremonies. Naming ceremonies, both at birth and as a rite of passage, mark a transition between one stage of life and another. Purification ceremonies frequently include symbolic rituals involving water.

Jesus was baptized by John in the River Jordan at the start of his ministry. Although there is no record that Jesus performed any baptisms himself, it is written that he commanded all who believed in him to be baptized (*Matthew 28:19*). Baptism was – and still is – a way of showing that a person's sins are forgiven, and that they have passed from their old life into a new life as a Christian.

In the Church there are two forms of baptism: infant and adult baptism. Infant baptism traditionally takes place at a font in a church. Water is poured over the child's head

as it is baptized "in the name of the Father, Son, and Holy Spirit." Reference is also made to the baby's passing from darkness to light. Sometimes godparents, Christian adults chosen to oversee the child's spiritual development, play a role in the ceremony.

There is no specific reference to infants being baptized in the New Testament, but those who practice infant baptism refer to the household baptisms mentioned in the Acts of the Apostles *(16:15,33)* which they believe would have included children of all ages. Advocates of infant baptism argue that it is the way children of Christian parents should be received into the Christian family.

Adult baptism

The baptism of adult converts is practiced throughout Christianity. With some Christian denominations, notably the Baptists, the baptismal ceremony is exclusively for adults who have made a personal choice and commitment. A Christian called Alison Beesley tells of her own experience of baptism at the age of eighteen.

in the sight of God. The baptismal pool itself symbolizes a grave. Being laid back into the water symbolized the death of my old life and the resurrection to a new life where my relationship with Jesus and God was important. In baptism I was identifying myself with Jesus' death and showing that because Jesus died I was no longer condemned to eternal death, but that in becoming a Christian and identifying with Jesus through baptism, I would, like Jesus, be resurrected to enjoy an everlasting life with God.

After the baptism the minister laid his hands on my head and prayed that I would receive the Holy Spirit. Looking back, my baptism was the real starting point in my Christian life. I can see the times when God, through the power of the Holy Spirit, has given me guidance and strength in my life."

"When I became a Christia███████████████ give me all the wrong things th███████████████ ieve that at that moment God ███████████████ my life marked a new beginn███████████████ Him. In some way I wanted to s███████████████ what had happened to me. Bapt███████████████ king this change in my life. It al███████████████ esus' words in Mark 16:16, 'V███████████████ ized will be saved.'

The symbolism of ba███████████████ fully immersed into the water b███████████████ vater symbolized that I had bee███████████████ sin. I also wore white to sho███████████████ clean

Baptism has the same symbolic███████████████ away the original sin that Christians███████████████ m and Eve. The ceremony takes dif███████████████ st common (above), but some ch███████████████ eft), reserve the ceremony for adult███████████████ ment to Christianity. Some African███████████████ of a church service and make███████████████

CHRISTIAN RITES

Confirmation

Denominations that practice infant baptism almost always have a further ceremony where a person can "confirm" or renew the promises that were made on their behalf by other adults and godparents. Among the denominations that have confirmation services are the Roman Catholic, Methodist, Anglican and the Greek Orthodox churches. The confirmation service takes place once a candidate is considered to be responsible for their own spiritual development and religious behavior. Many denominations regard this as occurring at around the age of 14, corresponding with the onset of puberty and the development of physical maturity, though it can occur at any age.

In the weeks or months leading up to the service, candidates will often go to classes to learn more about the Christian faith and the vows that they will be taking. This helps to ensure that they know what they are undertaking, and that they are happy with the promises thay will make during the ceremony. In the Catholic service, candidates are anointed with oil in the sign of the cross, and they are gently slapped on the cheeks to symbolize that all their previous sins have been forgiven.

In most denominations, the ceremony is performed by a high-ranking member of a hierarchy, often a bishop. The most important part of the service involves the bishop laying hands on the head of the candidate. The laying on of hands is an ancient and important ritual, symbolizing "apostolic succession," the passing on of the Spirit from one generation to the next, reaching back to Jesus.

Confirmation takes place when a candidate feels ready to make his or her own decision about being a member of the Church

Holy Communion

For most denominations o███ ████████ ██████ ████ the
exceptions of the Salvati█████████ ███ ███ ███████ the
sharing of bread and win███████ ███ ██████ ██ ████████ s of
deep significance. The ce████████ ██ ████ ██ ████ ██████ical
account of the last meal J██████ ███ █████ ██ ████████ fore
he was put to death, and t███████ ██ █████ ███ ████ e go
far back into history. The sh████████ ██ ████████████ ding
Holy Communion, the Lo█████████ ███ ███████ Mass,
and the Divine Liturgy. T██████████ ██ ███ █████████ ony
lies in the fact that it ena███ ███ ███████ ██ ████████ ber
and share symbolically in███ ███████ ██ █████ ██ ████ irm
belief in Jesus as the Savi██████ ███ ████████ ███ ████ e to
achieve a place in heaven.

In the Orthodox and C█████████ ██████████ ███ ████████ ony
has an element of the mir██████ ██ ██████ ██████████ that
the bread and wine actual████████ ███ ████ ███ █████ d of

This window in Buckfast Abbey depicts the Last Supper, when Christ
shared a meal of bread and wine with his disciples and asked them
to do the same regularly in his memory

Jesus. In Christian theology the term for this is "transubstantiation." Not all denominations believe this; for many
Christians the purpose of taking the sacraments is simply
to remember all that Jesus did for them by dying on the
cross, and to show their allegiance to him. The bread and
wine serve as a visual reminder to help the believer comprehend the depth of what Jesus achieved.

As with other aspects of worship, the form of the ceremony varies. In some churches, all participants take both
bread and wine. In others, only the priest will take wine,
on behalf of the rest of the congregation. Whatever the form
of service, by participating in the ceremony the believer
feels he or she is observing the custom Jesus commanded
his disciples to continue after his death, in his memory.

CHRISTIAN FESTIVALS

Like most other religions, Christianity has a cycle of festivals to mark out key points in the year and celebrate important events. The timing of most Christian festivals is closely linked to the seasonal cycle rather than the dates of actual events; indeed, the festivals are often celebrated on different dates in different regions and by different denominations. Usually the timing of the festivals reflects their displacement of earlier religious festivals with similar symbolic meanings. For example, the timing of Christmas – a festival of birth – coincides with the winter solstice. Easter, in the middle of spring, celebrates rebirth and fertility through the death and resurrection of Jesus.

Children frequently celebrate Christmas by re-enacting the events of the Christmas story, like this group in Andalusia, Spain

Christmas

The feast that celebrates the birth of Christ – Christmas – is held in the northern hemisphere's winter. In the modern world it is sometimes difficult to remember that this is a religious festival, because the Christian meaning of Christmas has been overlaid by other activities and traditions. For example, to the majority the most instantly recognizable symbol of Christmas is Santa Claus, or Father Christmas. He is based on the historical figure of Saint Nicholas who gave gifts to poor and needy children, but he has also taken on a number of pre-Christian Scandinavian traditions.

The period leading up to the Christmas celebration is called Advent, meaning "coming." It begins on the fourth Sunday before Christmas, and Christians are encouraged to think about how Jesus came into the world and about his return in the future.

Children are often given an Advent calendar, or an Advent candle, to help them count down the days to Christmas. In some churches Advent wreaths are hung up. These have five candles and

A 16th-century altarpiece showing the three wise men

evergreen leaves. One candle is lit on each Sunday during Advent, and the fifth candle on Christmas Day itself. The candles symbolize the light that came into the world with Jesus' birth. Advent services include the singing of hymns, and Bible readings that look forward to the coming of the Messiah. The purpose of such festivals of preparation as Advent is to heighten the awareness of the believers and to create a sense of expectation, which is then fittingly fulfilled at the climax of the festival.

Christmas was not instituted as a festival until the 4th century C.E., when Christians adapted elements of several existing Roman festivals, including one celebrating the birth of the pagan god Mithras, and changed them to the celebration of Jesus' birth. December is considered a good time to celebrate the coming of Jesus, the "Light of the World," because it is at this time of year (following the winter solstice in the northern hemisphere) that the days start to become lighter again as spring approaches. Many churches hold special services at midnight on Christmas Eve. Churches are decorated with

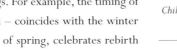

evergreen plants, such as ▨▨▨▨▨▨▨ the eternal nature of Jesus.

After Christmas come ▨▨▨▨▨▨▨ which falls early in January. This ▨▨▨▨▨▨▨ the wise men, or Magi, to Jesus ▨▨▨▨▨▨▨ ese were the first non-Jewish ▨▨▨▨▨▨▨ it is possible that they were fo▨▨▨▨▨▨▨ The

festival of Epiphany reminds Christians of their belief that the birth of Jesus was special for all the people of the earth, and not just for the Jews.

The Virgin and Child, here represented by Giovanni Paolo's 15th-century painting, is the most popular and enduring theme of early Western art

LENT
AND
EASTER

Lent is a time of denial, preparation, and purification leading up to the celebration of Easter, the major feast in the Christian calendar. Lent lasts for 40 days, reflecting the time that Jesus spent fasting in the wilderness before embarking on his ministry (*Matt. 4:1-11; Luke 4:1-13; Mark 1:12,13*). In the Early Church, converts to Christianity used to fast for 40 days before being admitted to the Church through mass baptisms held at Easter. This practice caught on as a beneficial way for all Christians to prepare for Easter.

Easter eventually supplanted earlier pagan festivals of rebirth and fertility, particularly the festival of the goddess Oestre, to which Christians owe the name Easter and the traditional seasonal symbol of the egg.

The day before Lent begins is commonly known as Mardi Gras (Fat Tuesday). In many parts of the world it is a day of great festivity because, in medieval times, Christians would eat up their remaining stocks of rich foods and wine or beer, all of which were forbidden during Lent. On this day believers also went to church to confess their sins and ask to be "shriven" (forgiven), hence the name Shrove Tuesday.

The re-enactment of Christ's triumphant entry into Jerusalem on Palm Sunday is a tradition brought from Spain to Latin America

In preparation for his coming ordeal, Christ spent a period in prayer and fasting in the wilderness, depicted in this 19th-century Russian painting

Ash Wednesday is the first day of Lent. On this day palm crosses from the previous year are burned, and in some churces the ash is used to mark a cross on worshipers' foreheads. This is a sign of penitence, and a reminder that human beings come from dust and will return to dust. Nowadays, few Christians fast rigorously, but many give up indulgences, such as cakes or candy, so as to share in Jesus' experience of sacrifice and temptation.

Holy Week

Palm Sunday marks the start of Holy Week, which culminates in the festivities of Easter Sunday. During the course of Holy Week, Christians remember all the events leading up to the Resurrection. According to the biblical account, Jesus went to Jerusalem on Palm Sunday to celebrate the Jewish festival of Passover. He entered the city on a donkey to the cheers of the crowds. The Gospels tell of the crowd waving palm leaves and strewing the roads with them to make a carpet in honor of Jesus. In memory of this, palm crosses are blessed and given out in some churches on Palm Sunday to be kept until the following Ash Wednesday.

The Thursday of Ho............dy Thursday, celebrates the fin............sciples – the Last Supper. D............his disciples bread and wine, an............im after his death by meeting............he Communion service on Ma............s a very special significance.

Later on the same day,............as, arrested by the Jewish autho............ir-rection and blasphemy. The............ed is known as Good Friday, ...or Christians, they believe tha............of death could Jesus atone for............

Christians commemorat............ial services, and processions. I............, a mock funeral is held. Catho............he

Cross, remembering all the events leading up to the Crucifixion through prayers and Bible readings.

Easter Sunday is the climax of the Christian year. This is a day of joy, when Christians celebrate the resurrection of Jesus. Some churches hold services at around midnight on Saturday to commemorate the discovery that the tomb Jesus had been buried in was empty. The church is dark at the start of the service, and candles are lit as a symbol that Jesus has conquered death and brought light into the world.

145

CHRISTIANS IN WORLD HISTORY

Christianity began as a distinct religion soon after the death of Jesus. The accounts given in the Acts of the Apostles record the way that Christianity spread quickly from Jerusalem to all parts of the Roman Empire. The missionary journeys of Paul were especially influential in the creation and development of Christian communities around the Mediterranean.

Christians suffered persecution during these early days, at the hands of both the Jewish and Roman authorities, but the religion continued to grow in size and influence. In 312 C.E., the emperor Constantine declared himself to be a Christian, and removed the laws prohibiting Christians from observing their religion. This paved the way for Christianity to become the established religion of the empire, bringing great political and social advantage to the Church.

When the Roman Empire divided into eastern and western branches, the Church also became divided, with one center of authority in Constantinople and another in Rome. From the Roman branch came the Roman Catholic church and ultimately the Protestant churches; from the eastern branch came the Orthodox churches of Greece, Russia and Eastern Europe.

During the Middle Ages, from around the 11th to the 14th century, Christianity established itself strongly in Europe. It was a very productive time, with the rise of new monastic orders, an abundance of inspirational mystics and great scholars and the erection of beautiful cathedrals. The Popes in Rome grew in authority and power, as the Church developed a political and economic role, in addition to its spiritual role. But towards the end of the Middle Ages, many felt that the Church had become corrupted by worldly power and that reform was necessary. Religious thinkers, such as Waldo in France, Wycliffe in Britain, and Hus in Prague, preached reform and began to translate the Bible from Hebrew, Latin, and Greek into the vernacular, so that its message was accessible to all.

The 16th century saw two great changes for the Roman Catholic church. The first, known as the Reformation, began

Christianity has inspired many architectural forms, from the magnificent Renaissance dome of the cathedral in Florence, to the elegant simplicity of the early New England clapboard churches, to the solid dignity of the Norman parish church in England

in 1517 when a German Augustinian monk, called Martin Luther, spoke out against the shortcomings of the Church, and precipitated a movement which led large numbers of Christians, particularly in northern Europe, to establish new movements. Known collectively today as the Reformed Churches, they look to the Bible for their primary authority, while the Catholic churches look to the authority of the Pope and established traditions.

La Chapelle de Notre Dame du H━━━━━━━━━━━━ by
Le Corbusier, was inspired ━━━━━━━━━━

The second great event f━━━━━━━━━━━━ng
up of the American continen━━━━━━━━━━━at
expansion for the religion, ━━━━━━━━━━he
geographical distribution of i━━━━━━━━━━g,
the northern part of the Am━━━━━━━━━t,
and the southern part is Ca━━━━━━━━━ns
have developed distinct re━━━━━━━━━of
Christianity which do not al━━━━━━━━━er
established European traditi━━━━━━━━━ty
in the African continent in the━━━━━━━━nt

great expansion, and the world community of Christianity has much to do to incorporate the vitality that Africa and the Americas bring to the religion.

In recent decades, Liberation Theology has developed in these areas of the world to try and combat poverty, racism and destitution. This has been particularly important for Christians in South America and South Africa, though there is also a branch that looks at oppression in Northern Ireland. Liberation Theology celebrates the oppressed as the shapers of the Kingdom of God, and aims to resolve problems with the guidance of scripture. Liberation Theologians focus on the image of Jesus in the Gospels as liberator of the poor, oppressed, and marginalized of society.

CHRISTIAN MOVEMENTS

Over the centuries, theological differences of opinion, variations in the way people wish to worship, and cultural differences have all led to the creation of a variety of denominations and practices within Christianity. Although in some cases differences have, and sometimes still do, lead to conflict, most modern Christians would see that what unites them – the belief in the saving power of Jesus – is more important than that which divides them. The ecumenical ("coming together") movement is a strong and growing force for unity. Even so, there remain many thousands of different branches, denominations and sects within Christianity. In many ways Christianity is a very dynamic religion, and anyone can – and many people do – set up their own Christian group, which may owe no allegiance to an established church.

Many Nonconformist churches, such as the Methodists, broke away from established churches during the upheaval following the Reformation

The Coptic Christians of Egypt split from the rest of Christianity in 451 C.E. and have evolved their own rituals

The Roman Catholic church

The head of the Roman Catholic church is the Pope. Catholics believe the lineage of the papacy can be traced from Saint Peter, the traditional first Bishop of Rome, on whom, Jesus said, the Church would be built. Catholics hold the saints and the Virgin Mary in high esteem, believe in Heaven, Hell and Purgatory, and believe that the bread and wine of Communion become the flesh and blood of Christ through a mystical process called "transubstantiation."

The Orthodox church

The division of the Roman Empire into Eastern and Western branches also led to a split between the Latin and Orthodox churches which became permanent in 1054 C.E. The Orthodox church includes the churches of Greece, Armenia, Serbia, and Russia. Their elaborate, and sometimes mysterious, ceremonies are designed to give God "the correct Glory." Communion is known as the Divine Liturgy, and is believed to be a re-enactment of Jesus' death and resurrection. Icons of Jesus and the saints are an important artistic and creative focus for worship.

The Episcopalian churches

Episcopalian churches are distinctive in that they are led by a hierarchy of archbishops and bishops. Episcopalian beliefs and practices often have much in common with Roman

Many Christians see th[...]
and Latin America as [...]

Catholic beliefs, but th[...] not accept the primacy of the [...] with branches and offshoots ac[...]ple. There are many churche[...]ines, though they have no form[...] one common form of organiz[...]

Worship in Episcopa[...]usly. Some worship follows [...] are also many "charismatic" [...]larly in areas of the world su[...]rches have been established re[...]

Nonconformist [...]

A Nonconformist churc[...]rm to the rules, organization [...]ished church. The term can the[...]istians that breaks away from a[...]re are

many thousands of Nonconformist churches. Some are long established, and have their roots in the fragmentation of Christianity that followed the Reformation. They include the Methodist, Baptist, Lutheran, Calvinist, and Quaker churches. Each group has its own organization, theology, and pattern of worship. For example, the Quakers are renowned for silent worship and for allowing anyone who feels "led" to speak within a service.

The charismatic movement

The word "charismatic" comes from the Greek "charisma," meaning "gifts." There has always been charismatic worship, but in the past few decades, particularly in North America, charismatic worship has been on the increase. Charismatic worship places great emphasis on practising the gifts of the Holy Spirit, such as healing and speaking in tongues. Services are characterized by uninhibited singing, dancing, clapping and the raising of hands. Charismatic services can be found in many denominations, but the Pentecostal church is especially renowned for this kind of worship.

THE NATURE OF ALLAH

"I ⸻ no ⸻ness that ⸻ r of Allah ⸻ that Musl⸻ day, espec⸻ It is the first statement spoken⸻ into a Muslim family and the l⸻ utter before death. By making⸻ rely believing in it, a new Mus⸻ This is the first of the five ba⸻ther known as the "five pillars o⸻ adah (declaration of faith).

The one and onl⸻ existing beyond ⸻

The bedrock of Islam is tha⸻thing shares divinity with Him,⸻ and nothing besides Him des⸻e has no partner and no family.⸻man beings as there is nothin⸻ssertion of the absolute onen⸻rous passages of the Qur'an an⸻eachings rests on it:

"Say: 'He is Allah, the ⸻.
He does not beget, nor ⸻
nothing that is like Hi⸻

It is argued in the Qur'a⸻n one god, there would not be⸻tinual conflict would arise fr⸻arious deities:

"they would surely hav⸻
another" (Q. 23:91).

Following the Qu'⸻ art as a deligl⸻ flower⸻

Muslims believe that of all sins, the worst and most unforgivable is to attribute divinity to anything other than Allah, whether through the worship of idols, natural forces, ancestors, heroes, angels, or even one's own desires (Q. 25:43; 45:23). The Christian doctrine of the Trinity is specifically rejected (Q. 4:171; 5:73). Believing in or worshiping two gods is also strictly forbidden (Q. 16:51).

For Muslims, Tawhid – the strict monotheism of Islam – strengthens their self-confidence because it frees them from slavery to a created being, or a superstition. It enables believers, as their Creator wills, to use their capabilities to the full in their role as trustees given guardianship and responsibility over the rest of Creation on earth.

Allah's attributes

Muslims are expected to think about the qualities of Allah and appreciate His deeds rather than concern themselves with the form in which He exists. There is frequent reference in the Qur'an to Allah's 99 Beautiful Names (*al-asma al-husna*) which describe His attributes:

*"The Creator, The Sustainer, The Most Compassionate,
The Most Merciful and The King; He alone is Holy;
from Him comes Peace; He is The Protector and
The Guardian; He gives life and causes death;
He sees everything and hears what everyone says;
He knows what everyone thinks; He neither slumbers
nor sleeps" (Q. 2:255).*

"He is closer to human beings than their jugular veins (Q. 50:16) and He answers the prayers of those who believe in Him and call on Him (Q. 2:186; 27:62). Although He punishes the wicked and disobedient and can be severe in doing so (Q. 5:98), He is quicker to forgive and show mercy; indeed, He has willed the law of grace and mercy upon Himself (Q. 6:12,54) and His mercy extends to all things (Q. 7:156)." Belief in these divine attributes strengthens trust in Allah and His limitless powers, as well as hope in His mercy and help.

THE LAST OF THE PROPHETS

Muslims believe that Muhammad (born in 570 C.E.), was mentioned by the prophets who came before him (Q. 7:157). He was born in Makkah, in Arabia, the town where Prophet Ibrahim, his ancestor, had prayed to Allah to raise a messenger (Q. 2:129).

As was customary at the time, Muhammad was raised by a paid foster-mother, a tribeswoman named Halimah. She and her family believed that fostering him brought them many blessings. Muhammad was returned to his mother Aminah a few years later, but she died when he was only six years old. Muhammad's father had died before he was born, so he then went to live with his grandfather, Abd al-Muttalib, for two years.

On his death Abu Talib, Muhammad's uncle, took over the task of caring for the boy. Muhammad helped to look after the animals and soon became so well known for his good conduct that he was nicknamed al-Amin (The Trustworthy). Later, he went to work as a trader for a rich widow named Khadijah, who was greatly impressed by him. When she was 40 and he was 25, they married at her request and had six children.

Muhammad was highly respected by the people of Makkah and was acknowledged as a wise peace-maker, but he disapproved of the way his fellow citizens were living. The Makkans no longer worshipped Allah, but prayed instead to all sorts of objects which they placed in and around the Ka'bah (the sacred house in Makkah). They were very materialistic and greedy, and the rich and strong oppressed the poor and weak.

The Qur'an contains the words of Allah revealed to Muhammad by the Archangel Jibril (Gabriel) over a period of 23 years. His companions wrote them down and they were compiled into a volume shortly after his death

Unhappy about the si............ from time to time, leave the tov............ alone and think in peace. He sp............ cave on a high mountain side, v................nding quiet and solitude.

The Qur'an

When he was 40, Muhar..............n the Hira Cave. There he was v..............riel), who brought a message f...............of the revelations recorded in t...............tinue for 23 years, commandi...............e only true god. The revelation...............y kind and warned of punishm...............d and rejected these commands, as well as blissful rewards for the obedient and righteous.

When Muhammad relayed Allah's message, most people opposed him. In time, however, the growing number of Muslims made the Makkan aristocracy increasingly worried that Muhammad's teaching was going to destroy their religion, their position among the Arabs as custodians of the Ka'bah, and the trade which they relied upon for their livelihood. As a consequence of this, the Makkans tried various means to stop Muhammed, offering him a number of incentives, but he flatly refused all offers. They then resorted to harsher persecution, both of Muhammad and his Companions. Many of his Companions were arrested and tortured, and some were actually killed. In the face of such hostility, Muhammad sent some of the Muslims away to Abyssinia where the Christian king protected them, true to Muhammad's expectation, and against diplomatic pressures from Makkah to send them back.

PERSECUTION AND ACCEPTANCE

Sanctions imposed in Makkah included an order that no one was to have anything to do with Muhammad, his family, or his Companions. As a result, Muhammad and his followers lived in great hardship for three years. The Muslims endured these various forms of ill-treatment with a great deal of courage. In spite of all the odds, they tried hard to live as true believers, the way Allah had commanded.

With the death in the same year of his wife and his uncle, both of whom had given him unflinching support, Muhammad visited other cities to see if the people would accept him and give him and his followers protection. He was stoned and turned back from Ta'if, another important city southeast of Makkah, but the people of Yathrib, to the north, were impressed by what they had heard about the Prophet and his Companions. They invited Muhammad to their city to give them just and honest leadership, and

pledged to give him and his followers protection. He sent a teacher to instruct the people in the ways of Islam and many of his Companions in Makkah left for Yathrib.

Finally, when his life was in danger, Muhammad received Allah's order to leave Makkah and emigrate to Yathrib. This migration is called the Hijrah and it is the event from which the Muslim calendar is calculated.

A fresh start in Yathrib

When the Muslims from Makkah arrived in Yathrib, they had no houses and very few possessions. In response to the Prophet's appeal, their fellow Muslims in Yathrib invited them to share their homes, gave them food and clothing and treated them as honored guests. Thus the Muslims from Makkah were at last free to worship Allah without fear of persecution. Many of them soon started to work for their living

The message of Islam changed former enemies to converts, so that the Muslim army was able to take the holy city of Makkah without bloodshed

Draped in black velvet, th[...]
house ever built for the worship [...] nual
Makk[...]

through trade. The city [...] al-
Nabiyy (City of the Proph[...]

The Prophet was chos[...]ling
to the commandmen[...] lso
gave the few Jews livin[...] to
worship according to the[...]ent
that was dictated by the[...]ons
among the various groups[...]ling
the Jews, is recognized as[...]sti-
tutions in human history.

The Hijrah did not sto[...]ans.
They made several unsucce[...]hen
Muhammad led some Musl[...]ake
a pilgrimage to Makkah, [...] but

agreed to a truce, and it was during this cessation of hostil-
ities that the message of Islam spread rapidly throughout
Arabia, changing former enemies to friends.

The Makkans soon broke the truce, so the Prophet
Muhammad led a large band of his Companions to the
city, which they were able to take without bloodshed.
Muhammad returned the Ka'bah to what it had been at the
time of Ibrahim – the place where only Allah could be
worshiped. It has since become the focal point for Muslims
throughout the world. Muhammad granted an amnesty to
his enemies, ignoring their past atrocities, and many more
of them became Muslims.

In the last year of his life, in 632 C.E., Muhammad led
a great pilgrimage to the House of Allah. He gave a final
speech to the Muslim community, urging kindness and
respect, especially towards women. He entrusted them to
the reliable guidance contained in the Qur'an, and to his
own example. Back in al-Madinah, he died and was buried.

TWO MAIN SOURCES OF TEACHING

Muslims believe that the Qur'an is Allah's own Word, not that of any human being. Allah revealed the Qur'an to Muhammad through the Angel Jibril (Gabriel), little by little, over a period of 23 years. The purpose of the Qur'an is to guide human beings until the end of life on earth. Muslims believe Allah Himself taught Muhammad how to recite the Qur'an (Q. 75:18) and arrange it into 114 Surahs (divisions).

As Muhammad received each portion of the Qur'an, he learned it by heart, and never forgot it (Q. 87:6). Many of his Companions also learned it by heart, and it was also written down. Whatever had been revealed was recited in the daily prayers (the word "Qu'ran" is derived from the Arabic word for recite), and the Muslims were soon able to say it by rote. Every year, the Prophet Muhammad recited all that had been revealed to him in front of the Angel Jibril to make sure it was correct: "We have, without doubt, sent down the Message and We Ourselves will guard it from corruption" (Q. 15:9).

As well as truths revealed by Allah, the Qur'an contains Muhammad's instructions on all aspects of religious life

The compilation of the Qur'an

After the death of Muhammad, Muslims were led by Abu Bakr, the first khalifah (caliph). He asked Zayd ibn Thabit, the Prophet's chief scribe, to compile a full written version of the Qur'an from all the various written records and from those who knew it by heart; then they confirmed that the compilation was accurate.

Thirteen years later, Khalifah Uthman ordered a committee, headed by Zayd ibn Thabit, to recheck and confirm the accuracy of the written version of the Qur'an and to make several copies of it. He sent these authorized copies to different parts of the Muslim world, and two have survived to this day. They are regarded as representing the only definitive version of the Qur'an in existence although all copies have exactly the same content. The Qur'an has been translated into many languages, but these are never regarded as substitutes for the original Arabic version.

Sunnah

The Qur'an covers all aspects of Muslim life, public and private. It is supplemented by a second source of guidance, called sunnah. Sunnah is concerned with the model behavior and practice of the Prophet Muhammad, and it consists of a record of his sayings, actions and the things he approved.

Muslims believe that, along with revealing the Qur'an to Prophet Muhammad, Allah also gave him special wisdom so that he could explain the things Allah revealed to him (Q. 62:2). Muslims are therefore directed to follow his example in all matters (Q. 33:21) and to carry out his instructions and advice (Q. 59:7).

Statements reporting the sunnah are called *ahadith* (singular, *hadith*). They were narrated by Companions of the Prophet who heard him say, or saw him do, what they reported. Those who heard the ahadith from Companions passed them on to others. Most ahadith were thus handed down verbally through chains of narrators.

Later, pious and meticulous scholars collected thousands of ahadith into large volumes, rejecting thousands of others because they were of weak authority. The authenticated collections made in the 9th century C.E. by al-Bukhari, Muslim, Abu Dawud, al-Tirmidhi, Ibn Majah, and Al-Nasa'i are accepted by the vast majority of Muslims as the most reliable and important texts, in that order.

...ad, the Prophet's chief scribe compiled ...ur'an using oral and written traditions

THE SPREAD OF ISLAM

After the death of Muhammad, his Companions carried the message of Islam further and further into the world. From 632 to 661 C.E., under his first four successors – Abu Bakr, Umar, Uthman, and Ali – Islamic rule expanded into countries west, north, and northeast of Arabia. Large numbers of the people in those places accepted Islam and were converted.

Sometimes Muslims had to fight to protect themselves and their religion from attack, and for the right to carry on preaching the message of Islam. Many people converted because they preferred the way of Islam to the lives they had experienced under their former rulers.

When Muslims took charge of any place, they preached Islam to the people, but allowed them to make a choice: to accept Islam, or reject it and pay a moderate tax to the Muslim state. In return, the state protected the people and took care of them.

From 661 to 750 C.E. the Islamic state was ruled by members of a clan, known as the Umayyads, who introduced hereditary dynastic rule to the Muslim world. They moved the capital from al-Madinah to Damascus, which is now in Syria. It was during their rule that Islam spread as far as Morocco and Spain, in the West, and beyond India, in the East.

In 750 C.E., the family of the Prophet's uncle, Abbas, took over from the Umayyads. Baghdad became the capital of the Islamic state. Under the Abbasids (750–1258), Islam was carried first into Central Asia and then further still, into India, by Turks from Central Asia who had themselves accepted the religion.

Mongols and Turks

The Mongols seized Baghdad in 1258 C.E., and caused great destruction in the Muslim world. They soon became Muslims themselves and, with them, most of the people they ruled. Later, part of Anatolia (now Turkey) also became part of the Muslim world. The Turks and the Mongols were now the effective rulers of most of the Muslim commu-nity, but they retained the Abbasid khalifahs as spiritual leaders until 1517.

During this period, Islam was carried by traders, leaders, and sufis (Muslim mystics) to East and West Africa and southeast Asia. In the 14th century Ibn Battuta visited the West African Muslim state of Mali. Indonesians still remember the Waliyys (friends of Allah) who taught them all about Islam.

From the 15th century to the end of the First World War, the Ottoman Turks ruled the Islamic world, extending

their territories even into E[...]he Muslim world has faced [...]om European power and though[...]ad throughout the world.

During the early Middle Ages[...]providing a force for order, lear[...]l (former Constantinople), the chu[...]st Christian emperor, was converted[...]ols of Central Asia, who initially att[...]in the 13th century, as is evic[...]

THE FIVE PILLARS OF ISLAM

Muslims are required to observe five basic acts of devotion known as "pillars." These are al-shahadah (the declaration of faith – *see page 153*), *salah* (ritual prayers performed five times daily), *zakah* (the payment of welfare dues), *sawm* (fasting in the month of Ramadan), and *hajj* (making a pilgrimage to Makkah at least once in a lifetime for those who can afford it). Each of these duties has moral and social benefits.

Ritual prayer

For salah (prayer), worshipers must be ritually clean; indeed, cleanliness is a very important part of Muslim daily life. Before prayer, Muslims must wash certain parts of the body with water. This ritual cleansing, called *wudu*, means

Muslims pray five times a day as a means of renewing their contact with Allah, and are called to prayer by the mu'ad-hdhin *(bottom); such regular prayers are a means of ensuring that spiritual matters are not neglected in the rush and bustle of modern life*

more than the cleaning of the body – it symbolizes the cleansing of the soul from sin. Under certain conditions, Muslims must wash the whole of the body in a particular way before praying. This is called *ghusl*. If they are unable to use water, *tayammum* (dry ablution) is allowed using clean dust, stones, or sand (Q. 5:6).

Salah is always conducted in Arabic, the language of the Qur'an, so Muslims from different countries can worship together, and the required passages or utterances are said to be quite easy to learn.

The five times for daily prayer are: just after dawn (*fajr/subh*), at noon (*zuhr*), in the mid-afternoon (*asr*), at sunset (*maghrib*) and at night (*isha*). Thus the link with Allah is renewed regularly during waking hours. These times are

Special areas of the mosque are reserved for women and children, though all perform the same prayers and devotions

Friday is the day for weekly con███████████████████████l. All males are required to attend █████████████████gs of the Imam, who then ████████

announced by the *adhan* (the████████████████████ich reminds Muslims of the nee████████████████████ey are busy with daily life.

In communal worship, ███████████████████en and women separately, beh█████████████████the Prophet Muhammad, the ████████████████on recite parts of the Qur'an, f████████████████ns, which include bowing and████████████████is-sion to God) and say prayer████████████████lar intervals during the day, M█████████████████er

and praise Allah Most High and ask Him for what they need, so that it becomes a matter of habit.

For Muslims, observing salah frequently throughout the day is considered to have many benefits. It is a regular reminder of Allah and a direct communication with Him, keeping material concerns in proportion (*Q. 20:14*).

Prayer is also a constant reminder of other duties: "Salah keeps one away from shameful and evil things" (*Q. 29:45*). "The remembrance of Allah brings rest to the hearts (of believers)" (*Q. 13:28*).

Salah offers the chance to ask Allah constantly for forgiveness and to pray for your needs (*Q. 1:5; 2:45, 153*). It helps Muslims to do things regularly and punctually: "Salah is a duty to be done at prescribed times" (*Q. 4:103*).

Observing salah promotes a feeling of fellowship and equality among diverse worshipers as they stand so often side by side before Allah (*Q. 49:13*). The Prophet Muhammad said that salah performed communally is 27 times more meritorious.

On Friday, Muslims try to perform the *jumu'ah* (congregational) prayer in the mosque. Before the prayer, the Imam (leader) gives a speech (*khutbah*), and then leads the group in the prayer. Attending the Friday prayer is obligatory for men but optional for women.

THE PAYMENT OF DUES

Muslims believe that everything in the universe belongs to Allah and that whatever we are given, plenty or little, is held in trust for Him: "His are the keys of the heavens and the earth. He gives abundantly to whom He wills and sparingly to whom He pleases" (Q. 42:12). Allah watches to see how we use these gifts. Muslims should be thankful for what they are given and show this thankfulness by using what they have in the right way. Part of this is to pay zakah: "Do prayer regularly and give zakah" (Q. 22.78).

In Arabic, zakah means growth, blessing, or making something pure. In Islam, zakah is the act of setting aside a specific portion of your wealth for the poor and needy, doing this happily and hoping only for Allah's pleasure, not for praise or thanks from the beneficiaries. (Q. 2:262).

Responsible guardianship

Some people have more possessions and money than they need. Islam requires such people to pay at least a small part out of whatever they have left after fulfilling their needs. The Prophet Muhammad said: "I have been commanded to collect zakah from the rich among you and distribute it to the poor among you" (Hadith: al-Bukhari); "A charity puts out sin as water puts out fire" (Hadith: Mishkat al-Masabih).

Shepherds in Afghanistan tend their flocks of goats and sheep; Muslims believe that all things are held in trust for Allah

Muslims share the good th░░░░░░░░░░░░░░░░░░░░░e
poor through the payment o░░░░░░░░░░░░░░░░░░░░░sets

In addition to pleasin░░░░░░░░░░░░░░░░░░░░slims
believe they free the░░░░░░░░░░░░░░░░, and
cleanse their souls from s░░░░░░░░░░░░░░░chan-
dise is paid once every N░░░░░░░░░░░░░░ops is
paid at the time of harv░░░░░░░░░░░░░every
Muslim who has more ░░░░░░░░░░░░░ property (*nisab*): "O you wh░░░░░░░░░░░░ good
things which you have ░░░░░░░░░░░d give
[out]of the fruits which░░░░░░░░░░ of the
earth for you" (*Q. 2:267*░

Muslims are not all░░░░░░░░░░░rough
unlawful means, such as░░░░░░░░░░g. Any

zakah paid out of wealth earned in this way is unacceptable
to Allah because the source is impure: "Allah, the Almighty,
is good and accepts only that which is good" (Hadith:
Muslim). Muslims give and share the good things they receive
from Allah in all sorts of other ways besides zakah. Sometimes
they do this to make amends for their misdeeds, or for good
deeds left undone.

Voluntary charity (*sadaqah*) is recommended at all
times. Any act of kindness, even a smile, or kindness to
animals, can count as sadaqah for which Allah gives great
rewards and blessings. Muslims see zakah and sadaqah as
helpful to the giver, the receiver, and to society: they relieve
the giver's mind of greed and selfishness, provide sustenance
to the receiver, and induce friendship between the rich and
the poor which is good for society.

RAMADAN AND EID AL-FITR

"F" ... as ... so that y... (Q. 2:183 ... ut food, ... ne, and t... to remember Allah and be obe... ims fast regularly on certain day... ims must fast in Ramadan, th... lim calendar (Q. 2:183-5).

The Islamic calendar

It was Ramadan, in the yea... rds of the Qur'an were made k... nad. Each year thereafter, duri... e all that had been revealed up ... isha (night) prayer, many Im... the Qur'an, one for each eveni... ecial tarawih prayers at the mc...

The anniversary of th... first words of the Qur'an were ... Qadr, the Night of Power (Q. 97 ... f the last five odd-numbered ni... slims do their best to stay awa... g the Qur'an and praying, he... from Allah. Some Muslims sta... t ten days of Ramadan. This ac... kaf.

Muslims fast from da... r the whole month – 29 or 30 ... n the Qur'an that: "Allah wish... not difficulty," even in the ma... Some people who are unwell, ... here-fore excused fasting in t... ke up the missed days later, o... each day they do not fast. The... n the new moon is seen.

Muslims believe fast... t they are always in the presen... gthen their willpower so that t... haytan (Satan). Another benefit ... xperi-

Devout Muslims spend the whole of Ramadan in prayer and fasting at the mosque; the picture opposite shows the square outside the Dome of the Rock in Jerusalem. At the end of Ramadan, marked by the new moon, Muslims break their fast with prayers of thanks to Allah and a family banquet.

ence hunger and thirst like the poor, and therefore understand their needs better. The Prophet Muhammad said Allah would forgive the sins of those who fast properly, and reward them in this world and when they return to Him.

Eid al-Fitr – The festival of breaking the fast

Once the new moon for the next month is sighted, Ramadan ends and the fasting stops. The next day is the festival of Eid al-Fitr. On, or before, this day the head of each family must give to a poorer person food enough for a day's meals, or the money to buy it. This makes it possible for everyone to celebrate the festival happily.

On the day itself, special salah takes place in large mosques or open spaces and everyone is encouraged to be there to celebrate. Wearing their best and newest clothes, Muslims rejoice that the fasting is over, and they greet their friends, relations and others, saying *Eid mubarak* – happy festival.

They chant words of praise and glory to Allah as they go to the mosque and before the prayers start. The Imam leads the people in a special salah and gives a speech (khutbah) afterwards. Then the congregation goes to join their family and friends for their first midday meal since the beginning of Ramadan.

PILGRIMAGE

At least once in their lifetime, Muslims have a duty to do hajj (pilgrimage) if they can find a way. If they are able to make the journey, intending pilgrims recite a special prayer, called the talbiyah, which begins: Labbayk allahumma labbayk (I respond to you O Allah, I respond to you).

Hajj takes place during the Islamic month of Dhul-Hijjah, the last month of the calendar, but *umrah* (a lesser hajj) can be made at any time during the year. Hajj is the largest gathering of its kind in the world. Muslims of different races and languages assemble in one place, worshiping Allah together and living as brothers and sisters, reflecting their true relationship as children of Adam (*Q. 49:13*). Traders find a big market for their goods. Animals are sacrificed and the meat is sent to help poor Muslims in other countries.

Pilgrims once traveled for several days or weeks to reach Makkah in time for the hajj. Nowadays they come more quickly by aeroplane, ship, or car. Before they arrive, all male pilgrims, rich and poor, change into simple *ihram* clothes (two seamless pieces of white cloth) and everyone, both men and women, dedicates themselves to Allah. This marks their intention to do the hajj, to be good, and to refrain from certain things while in the state of ihram, as Allah has commanded (*Q. 2:197*).

The rites of hajj

Near the Ka'bah lie the small hills of Safa and Marwah. When the Prophet Ibrahim left his wife Hajar and his son Isma'il in Makkah, Hajar ran up and down between the two hills seven times, looking for water, leaving Isma'il on the ground. The tradition states that while she was away, his heel dug into the sand and water miraculously came up. Muslims believe this water is still flowing and call it Zamzam.

Pilgrims re-live Hajar's search by doing *sa'y* — walking, and in some places trotting, seven times between Safa and

Hundreds of thousands of Muslims gather every year in Makkah for the hajj

*Pilgrims journeying to Mak..................................,
Leon Auguste ....*

Marwah. Sa'y is an essent..................... hajj. A huge, air-conditioned c..................... on to the mosque to shade the ....jar's distress and relief.

Muslims believe the I.....................s the first house built on earth ....:96). When Muslims visit the I.....................d his son Isma'il on Allah's i..................... go round it seven times, ant.....................rner where the sacred Black St.....................ame. As they go, they recite pr.....................lking round is called *tawaf*, an.....................jj and umrah. Each year the wh..................... black velvet cloth, called the ....gold with passages from the.....................part covering the door.

On the eighth day c.....................ve out to stay in tents and hos.....................ainous edge of Makkah. On th.....................rayer, pilgrims start to go tow.....................nearly 20 kilometres (12.5 mi.....................t is the most important part of.....................

At noon, when eve.....................plain is covered with millions o.....................he zuhr and asr prayers toget.....................amirah Mosque. This is followed by a sermon by an Imam, following the example of Prophet Muhammad who gave his last speech on the day of Arafat. After the salah, pilgrims stay on the plain, praying and asking for forgiveness, remembering that one day all human beings will be gathered together like this before Allah for judgement.

After sunset, the crowd begins to move away towards Muzdalifah, another plain half way between Arafat and Mina. Here they perform the maghrib and isha salahs combined, before picking up small pebbles to take back to Mina for the next part of the hajj. They then settle down to rest, and devote themselves to remembrance of Allah.

The Festival of Sacrifice

The next day, the tenth of Dhul Hijjah, is Eid al-Adha (the Festival of Sacrifice), when Muslims all over the world remember the obedience of the Prophet Ibrahim to Allah's command that he should sacrifice his only son (Isma'il). Such obedience conveys the essence of Islam – surrendering your whole self to Allah (*Q. 2:131*). The pilgrims remember how Ibrahim was tempted not to obey. They throw pebbles at the largest of the three stone pillars in Mina, which is called the Jamarat, to symbolize rejection of the Shaytan (Satan).

Most pilgrims pay for an animal to be sacrificed to Allah, as do those at home who can afford it, to commemorate Ibrahim's obedience to Allah when He gave him a ram to sacrifice instead of his son. The meat is shared with the poor, and many pay to send meat to Muslims in other countries.

The pilgrims then return to Makkah and perform another tawaf (walking round) before changing out of their ihram clothes and into their normal garments. Some of the men have their heads shaved, while others cut some of their hair, as do the women. After this, nearly everything given up during *ihram* becomes allowed again.

Before leaving Makkah, it is important to take one last walk round the Ka'bah to say goodbye to the holy place. The hajj is now over, but pilgrims try to visit the mosque in al-Madinah, where the Prophet's tomb is located, to do salah and pray for his soul.

SCIENCE AND ISLAM

The Qur'an states that all things belong to Allah (*Q. 24:64; 3:109*) and must obey His laws (*Q. 30:26*). In the end, all will return to Him (*Q. 3:109*). The wonders in creation are "signs" of Allah's limitless power, wisdom, mercy, and care. Muslims must not abuse these "signs" but use them only as Allah approves.

Allah says in the Qur'an that He has provided everything people need and showered His favors upon them: He has made the skies and the seas serviceable to human beings (*Q. 16:12-14*), along with the various kinds of domesticated animals (*Q. 36:71-2*).

Although they are trustees and managers, Muslims believe that human beings are only a part of creation; the other creatures too are "communities like you" and have their own functions. In our greed, arrogance and rebellion, human beings have corrupted or even destroyed much of the environment. Those who do these things often claim that they are "improving things." But Allah says: "it is they who are making mischief, but they do not realize it" (*Q. 2:11-12*). In the end, we are accountable to Him for the way we treat other creatures and the environment. Nevertheless, Muslims believe the mercy of Allah is such that He makes us taste the consequences of only "a part of what we have done," so that perhaps we will "see reason and return from evil" (*Q. 30:41*).

The Qur'an encourages Muslims to examine themselves and their environment closely. Muslim scholars have made important contributions to various areas of expertise, many of which have helped European scholars to develop the empirical sciences, astronomy, medicine, and mathematics as we know them today.

Early scientists

Ibn Sina and al-Razi were among the most prominent Muslim physicians; while his chief contribution to science was to medicine, Ibn Sina was also a very important philosopher. Ala'al-Din ibn al-Nafis (who died in 1288 C.E.) explained how blood absorbs oxygen in the lungs four centuries earlier than William Harvey, the English biologist who completed the scientific picture of blood circulation.

Ibn al-Haytham put the science of optics on a new basis in the 10th century C.E. He traced and described the functioning of the eye from the optic nerve originating in the brain to the eye itself. He was the first to demonstrate the second law of refraction of light, and his work was consulted by Sir Isaac Newton centuries later.

Muslim alchemists made use of the technology of ancient Babylon and Egypt, especially in glass-making, dyeing and metallurgy. They developed scientific instruments which they used to carry out various chemical processes (including sublimation, distillation, and crystallization). Muslim craft industries applied techniques derived from alchemy to decorate glass, pottery, and metalwork.

Muslim astronomers built observatories, compiled tables of planetary motion and calendars, and provided much of the vocabulary of modern scientific astronomy. Such precise knowledge, together with highly skilled metalworking, enabled astrolabes, which were a vital contribution to navigation in the age of European exploration, to be constructed.

Modern astronomy and space exploration owe a great deal to the observations and experiments of early Muslim astronomers

...concave mirrors to magnify the stars was
...Din al-Tusi at his observatory in Merega

FAMILY LIFE IN ISLAM

Islam attaches great importance to the family. It is believed that the continuity of the human race depends on the love, compassion, and mutual support that exists between members of the family, because this ensures a secure upbringing for children, and a strong society, based on stable, peaceful homes.

For Muslims, a valid marriage is the only acceptable basis for the family. Sex, except in marriage, is forbidden in Islam. Muslim parents believe they have a responsibility to see their children well married, so marriage is brought about through co-operation between the generations.

The marriage ceremony is quite simple and can be conducted by anyone learned in Shari'ah (Islamic Law). The parties give consent in the presence of two male Muslim witnesses, and the bride receives a dowry from the groom. This is followed by celebrations, known as *walimah*, to publicize the lawful nature of the union.

Divorce and polygamy

The Prophet Muhammad said: "The most hateful to Allah of all things lawful is divorce." However, Islam does allow divorce if, despite efforts at reconciliation, the couple can no longer live together peacefully. Either the husband or the wife may initiate the divorce. If there is agreement, this can be achieved with few formalities, but if the husband is unwilling, the wife may need the help of a court. A waiting period, lasting three menstrual cycles, is required before the couple separate, to establish whether there is a pregnancy and to encourage reconciliation. The emphasis is on mutual agreement, reasonableness and kindness between the couple. Muslims obey laws regarding divorce in countries where they are resident.

Polygamy can be practiced in Islam, to a maximum of four wives at a time, but only if the man can treat them all

Muslim marriage ceremonies are simple, and there are celebrations afterwards to publicize the union

*Muslim parents try to gi[...]
well as boys, t[...]*

equally; otherwise he sho[...] 3).
Polygamy in the right circu[...] ar-
antee protection and dignity[...]wise
be left unmarried, as well[...]er-
wise be born outside marr[...]

Children and parent

Islam encourages the fulfi[...] for
children. A Muslim coupl[...] tra-
ceptive under certain cond[...]ally
choose to remain childl[...] as a
serious sin, and a crime,[...]r is
confirmed to be in real da[...]

A newborn baby is we[...] the
call to prayer is whispere[...] the
baby is marked with t[...]ing.
A male child is circumcis[...] the
prophets of Allah.

The Prophet Muhammad stressed that showing kindness and affection towards children was part of being a good
Muslim. Good parenting includes giving children good
names, treating them equally, and providing a good religious and general education to both boys and girls. Men
are fully responsible for the upkeep of their wives, children
and other womenfolk (*Q. 4:34*).

Old age and death

Muslims are urged to be kind and respectful to their parents,
particularly their mothers, who go through so much trouble
to give birth to them and care for them. Children should
obey their parents (unless their parents are so dishonorable
as to try to make them go against Allah's commands). They
should look after parents, and be patient with them when
they grow old (*Q. 17:23-4; 31:14-5; 46:15*).

When parents die, their children and grandchildren pray
for them and show kindness to their relatives and friends.
They try to fulfill for them any outstanding obligations,
whether religious (performing the hajj and zakah), or
personal (repaying debts or promises).

MOSQUE DECORATION

The strict monotheism of Islam leads Muslims to avoid the realistic representation of human and animal forms, especially in places of worship, believing that this can lead to idolatry. Therefore, Islamic art is non-figurative, consisting principally of calligraphic representations of the words of Allah from the Qur'an, as well as arabesques and geometric patterns. These patterns reflect the fundamental harmony in the universe, and in the natural world, which in turn derives from the Islamic belief that Allah is One.

Within these guidelines, the styles of mosque architecture and decoration vary widely according to local esthetic taste and period, and according to the resources available.

Muslim places of worship are called mosques, from the arabic *masjid*, meaning place of prostration. Mosques are places where Muslims perform regular salah (ritual prayer), standing before Allah and bowing and prostrating before Him (*Q. 22:78*). During the salah, Muslims of different races, rich and poor, young and old, pray side by side behind the Imam. The spirit of fellowship and equality is thus fostered in the mosque, and Muslims believe that salah performed in congregation brings greater rewards from Allah than salah performed individually.

The mosque is also a center for education, where people can learn about Islam. There are usually scholars there who can advise Muslims from the teachings of the Shari'ah (Islamic Law). Great mosques in history and around the world have schools and libraries attached to them.

The components of a mosque

Muslims pray facing the direction of the *qiblah* – that is the Ka'bah, the House of God, in Makkah. To show where this is, there is usually a *mihrab* (niche) in the middle of the front wall of the mosque. To the right of the *mihrab* is the *minbar*, a platform with steps. It is from the minbar that the Imam addresses the worshipers during the khutbah (talk), mainly on Fridays and festivals.

Many mosques have a dome, a hemispherical roof representing the Universe and Creation. Some mosques also have a tower, called a minaret, which is where the *mu'ad-hdhin* (caller) makes the call to prayer (adhan) five times a day, reminding the faithful of their duties.

Men and women pray separately, so most mosques have special sections, or galleries, for women. In addition, mosques have facilities for worshipers to perform wudu (ritual washing) before salah; some have a decorative fountain, and some have separate showers and toilets for men and women. Shoes are not worn in the mosque, because they are regarded as unclean, and the Prophet Muhammad said, "Cleanliness is part of faith."

Muslims believe that "All of the earth is a mosque," and as salah must be performed at specific times, a Muslim who cannot get to the mosque for a particular salah, may perform it at home, in the office or, with a few exceptions, in any clean place.

A distinctive form of Islamic art and architecture developed in the early Middle Ages, rooted in strict geometry but breaking out into intricate patterns, inspired by flowers and leaves, and incorporating inscriptions from the Qur'an; lavish use is made of precious materials, as seen in the gilded and tiled domes of the Regent's Park mosque in London (far left), the Sheik Lutfullah mosque in Iran (center left) and the Majjed-e Jame in Esfahan (left); since the 1300s mosque architects have experimented with bold sculptural forms, as in Cairo (above)

SHINTO

" **In times of need, approach the kami for help** *Buddhist temples and Shinto shrines are seen in every Japanese city, town and village. Buddhist temples are mainly concerned with funerals and ancestor rituals. Shinto shrines, on the other hand, mark a sacred place identified with one or more* kami *(spirit entities). Shrines do not relate to a deity elsewhere; they mark the actual abode of the kami of that place, so to approach the shrine is to approach the kami. Shrines are often set in attractive wooded surroundings. The approach path is marked by one or more* torii, *distinctively shaped archways. Shrines are the setting for a variety of rituals and festivals (*matsuri*). These are mainly to do with the lifecycle of family members and the well-being of the community.*

Shinto shrines are instantly recognizable because of the distinctive form of their torii, *the entrance gateways that frame the approach. At the famed Itsukushima shrine the approach is from the sea*

Before 1868, shrines o_____in-guishable from Budd_____nks performed rites for the ka_____ami were represented in Buddh_____oth shrines and temples. Ho_____nto "cleansed" of Buddhist ele_____ate-19th century by the Japane_____out to transform feudal Japan_____ial-ized nation. To mobilize th_____ate Shinto" which was taught_____elf-less devotion to the divi_____was defeated in 1945, the natio_____nto

were formally abandoned, and Shinto shrines, like Buddhist temples, now have to work hard to adapt their spiritual wares to the "marketplace" of Japanese religions.

There is little agreement in Japan on exactly what "Shinto" means, but many of Japan's 100,000 shrines are well-supported by their local communities, and numerous colorful and exuberant festivals bear witness to the contin-uing appeal of shrine rituals to the Japanese people.

ORIGINS AND HISTORY OF SHINTO

It is often assumed that Shinto is Japan's ancient indigenous religion, but this idea is largely a legacy of 19th-century Japanese nationalism. Throughout most of Japan's history, shrines and their kami (spirits) were closely associated with Buddhist temples and understood within a predominantly Buddhist-Confucian world view. Many of the ideas and practices now regarded as "Shinto" were imported from China or Korea.

Although very early Chinese records of Japan tell of women acting as shamanic rulers, women have no significant role in modern Shinto. It seems likely that certain places (for example strange rocks, waterfalls, mountains) were regarded as sacred or the abode of spirits before Buddhism entered Japan, and these places developed into Shinto shrines. Some important ancestral cults, based at shrines, worshiped the protective deities of clans, such as the imperial family and the Fujiwara regents. These were soon absorbed into Buddhism.

As Buddhism spread within Japan, the trend was always to integrate local beliefs and customs into Buddhism rather than displace them. The local kami were offered rites to help them attain spiritual liberation. Because of this recognition within Buddhism, they were eventually seen as almost equal in rank to Buddhas and *bodhisattvas* ("beings of enlightenment"). The deity Hachiman, for example, was identified as a bodhisattva in the 8th century and brought

to Nara with great ceremo███████████████████ of the Great Buddha statue at ██████████████

Interpretations of ████

In the medieval period, s███████████████████gs were developed by monk-p██████████████bu (Dual) Shinto, propounded b████████████████n, understood kami as local m████████████████nd bodhisattvas. Yui-itsu (One-████████████████ of Buddhist, Taoist and Confu█████████████ by priests at the Yoshida shrine █████████████mi as being inner spiritual q████████████gs propagated by the Watarai ██████████████he "Outer Shrine" at Ise, enco███████████e a

physical pilgrimage to Ise at least once during their lifetime to obtain spiritual blessings.

During the 17th century, in a bid to stamp out Western Christian influences, Japan became a "closed country" to outsiders, and every Japanese family had to prove that it was not Christian by registering with a Buddhist temple. Eventually, a reaction against Buddhism set in, linked to a growing disillusionment with the feudal rule of the Shoguns. Some outstanding scholars of "National Learning" rediscovered, and began to revere, ancient Japanese texts, such as the *Kojiki* (the "Record of Ancient Matters") of 712 C.E., which told the story of the descent of the imperial family from the sun goddess Amaterasu.

The transformation of Japan

In the 1850s pressure from the West forced Japan to open her doors to international trade. In a brief civil war the Shogunate collapsed and imperial rule was "restored." Japan was rapidly transformed into a Western-style industrialized society, but this difficult social transformation was carried out under the ideology of a "return" to a glorious mythical national past.

In 1868, shrines were "cleansed" of Buddhist elements and a national system of approved shrines and rituals emerged; at its apex was the shrine of Amaterasu at Ise. "State Shinto" from 1868 to 1945, though officially defined as "non-religious," taught that citizens should submit to the will of the emperor, who was considered to be divine.

After Japan's defeat in 1945, the new American-style constitution separated religion from government in order to guarantee the people of Japan the right of religious freedom. Shinto shrines today are independent religious bodies, on exactly the same level as any Buddhist, Christian, or new religious organization in Japan.

Every Shinto shrine has its own local deity, and since there are some 100,000 shrines in Japan today, there are many spirits in the Shinto pantheon; in this 19th-century woodblock print the goddess Amaterasu emerges from her rocky abode

THE SHINTO SHRINE

The Japanese word most commonly used for a Shinto shrine is *jinja*, meaning "place of the kami." Some important shrines are called *taisha* ("great shrine") and shrines connected with emperors are known as *jingu* ("palace of the kami"). The number of officially recognized shrines grew rapidly in the 15th and 16th centuries when the Yoshida priestly clan became responsible for granting shrine titles and ranks, in return for donations. By 1900 there were about 200,000 shrines in Japan, but this number was drastically reduced when a government program of *jinja gappei* ("shrine merger") closed many community shrines dotted around Japan, taking the number down to around 100,000 by 1927.

The presence of a shrine is always indicated by a torii, a distinctive wooden, stone, or concrete archway which marks the entrance or approach to a shrine. On entering a shrine visitors are expected to rinse, and thereby purify, their hands and mouths at a trough of running water. In many shrines the visitor then passes through a series of gates and over a small bridge, each one marking a further degree of proximity to the kami.

Shrine buildings are not really necessary to mark the presence of the kami, but most shrines do have buildings. A typical shrine has a *honden*, a main hall, which is seen, but not entered, by worshipers. The honden houses the "seat" of the kami. There might also be a hall of worship used by worshipers for their prayers and coin offerings, and a hall of offerings, or *heiden*. In the heiden, special offerings and rites are conducted by priests, or by a special group of worshipers, as distinct from the general public. Only large shrines can afford a full-time priest, and virtually all shrines rely on the active co-operation of members of the local community for their rites and festivals.

Who follows Shinto?

Since 1868, Shinto shrines have been administered separately from

Halls are set aside for worship and for offerings, but only priests may enter the inner hall where the spirit dwells

As well as nationwide festivals, a   kko
have their own calendar of rites   part

Buddhist temples, but the   nto
shrines are the same peo   to
Buddhist temples. Shinto   pa-
rate religions with differe
they represent complemen
religious life of most Japa

   At special festival tim
Year, more than 80 per
Japanese population makes
(*hatsu-mode*) to a Shinto
majority of these people
they are doing anything "re
New Year visit is seen as a
tradition. Nevertheless, n
visitors buy amulets at th
invoke the protection of th
the coming year, and mar
the opportunity to be rit
a simple ceremony perfo

As well as nationwide celebrations, such as New Year, each of Japan's 100,000 shrines has its own calendar of matsuri (festivals or rites). Most shrines have at least one major festival each year in which members of the local community take part. The "seven-five-three" festival in November (*see page 188*) involves whole families. Children are brought to the shrine to receive a blessing for the future.

Shinto priests perform a number of protective rites for different members of the community. A priest may visit a factory, or employees may visit a shrine to seek prosperity and safety at work. Mothers-to-be visit shrines to pray for a problem-free childbirth, and people often have their new cars blessed by a priest for protection against road accidents. Schoolchildren visit shrines, especially those dedicated to Tenjin, to pray for admission to the high school of their choice.

*A miko, or shrine assistant, lighting incense
at the Hagurosan temple*

SHINTO IDEAS AND BELIEFS

Shinto ideas have drawn on a variety of sources – mainly Buddhism, Confucianism, and Taoism – as well as local legends and oral traditions. Thus, for example, the influential shrine priest and scholar, Yoshida Kanetomo (1435–1511 C.E.), taught that the myriads of kami formed a single entity identical with our innermost essence. For him, Shinto, like Buddhism, meant cultivating the kami qualities of purity, honesty, and sincerity.

The Watarai priests at the grand shrine of Ise later offered a quite different interpretation of Shinto, one which required people to make a physical pilgrimage to Ise to attract the blessings of the kami there. In the Edo period (1600-1868), several remarkable spontaneous mass pilgrimages to Ise occurred when millions of people abandoned their work and family and converged on the shrine.

In the late 19th century, a body of new Shinto teachings was taught in schools. State Shinto had its roots in the National Learning movement of the 18th and 19th centuries.

Before 1945, generations of Japanese schoolchildren were taught that their divine emperor, and the land and people of Japan, were truly descended from the gods, and that Japan therefore had a special and superior destiny in the world. These nationalistic ideas were designed to underpin and justify Japan's attempts to colonize other countries in East Asia, and were largely discredited after the war.

Since 1945, Shinto theology has been almost non-existent; priests are trained in correct ritual, rather than expected to teach doctrine. Post-war Shinto writers sometimes even stress vagueness and a lack of doctrine as positive hallmarks of Shinto, distinguishing it from "rigid" belief systems, such as Buddhism or Christianity. In the 1990s comparisons have been made between Shinto and Western neo-paganism. As Japan acquires new national confidence, as a result of economic success, there has been a trend back to the "ancient" Shinto taught after 1868, that is to say, a

The Gods of the Sea festival at Okinawa: in modern Japan such festivals are increasingly seen as a way of maintaining community spirit

The rock shrine at Ise; visiti████████████████████████████████
the soul to its ███████████████

Shinto "cleansed" of Budd██████ ██████████ ████████zing
the mythology of the ancie█████ ████████ █████ ████nout
the jingoism of pre-war sta████████ ██████████ ████ople
freely combine Buddhist ███████████ █████ ██████es in
their religious life.

Purity and ritua

In local shrine worship, th████████████████████deas
– *harae* (purification) and█████████████████n be
discerned, though these ar████████████████ines.
It is widely understood t█████ ████ ██████ ████ away
moral corruption, evil in█████████████████ts. In
most cases, purification i████████████████priest
waves a *harai-gushi*, or pu███████████████paper
streamers attached) over██████████████████Vater
and salt are also comm███████████████████ents.

Purifications may take place several times a year, as occasion demands.

The underlying idea is that human beings are naturally in a state of purity, but we become "polluted" (*kegare*) by our actions, thoughts, and circumstances. Harae rites can restore us to our pristine state. The New Year visit to a shrine undertaken by most Japanese people can be seen in this light as a shared ritual of purification, in which the impurities collected during the past year are removed, allowing a fresh start for the year to come.

Matsuri (festival or ritual) means service to the kami. Festivals typically include solemn offerings of food and *sake* (rice-wine) to the kami, followed by colorful and (sometimes dangerously exuberant) processions, dances, contests and other entertainments of various kinds. Many festivals originally marked crucial moments in the agricultural calendar, though in modern urban Japan festivals are increasingly seen as secular affairs, designed to boost tourism and maintain community spirit.

THE MAKING OF A KAMI

Sugawara no Michizane (845–903 C.E.) was a brilliant and popular scholar, poet, and teacher. He was also a skilled administrator with a promising future in government. Before long he had become the personal tutor of the young heir to the imperial throne, given his daughter to the palace as an imperial consort and risen rapidly to high office. By 899, Michizane was the second-highest official in Japan. The only person above him in rank was the brother of the empress, a member of the ancient and powerful Fujiwara clan.

Envious of Michizane's influence at court, the Fujiwaras intrigued against him and persuaded the emperor to appoint Michizane as Viceroy of Kyushu. Kyushu was many days' journey from the imperial capital, Kyoto, so Michizane's new post was in reality a banishment to unhappy exile. Angrily protesting his innocence, Michizane shut himself away in the government residence at Dazaifu in Kyushu and spent his time writing poetry. He died two years later, on February 25 903.

Supplicants ask the gods for favors by writing their requests on wooden prayer tablets that are then hung in the shrine

A series of strange and terrible events then began to unfold in Kyoto. Some courtiers were killed when the palace was struck by lightning. Severe storms hit the city, followed by an appalling drought and thunderbolts. The imperial prince, and several of those who had plotted against Michizane, died in quick succession. A government minister "died" but came back to life three days later and declared that he had seen Michizane, 3 meters (10 feet) high, petitioning the king of Hell for an inquiry into his unjust banishment. Michizane had become an "angry spirit" who would continue to wreak havoc until he was pacified.

Deification

The emperor, repenting, reappointed Michizane posthumously to his former high office, but the tragedies continued.

*Purification rituals are cer̶̶̶̶̶̶̶̶̶̶̶̶̶̶̶̶̶̶̶̶,
water, and s̶̶̶̶̶̶*

*Local communities pay tribute to their spirits through music,
dance and drumming, as well as by more solemn rituals*

Several times Michizane s̶̶̶̶̶̶̶̶̶̶̶̶̶̶̶̶̶̶̶̶̶̶aling,
in 947, that 168,000 de̶̶̶̶̶̶̶̶̶̶̶̶̶̶̶̶̶e. In
response higher and h̶̶̶̶̶̶̶̶̶̶̶̶̶̶̶d on
Michizane's spirit and fi̶̶̶̶̶̶̶̶̶̶̶̶̶̶̶imate
title of Tenjin, or Heaver̶̶̶̶̶̶

Numerous shrines ha̶̶̶̶̶̶̶̶̶̶̶̶̶̶̶̶enjin,
and small Tenjin shrines̶̶̶̶̶̶̶̶̶̶̶̶̶̶cts of
other shrines. The Osak̶̶̶̶̶̶̶̶̶̶̶̶̶̶ded in
951 on the orders of th̶̶̶̶̶̶̶̶̶̶̶̶̶e saw
a miraculous light at a̶̶̶̶̶̶̶̶̶̶̶̶ halted
during his unhappy jou̶̶̶̶̶̶̶̶̶̶̶ Tenjin
matsuri (festival) takes̶̶̶̶̶̶̶̶̶̶olorful

parade through the city of Osaka is followed by an evening
floating procession down the Dojima river, with lanterns
and fireworks. Other well-known Tenjin shrines are the
Dazaifu Tenmangu, built at the site of Michizane's burial,
and the Kitano Tenjin shrine in Kyoto. Worshipers often visit
on the 25th of each month, the day on which Michizane
was born and died.

Because of his reputation as a brilliant scholar, Tenjin is
regarded as a kami who can grant scholarly success. At thousands of Tenjin shrines youngsters appeal for success in
their studies and ask Tenjin to help them get into the school
or university of their choice.

A popular means of communicating your wishes to Tenjin
(and to other kami) is to use the *ema*, a five-sided wooden
tablet about the size of a hand. It has a picture relating to
the shrine on one side while the other is left blank so that
supplicants can write their name, address and request to the
kami. Once filled in, the ema is hung on a rack provided for
the purpose at the shrine. Rows of ema remain on the rack
until New Year, when the old year's ema are ritually burnt,
and new ones are made available at the shrine.

SHINTO PRACTICES

At any large Shinto shrine the practices undertaken by shrine visitors will be many and varied. They include lifecycle rites, individual acts of prayer or worship, and rites and festivals for the community.

Lifecycle rites

Hatsu miya-mairi ("first shrine visit") takes place when a newborn baby is brought to the shrine, usually by the mother or grandmother, on the 32nd day (for a boy) or 33rd day (for a girl) after birth. The baby comes into the presence of the kami and becomes a parishioner of the shrine.

The *shichi-go-san* ("seven–five–three") festival is held throughout Japan on the nearest Sunday to November 15. Parents who have boys aged three or seven, or girls aged five, bring their children dressed in traditional kimono clothes to the shrine for a brief purification rite. In the similar *jusan mairi* ("13 visit") festival, children aged 13 are brought to the shrine for a blessing.

O-mamori and *o-fuda* (amulets and talismans) are purchased from the shrine for many purposes, from protection against traffic accidents to help with university entrance exams. Different shrines claim different *shintoku* (divine

Mount Fuji is held to be the sacred abode of both Buddhist and Shinto deities and white-costumed pilgrims visit the summit at sunrise

powers), so, for example, some shrines will attract those in search of healing, while others are popular with couples seeking the blessing of the kami on their marriage.

The *shinzen kekkon-sai* is a marriage ceremony before the kami. About two-thirds of wedding ceremonies in Japan involve Shinto rituals (the rest are mainly Christian in style, popular since the war). Shinto weddings became the norm in the early 1900s after the first ever royal wedding to be conducted by Shinto priests. Shrines often have a special hall to accommodate wedding groups.

According to the Chinese-Japanese zodiac, based on 12 animals, every 12th year of your life is significant, and purification rites for *toshi-otoko* or *toshi-onna* ("year-man" or "year-woman") are recommended. Women of 33 and men of 42 are in their *yakudoshi* ("unlucky year"), so many undergo harae (purification) ceremonies and carry protective amulets from the shrine.

Hatsu-mode, the first visit of the New Year, involves a visit to one or more shrines. The most famous shrines are packed with visitors during this period.

Household and business rites

The *jichinsai* ("ground-purifying ceremony") is conducted at the beginning of almost all building construction work. A Shinto priest invokes the protection of the kami of the land to make sure that no offence will be caused to the spirit by the building work.

O-harae (purification) rituals are carried out by priests on business premises, or at shrines in the presence of a deputation of staff from a company, to pray for business prosperity and ask for protection against accidents at work. Shrines dedicated to Inari, the god of rice and trade, are especially favored for these rites.

Communal festivals and rites

There are thousands of matsuri (festivals) based at shrines throughout Japan. Each matsuri has its own unique history, and members of the community take pride in participating in their special town or village festival. Larger matsuri usually involve resplendent parades of decorated floats, priests,

There are special shrine fest█████████████████████
that mark significant ████████████████████

retainers, and costumed ██████████████████████ the
mikoshi (sacred palanquin) ███████████████████ ied
to a temporary resting-plac████████████████████ om
the shrine, and solemn o██████████████████ ter-
tainments, such as music, ██████████████████ ests
involving the young men. I██████████████████ ows
freely. Some festivals ha██████████████████ ure
origins, while others have ██████████████████ rve
the needs of new urban c█████████

Shinto today

About 80 per cent of shri██████████████████ lun-
tary nationwide network,██████████████████ nes.
The figure of the emper██████████████████ ome
Shinto adherents, and the██████████████████ ts by
right-wing politicians to ██████████████████ kuni
war-memorial shrine in T██████████████████ atus.
However, each of the 100██████████████████ now
financially and legally ind██████████████████ owa-

days is far more on responding to local needs than aspiring
to a national leadership role.

Shrines in Japan are known for the benefits offered by
their resident kami (such as healing, educational success,
protection from accidents) and for the colorful festivals they
host. People attend shrines for rites of purification and to
receive help and blessings when required. The same people
who visit shrines also take part in Buddhist rites (mainly
funeral and memorial services) and about 40 per cent of
Japanese people are also involved in one or more of the
hundreds of new religions flourishing in Japan's post-war
climate of religious freedom. To a large extent, Shinto has
now reverted to its pre-1868 role of forming simply one
part of the broad tapestry of religious practices available to
the Japanese, albeit one that continues to have a strong appeal
to the people of Japan.

Perhaps 80 per cent of Japan's 125 million people participate at least occasionally in Shinto rites. For them, Shinto
is part of ordinary life. In an uncertain world, they could
argue, why not accept a little bit of extra help from the
kami? Relatively few people, however, think of Shinto as a
religion in which they personally "believe."

SIKHISM

Work hard, 66 adore the Divine Name and share the fruits of your labor

Sikhism is the youngest of the religions originating from India. It was founded in the 15th century by Guru Nanak and marked a radical departure from existing Indic traditions in its theological message and devotional practice. This break is reflected in the monotheism of Sikhism, its emphasis on the Formless Creator, and on the need to meditate on the Divine Name. The concept of God (Wahaguru), as outlined by Guru Nanak, is accompanied by a simple injunction to the believer to strive for union with God by working hard, by adoring the Divine Name, and by sharing the fruits of your labors with others. These simple precepts give Sikhism a distinctive vision and identity that contrasts sharply with some of the more ritualized traditions of southern and central Asia.

The plains of the Punja[...]n root, have historically [...]e between Central Asia and Indi[...]d fertile ground in Punjab beca[...]ly egalitarian social structure, a[...]t of many traditions.

Sikhism at the cro[...]

Since the late 1970s, ther[...]al interest in Sikhism arising fro[...]d India and the activities of Sik[...]s. In the early 1980s, a political r[...]y for the state of Punjab, where[...]t confrontation between the I[...]s. In June 1984, the Indian Ar[...]ib (the Golden Temple, the hol[...]in an operation codenamed Blu[...]s of about 1,000 people. Since [...]ve been killed in Punjab as the [...]a-rate Sikh state, and counter-i[...]d by the security forces. For a[...]4 and 1994, the Punjab was in[...]

The Golden Temple at Amritsar, the holiest of all the Sikh shrines, built in 1604

Sikh militancy, however, only partly explains some of the contemporary tensions within the faith. Historically, Sikhism's egalitarian message has had to contend with persistent caste prejudice within the faith, especially between Jats (yeoman farmers) and non-Jats. The circumstances in which the Sikh faith was established, and the long slow evolution of the faith, also created ambiguous boundaries between Sikhism and Hinduism. Many followers of Hinduism have, over the centuries, made selective appropriation of Sikh tenets, thereby encouraging lack of orthodoxy, or challenging the basic beliefs of Sikhism.

In the 20th century, Sikh beliefs and values have also been confronted by the experience of a sizeable Sikh diaspora (dispersal), with approximately two million Sikhs living in Western countries. The expansion of the Sikh faith to the West has brought forth new challenges and innovations – and new converts – away from the traditional Sikh homeland of Punjab.

THE HISTORY OF SIKHISM

Sikhism was founded by Guru Nanak (1469-1539) during a period of religious reform in Northern India that coincided with the establishment of Mogul rule. The reform movements of the time were opposed to the orthodoxy of Islam and Hinduism, and in favor of regional tradition, devotional practice, and folk heritage. Guru Nanak, who was aware of these movements and drew upon them, sought to transcend Islam and Hinduism by creating a new religion for a new age. "There is," he proclaimed, "neither Hindu nor Muslim."

Instead, Guru Nanak's message focused on the devotional formless Creator who graciously revealed himself through the spiritual True Guru, who is the manifestation of His message to humanity. Such a God, Nanak insisted, was not accessible through deities or rituals. Rather, the path to God lay through three simple commandments: *kirt karo* (hard work), *nam japo* (adoration of the divine name), and *vand cauko* (sharing the fruits of your labor).

Guru Nanak's revolutionary message soon attracted considerable attention. He was succeeded by nine other gurus who guided the development of the Sikh community. The second guru, Guru Angad (1539-52), is remembered for establishing the Gurmukhi script in which Punjabi is written. The word Gurmukhi literally means "from the mouth of the guru," and during this period Sikhs developed a special attachment to Punjabi written in this form. Guru Amar Das (1552-74), continued the teachings of Nanak and is remembered for founding the town of Goindwal, where Sikhs were enjoined to meet twice a year. During his lead-

The Golden Temple was completed in 1604, on land donated by the emperor Akbar in the 16th century

Akbar. By the time of the fifth guru, Guru Arjan (1581-1606), Sikhism had established a strong foothold in Punjab's central districts. Initial steps had been taken to institution-alize the development of the community, with the comple-tion, in 1604, of the Darbar Sahib (the Golden Temple), in Amritsar, and the compilation of the Adi Granth (also known as the Guru Granth Sahib, the Sikh holy book). These developments did not go unnoticed. Emperor Jehangir's efforts to check the spread of the new faith led to the execution of Guru Arjan in 1606.

A new militancy

The martyrdom of Guru Arjan marked the beginnings of the evolution of Sikhism from a pacifist reform movement to Sikh militancy. This transformation began with the sixth guru, Guru Hargobind (1606-1644). He built the Lohgarh fortress, at Amritsar, and the Akal Takht (seat of temporal authority), opposite the Harimandar Sahib (Temple of God) within the Darbar Sahib complex. Guru Hargobind wore two swords which symbolized the entwining of spiritual and temporal authority. This was a significant development, for it marked the inextricable linkage of polit-ical and spiritual affairs in subsequent developments within the Sikh commu-nity. The court of Guru Hargobind increasingly assumed independence from the established Mogul authori-ties, forming a base in Kiratpur.

ership, the Mogul emperor is _____ in the guru's *langar*, the con_____ the congregation attached _____ (Sikh place of worship).

The fourth guru, Gu_____ (1574-1581) is remember_____ writings, which are used i_____ Sikh wedding ceremony. _____ also founded the city _____ Amritsar and moved th_____ spiritual center of Sikhis_____ from Goindwal to the current site of the Golden Temple, which was built on land granted by the emperor

PERSECUTION AND MILITANCY

The leadership of the seventh and eight gurus (Guru Hari Rai (1630-1661) and Guru Hari Kishen (1656-1664) was largely uneventful as they tried to avoid direct confrontation with Mogul authority in Delhi. The ninth guru, Guru Tegh Bahadur (1621–1675), who took over the leadership of the community at a time when the emperor Aurangzeb began systematic persecution of the Sikhs, was arrested and martyred in Delhi in 1675.

The tenth guru, Gobind Singh (1658–1707), was faced with sustained attacks on Sikh institutions, and heretical schism associated with the rival claims to the guruship. In response, Guru Gobind Singh introduced two major innovations which were to lay the foundations of modern Sikh identity. On Basakhi (the Sikh New Year), in 1699, the guru baptized the first members of the Khalsa (the Pure), who were to undertake a fearless defence of the community. The Khalsa were to adorn themselves with the five "Ks:" *kesh* (unshorn hair), *kacha* (short drawers), *kirpan* (the steel

The Sikh cavalry gave spirited support to the British East India Company during the Indian Mutiny

dagger), *kara* (the iron bangle), *kanga* (the comb) – and all were to adopt the name Singh, if they were male, and Kaur, if female.

Secondly, upon his death Guru Gobind Singh invested the guruship in the Guru Granth Sahib (the Sikh holy book), thereby terminating personal guruship. These two changes drew the boundary around Sikh identity much more distinctly and clearly than it had been previously. The end to personal guruship succeeded in marking a break in schismatic pluralism, and the militant Singhs created by Guru Gobind Singh were destined to assume a pre-eminent position within the Panth (the Sikh community).

The Heroic Age

The 18th century is known as the Heroic Age, because it was during this period that the Sikh faithful faced and overcame many adversities. During this period the Sikhs sustained a fierce opposition to Mogul rule, which led to the development of a martial tradition and the creation of an independent Sikh state. Sikhism rose to political power in the Punjab at the same time as Mogul rule collapsed in Delhi, and Afghan influence declined in the province.

In 1801 Ranjit Singh proclaimed a "Kingdom of Lahore" that was able to subjugate Afghan territories to the West, taking in Kashmir and extending as far as Lhasa and Tibet.

Much of Lucknow was left in ruins after General Havelock's victory during the Indian Mutiny in 1858

Large numbers of Sikhs were r████████████████████my,
serving in Egypt, Burma, and t██████████████████lWar

This kingdom lasted until ████████████████ Singh led a powerful modern m████████████████ ████ated North-western India. F████████████████ l the reconstruction of the Da████████████████ dates from this period. Althoug████████████████ █ religious and secular institu███████████████ed for his reverence to Islam a████████████████ main traditions of the Punjab.

The annexation of th███████████████sh led to a change in the fortu██████████████ Prior to the Indian Mutiny (18████████████ much suspicion by the British████████████st India

Company during the mutiny helped crush the rebellion. In the century that followed, the status of the Sikh community changed: from having been the ruling community, it became the smallest of the Punjab's three main religious traditions. A further reason for the decline in the Sikh community at this time was the fact that many Sikhs relapsed into Hinduism.

This trend was arrested in the late 19th century by Sikh reform movements, the most important of which was called the Singh Sabha. The recruitment of large numbers of Sikhs into the Imperial Army also created a new pride in the Sikh heritage. Over 100,000 Sikhs served on the Western front during the First World War and many saw service in Africa, Burma and the Far East during the Second World War.

SIKHISM IN THE 20TH CENTURY

The work of the reformist Singh Sabha movement was completed by the Akali movement (1920–25). This established a system of control through gurdwaras (Sikh temples) which were in turn managed by the Shiromini Gurdwara Parbandhak Committee (SGPC) and the Akali Dal (its political wing). Since the 1920s the SGPC and the Akali Dal have been the premier institutions within contemporary Sikhism, controlling the religious affairs of the community and dominating its political life.

Before the withdrawal of the British from India in 1947, the Sikh population was divided equally between West and East Punjab. In the late 19th and early 20th centuries, many Sikhs moved to the new Canal Colonies (now in the Pakistani Punjab). The Akali Dal opposed the creation of Pakistan, but its formation in 1947 led to the mass transfer of members of the Sikh population to East Punjab. After 1947 the Akali Dal spearheaded a campaign for the formation of a Punjabi-speaking state (Punjabi Suba). In 1966, following the Indo-Pakistan War, the boundaries of East Punjab were redrawn to create a Punjabi speaking province with a 60 per cent Sikh population. This reorganization was incomplete and left many Punjabi-speaking areas in the adjoining states. In the late 1970s and early 1980s a movement developed around the Anandpur Sahib Resolution seeking greater autonomy for Punjab. This culminated in Operation Blue Star and the decade of violence that followed.

Sikhs around the world

Today, most of the Sikh population is based in the Indian state of Punjab where, according to the 1991 census, there are approximately 12 million Sikhs out of a total population of 20 million. In addition there are approximately two million Sikhs in other Indian states, mostly in northern India (Haryana, Uttar Pardesh, Rajasthan, and Himachal Pardesh).

Sikhs have been migrating from India since the late 19th century, with East Africa, the Far East, Australasia and North America the initial destinations. After 1945 there was large-scale migration to the United Kingdom, Canada, and the USA. In the 1970s, following the oil boom, many Sikhs also migrated to the Middle East. Because of the troubles in the Punjab in the 1980s and 1990s, many Sikhs settled abroad, seeking political asylum all over the globe. Today, Sikhs are present in large numbers throughout the European Union countries and small pockets of Sikh settlement are to found in most countries.

Current estimates suggest that there are approximately two million Sikhs outside India. The largest Sikh settlement is in the United Kingdom with 400,000, followed by Canada with 300,000, and the United States with 100,000. Added to the Sikh population in India, this gives a total of 16 million Sikhs worldwide.

Lahore, former capital of Pakistan, was the home of many Sikhs until 1947. The city was the capital of Maharajah Ranjit Singh's kingdom in the 19th century

The Sikh population of the Pun[...] f a
total of 20 million, while a[...]
northern Indian states of Ha[...] d
Himachel Pradesh, and a further [...] pora
— live in Europe, the Middle [...] a

The Sikh diaspora (wh[...]nity
of Sikhs living abroad an[...]d to
Sikhism) represents a gro[...]aith.
The diaspora has been act[...]ts of
Sikhs to a global audience[...]ages
of a community that is c[...]s of
terrorist activities. Within[...]dap-
tation of Sikh institutio[...]local
conditions, and a growing[...]n the
light of new challenges.

TEACHING, CONCEPTS, AND BELIEFS

Sikhs are monotheists. The opening hymn of the Guru Granth Sahib (the Sikh holy book) begins with the words of Guru Nanak: "There is one supreme eternal reality; the truth; immanent in all things; creator of all things; immanent in creation. Without fear and without hatred; not subject to time; beyond birth and death; self-revealing. Known by the Guru's grace." This statement is known as the Mool Mantar (the Basic Teaching).

Sikhs believe that God (Wahaguru), who created the universe and everything in it, is present everywhere. God is omnipresent and immanent (indwelling, inherent) as well as omnipotent and transcendent. God does not appear in the form of a human body, but spiritual union with God is possible during this present lifetime through the guru's grace, and by constantly remembering God and serving others. The concept of service (*seva*) is central to the Sikh faith. Through seva, Sikhs are encouraged to overcome selfish desires and

This 19-century painting from Rjastha shows Sikh Saldar giving instruction

ੴ ਸਤਿਨਾਮੁ ਕਰਤਾ ਪੁਰਖੁ ਨਿਰਭਉ ਨਿਰਵੈਰੁ ਅਕਾਲ ਮੂਰਤਿ ਅਜੂਨੀ ਸੈਭੰ ਗੁਰ ਪ੍ਰਸਾਦਿ ॥

ਜਪੁ

॥ ਆਦਿ ਸਚੁ ਜੁਗਾਦਿ ਸਚੁ ॥ ਹੈ ਭੀ ਸਚੁ ਨਾਨਕ ਹੋਸੀ ਭੀ ਸਚੁ ॥ ਸੋਚੈ ਸੋਚਿ ਨ ਹੋਵਈ ਜੇ ਸੋਚੀ ਲਖ ਵਾਰ ॥ ਚੁਪੈ ਚੁਪ ਨ ਹੋਵਈ ਜੇ ਲਾਇ ਰਹਾ ਲਿਵਤਾਰ॥ਭੁਖਿਆ ਭੁਖ ਨ ਉਤਰੀ ਜੇ ਬੰਨਾ ਪੁਰੀਆ ਭਾਰ॥ਸਹਸ ਸਿਆਣਪਾ ਲਖ ਹੋਹਿ ਤ ਇਕ ਨ ਚਲੈ ਨਾਲਿ ॥ ਕਿਵ ਸਚਿਆਰਾ ਹੋਈਐ ਕਿਵ ਕੂੜੈ ਤੁਟੈ ਪਾਲਿ ॥ ਹੁਕਮਿ ਰਜਾਈ ਚਲਣਾ ਨਾਨਕ ਲਿਖਿਆ ਨਾਲਿ॥੧॥ਹੁਕਮੀ ਹੋਵਨਿ ਆਕਾਰ ਹੁਕਮੁ ਨ ਕਹਿਆ ਜਾਈ॥ਹੁਕਮੀ ਹੋਵਨਿ ਜੀਅ ਹੁਕਮਿ ਮਿਲੈ ਵਡਿਆਈ॥ ਹੁਕਮੀ ਉਤਮੁ ਨੀਚੁ ਹੁਕਮਿ ਲਿਖਿ ਦੁਖ ਸੁਖ ਪਾਈਅਹਿ ॥ ਇਕਨਾ ਹੁਕਮੀ ਬਖਸੀਸ ਇਕਿ ਹੁਕਮੀ ਸਦਾ ਭਵਾਈਅਹਿ ॥ ਹੁਕਮੈ ਅੰਦਰਿ ਸਭੁ ਕੋ ਬਾਹਰਿ ਹੁਕਮ ਨ ਕੋਇ ॥ ਨਾਨਕ ਹੁਕਮੈ ਜੇ ਬੁਝੈ ਤ ਹਉਮੈ ਕਹੈ ਨ ਕੋਇ ॥੨॥ ਗਾਵੈ ਕੋ ਤਾਣੁ ਹੋਵੈ ਕਿਸੈ ਤਾਣੁ ॥ ਗਾਵੈ ਕੋ ਦਾਤਿ ਜਾਣੈ ਨੀਸਾਣੁ ॥ ਗਾਵੈ ਕੋ ਗੁਣ ਵਡਿਆਈਆ ਚਾਰ ॥ ਗਾਵੈ ਕੋ ਵਿਦਿਆ ਵਿਖਮੁ ਵੀਚਾਰੁ॥ ਗਾਵੈ ਕੋ ਸਾਜਿ ਕਰੇ

The first page of the scriptures known as the Guru Granth Sahib; Sikhs are defined as those who believe in God and in the teachings and writings of the ten gurus

undertake the responsibilities of family life. The present world and that of the divine are linked together in three popular injunctions: devotion to and adoration of the Divine Name, union of God through hard work, and sharing the rewards of one's labor with others.

It is in light of these beliefs that the code of discipline of the SGPC (the Shiromini Gurdwara Parbandhak Committee — the premier religious institution within Sikhism) defines a Sikh as a man or woman who: "Believes in God, in the Ten Gurus, in the Guru Granth Sahib and other writings and teachings of the Gurus, in the Khalsa initiation ceremony, and who does not believe in any other religion."

The Guru Granth Sahib, or holy book, is the contemporary embodiment of guruship. The Guru Granth Sahib provides a constant source of spiritual guidance.

Another core belief of S━━━━━━━━━━━━━es to God are gender neutra━━━━━━━━━━━e are forbidden. Guru Nanak i━━━━━━━━━━━every gurdwara (Sikh temple)━━━━━━━━━━vhere the *sangat* (congregatior━━━━━━

The story of Gu━━ ━━━━ and Bhai Lalo

The importance of Sikl━━━━━━━━━━strated by the story of Guru N━━━━━━━━━y high-lights the essence of G━━━━━━━━━virtues of hard work and integr━━━━━━━━on the dignity of labor, but th━━━━━━━━ith the

purity of thought if you are to obtain the guru's grace.

Guru Nanak used to visit the house of a humble carpenter named Lalo. Once the guru was staying with him when the rich man of that village, a man named Bhago, held a feast to which he invited all the saintly people. Guru Nanak refused to go.

Eventually Bhago himself went to fetch the guru. Guru Nanak acceded to his request, but took some food with him from Lalo's house. At the feast, Guru Nanak held in one hand the food from Bhago's house and in the other hand he held the food he had brought from Lalo's house. When he squeezed his hands, blood came from Bhago's food while from Lalo's came trickles of milk. Guru Nanak said that this difference between the two pieces of food was because of the sincerity and honesty of Lalo in contrast to the way Bhago had made his wealth, by exploitation.

THE DUTIES OF A SIKH

The Sikh code of discipline (the Rahit Maryada) prescribes precisely the duties of an adherent. Sikhs are required to follow the teachings of the gurus and to study the scriptures regularly. The Guru Granth Sahib, or holy book, is written in the Punjabi language, in the Gurmukhi script. A knowledge of Gurmukhi is therefore essential for a Sikh. A clear understanding of the scriptures and the history of the Sikh tradition, especially Sikh history, is also required.

The Rahit Maryada also prescribes a daily routine for the Sikh. A Sikh should rise early (between 3 and 6 o'clock in the morning) and, having bathed, should observe *nam japana* by meditating on God. Each day a Sikh should read or recite portions of scripture, as ordained in the *nit-nem* (the daily rule). This means reading the *japji, Jap* and the 10 Savayyas early in the morning, the Sodar Rahiras at sunset, and the Sohila at night, before retiring. At the conclusion of the morning and evening reading, the prayer known as *ardas* must also be recited.

The influence of the Guru's word, and of the scriptures, is best experienced in the gurdwara. Sikhs are therefore required to join a daily sangat (congregation) where, in addition to listening to scriptures, they must undertake and perform seva (service).

After rising early, bathing and preparing for the day, Sikhs read a section of the Gutka, the abbreviated scriptures

Members of the Sikh community are encouraged to eat together in communal dining rooms as a mark of equality, and refreshment tents are set up for the purpose during popular festivals

The Rahit Maryada also imposes additional injunctions that determine the way a Sikh's daily life is lived. Sikhs are only allowed to eat meat killed in accordance with Sikh practice of Jhatka (a clean strike). The use of intoxicants, especially alcohol and tobacco, is forbidden. The cutting of hair is strictly forbidden; a Sikh must wear the five "Ks" and a turban. In conformity with the virtues of honesty and integrity, Sikhs are not allowed to gamble, to be unfaithful to their marital partners, or to steal. As part of the concept of seva, all Sikhs are asked to give one-tenth of their earnings for the welfare of the community.

Variations in Sikh practice

Much of the conventional writing on Sikhism – especially by Western scholars – focuses on divisions within the community and the disjunction between official beliefs and actual practice. Scholars working within the Sikh tradition, on the other hand, have viewed such tension creatively, as providing a new point of departure for interpreting established practices.

Although the Sikh identity is now firmly established, the practices described above developed more than 200 years after Guru Nanak's birth. Many who were initially attracted

Intoxicants are forbidden to ▓▓▓▓▓▓▓▓▓▓▓▓▓▓▓▓▓▓▓▓ n
accordance with the ▓▓▓▓▓▓▓▓▓▓▓▓▓▓▓▓

by the message of Guru N ▓▓▓▓▓▓▓▓▓▓▓▓▓▓▓▓▓ dher-
ence to the emerging ins ▓▓▓▓▓▓▓▓▓▓▓▓▓▓▓ g the
turmoil of the 18th centu ▓▓▓▓▓▓▓▓▓▓▓▓▓▓ ts of
the 19th, many of these ▓▓▓▓▓▓▓▓▓▓▓▓▓ uism
or other faiths. It was in ▓▓▓▓▓▓▓▓▓▓▓▓▓▓▓ and
to face the challenge of Ch ▓▓▓▓▓▓▓▓▓▓▓▓ ism,
that the Singh Sabha Mo ▓▓▓▓▓▓▓▓▓▓▓ ssert
Khalsa identity. In the 20t ▓▓▓▓▓▓▓▓▓▓ been
challenged by the emerg ▓▓▓▓▓▓▓▓▓▓▓ pora,

established mainly in Western countries. As the 21st century approaches, Sikhism stands at a crossroad between its traditional construction, and on-going redefinition in the light of contemporary challenges, both in India and abroad.

Some writers mistakenly highlight pluralism within Sikh practice by reference to Sikh sects such as Nanak Panthis, the Nirankaris, Namdhari, and Radoswamis. These groups have questionable linkage within Sikh tradition and have, on occasion, openly challenged the mainstream beliefs and practice. Mainstream Sikhism does not consider members of these groups to be Sikhs, and most of these groups have their own living guru.

SIKH SUB-IDENTITIES

Within Sikhism there are four main sub-identities, each distinguished by different levels of adherence to core beliefs and practices. The premier position is occupied by the *amrit-dhari* Khalsa (baptized Sikhs, "Singhs") who are few in number but represent the orthodoxy. Those Singhs who are not baptized, but who wear the five symbolic "Ks" (known as the *kesh-dari* Khalsa) constitute the majority of Sikhs. Baptized and non-baptized Singhs together account for nearly three-quarters of the Sikh population. The third category includes shaven Singhs (*mona* Sikhs) of baptized and non-baptized background who live in the Sikh diaspora. Finally, there are non-Singhs (Sahaj-dharis) who still follow pre-Khalsa pluralism and, in many cases, have assimilated practices from other religions.

There is a significant number of mona Sikhs within the Sikh diaspora. Many of them have shaved off their beards and cut their long hair because of the racism and hostility they faced in their host countries. Daily practices that are normal in Punjab (such as visiting the gurdwara) are often difficult to maintain in Western countries. Many Sikhs in the United Kingdom, for example, are only able to visit the local gurdwara at the weekend. The learning of Punjabi is also difficult. Many gurdwaras offer Sunday schools so that children can learn Punjabi and about Sikh traditions.

The challenge of the diaspora

The diaspora is also a microcosm of Punjabi society. Despite the injunction against casteism, caste still continues to play a significant role in Sikh society. The vast majority of Sikhs (nearly 70 per cent) are Jats (yeomen farmers). Non-Jat Sikhs have been active in establishing their own gurdwaras, which often service local or caste-based organizations. Many of these castes sustain an unorthodox form of worship, often sharing elements of the Sikh tradition with Punjabi folk worship or practices drawn from the many different varieties of Hinduism.

Sikhs on pilgrimage to Amritsar. Carrying arms is part of Sikh tradition

Rana Jawan Singh, show_____ in this 19th-century painting, car_____ extricable link between s_____

Custom and practice,_____ community, have been influe_____ There is
an increasing recogn_____ a rein-
terpretation of the p_____ ty. In the
management of gur_____ commu-

nity at large, young women are increasingly asserting their
rights to equal representation and regard. The lack of a
working knowledge of the Punjabi language among third
and fourth generation Sikh migrants has led to their
demands for the Guru Granth Sahib to be translated into a
variety of languages. Likewise, the expectation that you
should marry within your caste is increasingly being ques-
tioned, as young Sikhs reject arranged marriages and seek
to choose their own partners.

WORSHIP, RITUAL, AND FESTIVITIES

The gurdwara is the main place of worship for a Sikh. In the United Kingdom alone there are over 200 gurdwaras, often sited in industrial inner cities. A gurdwara is distinguished by a *nishan sahib* (a flag), and people who enter are required to remove their shoes and cover their hair. Sikhs and non-Sikhs are expected to kneel in front of the Guru Granth Sahib, and then the congregation sits on the floor to listen to hymns recited from the scriptures. The collective prayer (ardas) takes place at the conclusion of each reading. The congregation is served with *kara parsad*, a mixture of ghee, sugar, and flour, which symbolizes the equality of the congregation.

Sikhism plays a very central role in the lifecycle of a devout Sikh. A newborn baby is given a name in a cere-mony, often at a gurdwara, where, after a collective prayer, the Guru Granth Sahib is opened at random. The letter that begins the first verse of the hymn on that page is chosen as the letter with which the baby's name will begin.

Sikhs have a distinctive marriage ceremony know as *anand karaj*. This is normally held at the gurdwara. The bride and groom move clockwise around the Guru Granth Sahib four times, while hymns are read out from the holy book.

Following a death, a section of the scriptures known as Sukhmani Sahib is read. The deceased is dressed in the five "Ks" and the body is cremated on the day of the death, unless it is already very late in the day. During the funeral, the Sohila (part of the scriptures) is read. A special ceremony

Resplendent in scarlet and gold, the bride at this Sikh wedding ceremony covers her head as prayers are said

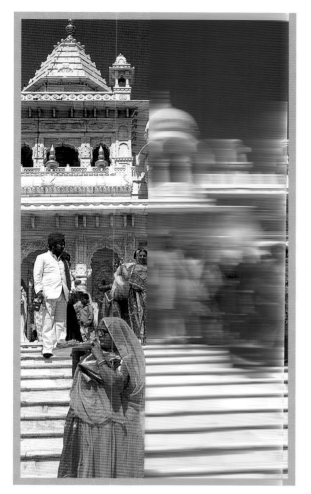

Festivities mark historical event_____e
birth and d_____

Above: *The Hola Moholla festival is held in Anandpur,*
and includes political gatherings and tests of physical strength
as well as musical competitions
Below: *Festive garlands of marigold, frangipani,*
and hibiscus in Amritsar

the popular traditions of the Punjab. The birth or death of a guru is called a *gurpurb*. The martyrdoms of Guru Arjan and Guru Teg Bahadaur are generally observed. The births of Guru Nanak and Guru Gobind Singh are universally celebrated with an Akhand Path, with popular gatherings and with processions through the cities.

Baisakhi marks the first month of the Sikh New Year and also coincides with the harvest season in Punjab. Baisakhi is important for Sikhs because it marks the time of the year when Sikhs traditionally assembled in the presence of the guru, from Guru Amar Das onwards, and when Guru Gobind Singh founded the Khalsa in 1699.

Sikhs also celebrate Diwali (the Festival of Light) which marks the release of the sixth guru, Guru Hargobind, from confinement at the Gwalior Fort. Sikhs celebrate Hola Mohalla, which commemorates a summons issued by Guru Gobind Singh, at the time of Hindu celebration of Holi (the Festival of Color), to test the loyalty of his followers. Today the Hola Mohalla is organized in Anandpur and includes celebrations of physical strength, political gatherings, and musical and poetic competitions.

on the ninth day after crema_____s.

To mark ceremonies su_____ other special occasions, Si_____ Path, an uninterrupted r_____ Granth Sahib, which norm_____ This reading usually ends o_____ day of celebration and co_____ special ceremony.

Sikhs celebrate many_____ related to the life and tim___ the gurus, marking particu____ historical occasions in t__ Sikh tradition, and reflect____

TAOISM

> Tao does nothing, but there is nothing it does not do

Taoism belongs to a tradition of thought that has much in common with Confucianism, but stands alone as a separate system of ethical and spiritual practices. Where Confucianism is primarily concerned with the secular values that ensure good order in human culture and society, Taoism is also concerned with religious issues. These are often mediated through the observation of nature. In early mystical strands of Taoism the sage gains immortality and spiritual freedom by emulating natural harmony, balance, and spontaneity.

TAO CHIA AND TAO CHIAO

T here ... to Ta... ...osophy (... ...m (Tao C... Ph... ...on the fol...

the Tao Te Ching (the Clas... attributed to the sage, Lao...

the work of the sage Chua... which date from the 4th c...

the work of the sage Lieh... materials in the 4th cent...

commentaries on these te... Learning" of the 3rd and...

According to Philosophical... ...who follows the way of heaven a... ...fish goals. He or she flows w... ...ting success or misfortune equa... ...ven a form of spiritual immor... ...nsequences of living withou... ...Such notions have inspired man... ...ists, recluses and craftsmen.

Religious Taoism

Religious Taoism is pra... ...and traditions which seek ac... ...eme reality. Followers seek i... ...tion, liturgy, alchemy, and ph... ...been concerned with the ritua... ...smic currents of yin and yang... ...tion, breath control, and mind... ...tures and training manuals we... ...Taoist Canon (Tao Tsang), a hu... ...vhich even in its reduced form, ...nsists of 1,120 volumes.

A 16th-century painting of Lao Tzu, author of the Tao Te Ching (the Classic of the Way and Its Power), source of Taoist philosophical thinking

All Taoists are concerned with harmonizing the fundamental energies in the universe. In Religious Taoism, energies are channeled in order to perform healing, exorcism and to regulate important festivals, such as the rites of cosmic renewal (Chiao). The traditional goal of Religious Taoism is immortality, through harmonizing yin and yang forces internally. This state may be interpreted literally as an imperishable subtle body, or metaphorically as a state of spontaneity and spiritual freedom.

THE TAO TE CHING

The Tao Te Ching (the Classic of the Way and its Power) is a pivotal text for all Taoists. It integrates a mystical path, of naturalness and unconstrained non-volitional action, with a political philosophy, in which the state embraces minimal interference and regal self-effacement. The text endorses a spiritualized vision of immortality arising from a non-acquisitive, natural, and harmonious life. Mystics, philosophers, and poets were quickly attracted to its teachings, interpreting the model of the disengaged, non-acquisitive Sage Ruler as a guide to life. It inspired many commentaries and interpretations, as well as works of art. In Religious Taoism it was given a more liturgical interpretation, with immortality conceived in more literal terms.

In places, the text appears to provide a view about the origins of life, the universe and everything. For example, chapter 25 reads:

"There was something formless yet complete,
Before Heaven and Earth, without sound or substance,
Standing alone unchanging.

Coursing everywhere witho_____
It can be regarded as the M_____
I don't know its name, but _____
If forced to name it I woul_____

To be great is to pass on,
To pass on is to be far away
To be far away is to return
So the Tao is great, Heaven_____
the King is great.
In the land there are four _____
one of them.

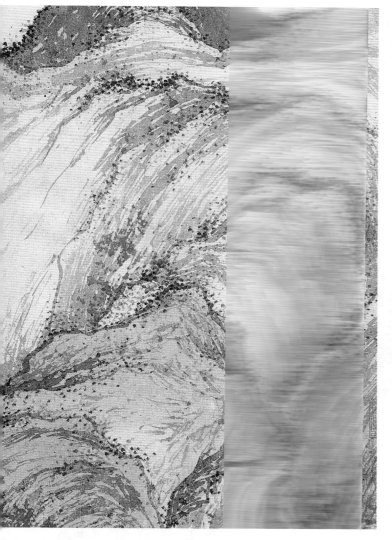

People model themselves on the Earth,
Earth models itself on Heaven,
Heaven models itself on the Tao,
The Tao models itself on that which is naturally so."

Rather like the answer to the mystery of life and the universe, it doesn't tell us very much. But it does suggest that people model themselves on Earth, Heaven and the Tao, and that Tao follows its own natural spontaneity. So it creates and gives rise to phenomena without purpose, or intention, or desire. And if we could be the same, it is suggesting that we would come to no harm. So without giving definitive answers, it has a way of suggesting what people do, or at least how they should do it.

Chapter 37 reads:

"Tao does nothing,
But there is nothing that it does not do.
If dukes and rulers could hold to this,
the myriad creatures would transform themselves.
If, after transforming, desires should arise,
restrain them with nameless, natural simplicity.
Nameless simplicity is freedom from desires.
If I cease from desire and remain tranquil,
the Kingdom under Heaven will be at peace
naturally."

Many chapters in the text shift with ease from statements about cosmic matters, such as the nature and origins of the universe and all phenomena, to statements about how the Sage Ruler (and by extension anybody) should act in the world so as to harmonize his or her life. Therein lies the universal appeal of the Tao Te Ching.

Amidst the splendors of the natural landscape, the Taoist sage T'ang Yin meditates on matters of immortality in this painting from the Ming Period; Taoist spiritual freedom is achieved through seeking detachment from extremes and through harmonizing yin and yang forces internally

THE ART OF MASTERING LIFE

With characteristic humor, Chuang Tzu delighted in taking examples of mastery of life from trades and skills that were looked down on by the Confucian scholarly elite. In his writings we find people such as carpenters, butchers, and animal trainers demonstrating the art of mastering life.

In one interesting passage, Chuang Tzu describes a hunchback cicada catcher assuming the role of teacher to Confucius himself. In doing so he emphasizes the importance of focused energy and attention to the performance of even apparently humble tasks.

Chuang Tzu's account of the excellence of cook Ting as a butcher provides a perfect model for the art of mastering life. Cook Ting, the Master Chef, was carving up an ox for Lord Wen-hui. As his hands moved, his shoulders relaxed and his knees bent. The knife slipped through the ox easily without resistance, in harmony with the body. It was as if he was performing the dance of the mulberry grove or keeping time to the Ching-shou music.

"This is wonderful," said Lord Wen-hui. "Imagine skill reaching such heights!"

Cook Ting laid down his knife and said, "What I care about is the Way (Tao) which goes beyond skill. When I first began carving oxen, all I could see was the ox itself. After three years I no longer saw the whole ox. And now I use the spirit (*shen*) not my eyes. My senses know where to stop and the spirit moves where it wants. I go along with the natural structure, striking into the big hollows, guiding the knife through the openings, and following things as they are. I never touch the smallest ligament or tendon, much less a main joint. A good cook changes his knife once a year, because he cuts. A mediocre cook changes his knife once a month, because he hacks. I've had this knife of mine for 19

An archery contest, in an 18th-century painting on silk from the Qing Dynasty

The Taoist approach to daily ta▓▓▓▓▓▓▓▓▓▓▓▓▓▓▓▓▓▓▓▓
skill and focused energy▓▓▓▓▓▓▓▓▓▓▓▓▓▓

years and I've cut up thousa▓▓▓▓▓▓▓▓▓▓▓▓▓he blade is as good as though it▓▓▓▓▓▓▓▓▓▓d-stone. There are spaces bet▓▓▓▓▓▓▓▓▓▓de of the knife has really no t▓▓▓▓▓▓▓▓▓▓has no thickness into such space▓▓▓▓▓▓▓▓▓▓m, more than enough for the▓▓▓▓▓▓▓▓▓▓hy after 19 years the blade of▓▓▓▓▓▓▓▓▓▓en it came from the grindstor

Whenever I come to a ▓▓▓▓▓▓▓▓▓▓ the difficulties, slow down and ▓▓▓▓▓▓▓▓▓▓hat I'm doing, work very slow▓▓▓▓▓▓▓▓▓▓lly, until the whole thing come▓▓▓▓▓▓▓▓▓▓m-bling to the ground. I stand▓▓▓▓▓▓▓▓▓▓ook around me, completely sa▓▓▓▓▓▓▓▓▓▓uc-

tant to move on. Then I clean my knife blade and put it away."

"Excellent!" said Lord Wen Hui. "I have heard the words of Cook Ting and learned how to care for life!"

Cook Ting's method of following the way of least resistance, never using muscular force or hacking with his knife, preserves both the blade and his energy and ensures that he achieves his objective effortlessly. A Taoist approach to life's problems uses exactly the same method. Cook Ting allows his spirit or consciousness (shen), along with tactile awareness, to guide his actions. The state he achieves is one which goes beyond that normally associated with the butcher's skills and techniques. It is an active meditative process involving a focused, attentive state of non-discursive awareness. In this state the appropriate actions to the task flow without recourse to intellectual analysis and without trying consciously to reproduce the conditions and actions of previous operations.

THE TAOIST VERSUS THE SHAMAN

The following story comes from the work of Chuang Tzu.

A famous shaman lived in the state of Cheng in ancient China. People feared and respected him for his powers of prediction. He could predict someone's fortune and lifespan, telling them their exact time of death. A Taoist student named Lieh Tzu was in awe of the shaman and was prepared to leave his master, the sage Hu Tzu, to follow him. Hu Tzu told Lieh Tzu that he did not yet know the Tao, and that he would like to meet this shaman and let him predict his fate.

The next day Lieh Tzu brought the shaman. After the meeting the shaman declared, "Your master is dying. He only has 10 days to live, his face already carries the damp ashen look of death."

Lieh Tzu wept as he told Master Hu Tzu the news. Hu Tzu smiled saying, "Just now I sat in the stillness and silence of the earth. He saw my inner power shut off. Bring him over another day."

Lieh Tzu brought the shaman the next day. After seeing Master Hu Tzu he reported, "Your Master is fortunate to have met me, his life and power are returning." Hu Tzu said, "Just now I meditated on bright Heaven, with the source of my power welling up from the heels. Bring him over another day."

Lieh Tzu brought him the next day. The shaman declared, "Your master is unstable, I cannot read him like this. Tell him to settle down and I'll try another day."

Going with the cosmic flow

Hu Tzu commented, "I showed him the equanimity of non-victory. He must have seen the source of my vital energy

The rock-cut caves of one of China's oldest Buddhist temples, now serving Taoists also, near Dunhuang, in Western Gansu province

Above: *This Taoist shaman use▮▮▮▮▮▮▮▮▮▮▮▮▮▮▮▮▮▮▮*
a state of trance in which he ▮▮▮▮▮▮▮▮▮▮▮▮▮▮▮
Right: *An elderly Taoist priest▮▮▮▮▮▮▮▮▮▮▮▮▮▮▮▮*
Gong, on top of ▮▮▮▮▮▮▮▮

alone like a clod of earth. Sealed against entanglement, he remained whole until the end.

Chuang Tzu comments: "Do not be an embodier of fame; do not be a storehouse of schemes; do not be an undertaker of projects; do not be a proprietor of wisdom. Embody what has no end, and wander where there is no beginning. Hold on to what is given you by Heaven but don't think you have attained something. Just be empty, that is all. The perfect man uses his mind like a mirror; pursuing nothing, welcoming nothing, responding but not retaining. He can win over things without injury."

in balance. The depths of ▮▮▮▮▮▮▮▮▮▮▮ of greater depths. There are ni▮▮▮▮▮▮▮▮▮▮▮ im only three. Bring him anotl▮▮▮▮

The next day, as soon as ▮▮▮▮▮▮▮▮▮▮zu, he fled in terror. Lieh Tzu ▮▮▮▮▮▮▮▮▮ch up. Master Hu Tzu said, "Ju▮▮▮▮▮▮▮▮▮ an empty, primordial state. U▮▮▮▮▮▮▮▮▮the wind and flowed with the ▮▮▮▮▮▮▮▮

After this Lieh Tzu re▮▮▮▮▮▮▮▮to learn anything. He went ho▮▮▮▮▮▮▮▮t go out. He took over his w▮▮▮▮▮▮▮▮ fed the pigs as though fe▮▮▮▮▮▮▮▮ picking and choosing and g▮▮▮▮▮▮▮ self-improvement. He mac▮▮▮▮▮▮▮

HEALTH AND LONG LIFE

Physical exercise has been recommended since ancient times as a means of channeling the vital cosmic force, known as ch'i, to various parts of the body

In Taoist theory and traditional Chinese medicine, the human body is thought of as an energy system consisting of patterned flows of *ch'i* (vital energy) and blood. It is usual to regard the flow of ch'i in the body as closely parallel to the flow of ch'i over the earth and landscape. From this insight, ideas about the detailed correspondence between the body and the landscape were developed. Since the human and the physical landscape are both composed of ch'i in varying configurations and degrees of refinement, such correspondences seem very natural to the Chinese.

The *ch'i* in the body is as subject to change and variability as are the forces in the weather. If ch'i is solidified and congealed, it is called *ching* (seminal essence). The gross forms of ching include the seminal fluids of men and the lubrication fluids of women. But ching also refers to the more subtle and insubstantial sexual energy, which is the emotional and psychological correlative of these substances. In its more refined form, ch'i is subtle air or breath. At an even more refined level, ch'i is referred to as shen (spirit or consciousness). Between these conditions there are, of course, many other degrees of refinement.

Physical exercise

These ideas led to the development of beneficial exercises called Tao Yin (literally "Guiding and Stretching"). Early forms of Tao Yin are described in the Chuang Tzu, in the form of animal postures and controlled breathing exercises. They are illustrated in a text named Tao Yin Tu, preserved on bamboo strips and discovered in the Ma wang tui tomb, dating from the 2nd century B.C.E.

Religious Taoist sects developed these methods of guiding and refining ch'i, in order to nurture and extend life, increase potency and resilience, and, in some cases, achieve immortality. Many later texts on these exercises are preserved in the Taoist Canon (the Tao Tsang). Their relative value and status, as guides to preparing for the quest for immortality, vary from text to text.

The archaic Tao Yin exercises have been developed and refined, and are practiced by millions of Chinese and Westerners around the world. Despite variations and changes, the emphasis

remains on thinking about ch░░░░░░░░░░░░░░░n,
and then directing ch'i as ░░░░░░░░░░░░░░░░us
parts of the body. The inter░░░░░░░░░░░░░░ct
a strong Taoist influence an░░░░░░░░░░░░░om
the ancient Tao Yin practice░░

Taoists seek to nurture░░░░░░░░░░░░░░yin
and yang, sexual activity ░░░░░░░░░░░░░░ By
arousing sexual energy, ch░░░░░░░░░░░░░nal
essence) can be increased an░░░░░░░░░░░░ale
does not ejaculate too fre░░░░░░░░░░░░░her
nurtures the ch'i of bot░░░░░░░░░░░░░ of
advanced Taoist sexual alc░░░░░░░░░░░░ted
up the spinal channel to n░░░░░░░░░░

*Elderly people in Daguan, Ch░░░░░░░░░░░░░░ave
recognized benefits in enc░░░░░░░░░░*

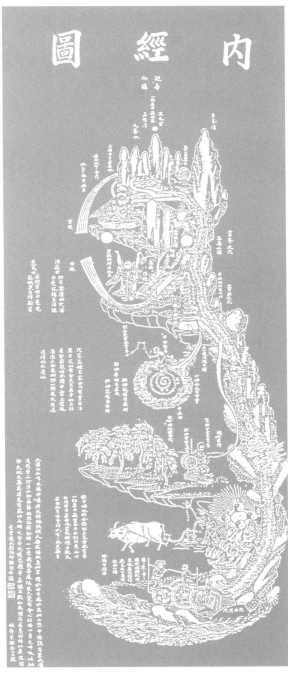

Traditional Taoist medicine portrays the body as a complex landscape, as depicted in this engraving from the walls of the Baigunguan Temple in Beijing; here the long mountain ridge represents the spine, the revolving circle of yin/yang symbols represents the balance of the elements, and the field being plowed symbolizes the cultivation of longevity

HEAVENLY MASTER MOVEMENT

Early Chinese thinking about immortality was often based on beliefs about remote locations in the Eastern seas or the Kun Lun mountains, and frequently involved the use of magical fruits or herbs. Such beliefs persisted in mythology and painting, even though more sophisticated and realistic beliefs about ways of achieving immortality were developed.

By the time of the Han dynasty (206 B.C.E. to 9 C.E.), several "hygienic cults" had developed. The followers of these cults interpreted the statements on immortality in the Tao Te Ching and Chuang Tzu literally, and they regarded Lao Tzu and the great cultural hero Huang Ti (the Yellow Emperor) as exponents of literal immortality. They believed that, by following strict dietary regimes, by using extensive breathing and physiological disciplines (Tao Yin), and by communing with spirits and immortals, the body could be gradually transformed from its mortal state to an immortal substance.

Creating the Great Peace

Groups of alchemists believed immortality was to be achieved by ingesting elixirs prepared through alchemy. One early synthesizer of such practices, who also found inspiration in the Tao Te Ching, was Chang Tao Ling, the First Heavenly Master of the Heavenly Master branch of Religious Taoism, who lived in the 2nd century C.E. Through a series of visionary encounters, including one with the Immortal Sage, Lao Tzu, he learned the secret names of hundreds of spirits, and the ritual method of healing the sick and governing the country in accordance

with the Tao. He mastered methods of longevity so as to sustain his earthly body and continue his mission. This involved establishing an era of order and harmony (the Great Peace) on earth, based around decentralized agricultural communities, led by ritual and administrative functionaries called "libationers." In these communities, people were expected to dedicate themselves to charitable conduct, ethical purity, and social order.

This early 18th-century jade landscape depicts pilgrims visiting a sacred mountaintop to worship at the Taoist temple of the gods of longevity, prosperity, and happiness

*The followers of the H_____
Lao Tzu, pictured he_____
to have b_____*

Chang acquired a lar_____ is new
Religious Taoist state in_____ olitical
independence was partl_____ central
Han imperial administ_____ central
control was accelerated_____ Yellow
Turbans" or "Way of Gr_____ r Taoist
ritual movement with_____ China.
The Yellow Turbans were_____ Chueh,
who was captured and_____ l forces
in 184 C.E., after lead_____ wers.

Chang Tao Ling's Heavenly Master movement developed more gradually, but survived. His grandson, Chang Lu, agreed terms with the Han imperial government, only declaring independence from it when he was militarily strong enough to do so. Even he was forced to surrender military and political control to a more powerful ruler in 215 C.E., but, in doing so he ensured that ritual and religious affairs were still controlled by the priests, or libationers.

The Heavenly Master lineage of Religious Taoism survives to this day in Taiwan and China. Its priests continue to practice the rites of healing and exorcism, as well as serving the community by officiating at rites of cosmic renewal. All these rites are designed to restore the harmony of the natural and social order and to banish malevolent forces.

THE ELEMENTS

Yin, yang and ch'i

The notion of ch'i (vital energy) is fundamental in Taoist thought and practice. In Chinese medical diagnosis and Taoist thought, ch'i is often classified in functional terms, as either yin or yang in quality. These terms carry with them a wide range of associations and meanings, some of which are suggested in the pictographic elements used to write the characters.

The character yin includes an element meaning hill, another meaning time, and another meaning cloud or shade. The basic meaning is therefore understood as the shaded side of a hill. It extends in meaning to imply the following qualities: cold, responsiveness, passivity, darkness, inwardness, and decrease.

The character for yang also has the element for hill, along with an element depicting the sun and an element depicting a waving flag. This is traditionally understood as the sunny side of a hill. It refers to the qualities of heat, brightness, stimulation, movement, vigor, light, and increase.

References to yin and yang in ancient texts, such as the I Ching (Classic of Change) and the Tao Te Ching, show that these concepts were first developed on the basis of observing the progression of time and the seasons, as the following passage from an ancient part of the I Ching illustrates.

When the sun goes the moon comes; when the moon goes the sun comes. The sun and moon give way to each other and their brightness is produced. When the cold goes the heat comes; when the heat goes the cold comes. The cold and the heat give way to each other and the round of the year is completed. That which goes wanes, and that which comes waxes. The waning and waxing affect each other and benefits are produced.

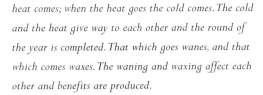

The Chinese characters for the yin quality (above) *and for its complementary yang quality* (below)

T'ai Chi and cosmology

The simplified t'ai chi symbol developed by the philosopher Chou Tun-yi (1017–1073 CE) perfectly illustrates the idea of the interdependence of yin and yang qualities. In this symbol, the dark force and the yang force are represented by complementary shapes that gracefully interweave either side of a curve shaped like a reverse letter "S." Each quality contains within itself the seed or potential of its opposite, represented by the circle of the opposite shade in each segment. The curve which represents the boundary between yin and yang suggests movement and a constantly changing relationship. Another passage in the Tao Te Ching emphasizes the creative and cosmological side of this relationship.

"Tao gave birth to one,
One gave birth to two,
Two gave birth to the ten thousand things.
The ten thousand things carry yin on their backs and embrace yang in their arms.
Through blending ch'i they achieve harmony."

This passage became very important in the development of Religious Taoist liturgy, which ritually reproduces the conditions of the emergence of all phenomena in the universe.

...elders alike are all caught up in contemplation of ...symbol in this 17th-century Chinese painting

THE BAHÁ'Í FAITH

Possess a pure, ❝ kindly, and radiant heart

In Baghdad in the spring of 1863, the friends and followers of a Persian nobleman called Mirza Husayn Ali Nuri met in an island garden on the River Tigris. Mirza Husayn Ali Nuri was known to his people as Bahá'u'lláh, meaning "The Glory of God." It was a farewell gathering, for Bahá'u'lláh, already banished from his native town of Tehran, was to be exiled yet again. In the rose-strewn tents, he made an announcement that proved to be the inauguration of a global religion – The Bahá'í Faith. The friends and family members who met on that island garden were followers of a contemporary of Bahá'u'lláh known as "the Báb," a title meaning "The Gate." In 1844 the Báb had told his followers to expect, "Him whom God shall make manifest," and shortly afterwards Bahá'u'lláh became one of his followers. In 1850, after six turbulent years, the Báb was martyred.

In 1853 Bahá'u'lláh* was ███████ █████ █████ ███ █████n-ished for following the ███████ ██ ███ ███ █████'is believe that, in prison, Bahá ████████ ███ ████ ██ ███ ████ld him of his mission. Ten year ████ █████ ██ ████ ██████ed that he was the Manifestatio ████████ ███████ ██ ██ ████.

Bahá'ís use the term "Ma██████ ███████ ██ ██████ be those people who are the fou████ ███ ████ ███ ██████ns. Moses, Buddha, Jesus, and ████████ ███ ██ ████████ed by Bahá'ís to be among th██████████ ██ ████ ─or Bahá'ís, it is a unique feature ████ ██████ ██████ ██ ████████ed by one Manifestation of Go██████ ██ ████ ██████ by another, Bahá'u'lláh.

In 1992, in New York, ████████ █████ ███████ ████'is attended the second Bahá'í ██████ ████████ ████ ████ ─as held in London in 1963). ███ ██████████ ███ ████ ██ to commemorate the centenar ██ ███ ██████ ██ ████ ██ ─áh (1817–92), to reflect on hi████ ███ ██████ ███ █████ge, and to celebrate the achiev█████ ██ ██████ █████ in the century since his passin ████ ████████ ███ ██████ed different ethnic and tribal g███████ ██████████ ██ ██ ─he Congress, a reflection of the████████████████ ██ ████ ██████'s mission: to bring unity and ████████ ██ ███ ██████ █████les of the world.

Bahá'u'lláh was born to ████████ ██████ ██████ ██ █─17. At the age of 27 he turned ██████ ██ ██████ ██ ██████on to dedicate himself to the r███████ ████ ██████ As a Bábí (a follower of the Bá███ ████████████████ ██████en on the soles of the feet), imp██████ ████████ ██ ██████ ─rst

Delegates from all over the worl█████████ ████ ███ ██████████ *er*
the Bahá'í cause of b████████ ████ █████

Mirza Buzurg-I-Nuri, father of Bahá'u'lláh, who served as Governor of Burujird and Luristan

to Baghdad, then to Istanbul, then to Edirne, and finally to Akka, now in Israel.

After openly declaring his mission, at first privately and later to monarchs, rulers, and leading ecclesiastics of the time, Bahá'u'lláh spent over 30 years revealing the religious explanations, laws, and prayers that form the basis of Bahá'í belief.

In 1890, a Cambridge orientalist, Professor E. G. Browne, met Bahá'u'lláh and described him in the following terms: "The face of Him on whom I gazed I can never forget, though I cannot describe it. Those piercing eyes seemed to read one's very soul; power and authority sat on that ample brow … no need to ask in whose presence I stood, as I bowed myself before one who is the object of a devotion and love which kings might envy and emperors sigh for in vain."

*The accents in Bahá'í and other proper names indicate that the vowels are long.

THE BÁB

The Báb's brief but eventful ministry began in Shiraz on May 23 1844 when he announced himself to be the "Lord of the Age." In the space of six years his following in Iran had spread to many tens of thousands, which alarmed the ecclesiastics and authorities in the region. Many thousands of the Báb's followers were killed in sieges and battles, and through persecution. The Báb was arrested, and spent the final three years of his six-year mission in remote mountain prisons.

The Báb and a companion were executed by firing squad. The circumstances of his martyrdom in 1850 have an element of the miraculous. The first regiment to fire on the Báb did not kill him and the soldiers refused to continue. A second regiment was more successful, and 750 bullets fused the bodies of the Báb and His companion together. The event attracted such attention that an account was even sent to the British Prime Minister, Lord Palmerston.

The remains of the Báb were discarded outside the city walls of Tabriz, but were retrieved by devotees. They were kept hidden for over 60 years, after which they were taken to Palestine by Abdu'l-Baha, the eldest son of Bahá'u'lláh. In 1909, Abdu'l-Baha placed the remains of the Báb in a simple brick mausoleum built on Mount Carmel. The mausoleum, known as the shrine of the Báb, also contains the remains of Abdu'l-Baha. The building has been embellished over many years, and is now a striking white marble building with a golden dome, visited by Bahá'í pilgrims from all over the world.

Abdu'l-Baha

Abbas Effendi was Bahá'u'lláh's eldest son. He knew well the sufferings of his father; at the age of eight he was taken to see Bahá'u'lláh, weighed down by chains and under threat of execution, in a filthy, underground dungeon in Tehran. Abbas Effendi went into exile in Baghdad with his parents and younger sister. As an adult he decided to serve his father in whatever way possible, and took the title Abdu'l-Baha, which means "Servant of Baha."

Bahá'u'lláh appointed Abdu'l-Baha the "Center of the Covenant" and the "Interpreter of His Writings." In 1892, after the passing of Bahá'u'lláh, Abdu'l-Baha took over the leadership of The Bahá'í Faith. He wrote explanations of Bahá'u'lláh's scriptures, developed the Bahá'í World Center on Mount Carmel, established shrines for his father and the Báb, received pilgrims, and directed the development of the Bahá'í faith.

For most of his life, Abdu'l-Baha's movements were restricted by the Turkish authorities. In 1911, he was allowed to travel, and he made the first of two journeys to the West, visiting Paris and London. In 1912 he traveled across the United States and through Europe, speaking in Bristol, Oxford, Edinburgh, London, Paris, Stuttgart, Budapest and Vienna. The Bahá'í Faith was already established in the United States and Europe, but these visits gave it a major boost, leading Abdu'l-Baha to plan for further growth. The Bahá'í Faith now claims six million followers in over 233 countries and their dependencies.

In 1921, shortly before his passing, Abdu'l-Baha was knighted by the British Government for his work to alleviate famine in the Middle East during the First World War. Abdu'l-Baha's way of life is seen as a model for followers of The Bahá'í Faith. Many members of the Bahá'í community display his photograph in their homes.

Above: *The home of "the Báb," who founded the Bahá'í faith in 1844.* **Right:** *Abdu'l-Baha, leader of the Bahá'í religion from 1892 to 1921, established the Bahá'í World Center in Israel*

THE BAHÁ'Í FAITH

After the passing of Abdu'l-Baha in 1921, his grandson, Shoghi Effendi (1896-1957) was appointed "Guardian" of the Bahá'í faith. Shoghi Effendi continued his grandfather's work, developing the Bahá'í World Center in Israel and directing the development of the global Bahá'í community. He also set the standard for the translation of Bahá'u'lláh's writings into English.

Almost all established religions have an organizational system which provides administration, direction and leadership for its followers. For Bahá'ís, this organization is called the "Bahá'í Administrative Order." It was set up by Shoghi Effendi, based on Bahá'u'lláh's instructions and Abdu'l-Baha's explanations. There are no priests in The Bahá'í Faith and the Administrative Order consists of elected "spiritual assemblies" at local and national level. Elections to the assemblies take place annually and each body has nine members. Every adult Bahá'í is eligible to vote and to stand for election. Voters write down the names of the nine people they feel most suited to the task. No canvassing takes place. Bahá'ís of all ages have access to their local spiritual assembly during a regular meeting

called the "Nineteen Day Feast" (because it takes place every 19th day), where there are opportunities for devotion, resolving administrative issues, and socializing.

Shoghi Effendi passed away in 1957 without appointing a successor. His appointed representatives, the "Hands of the Cause of God," decided that the time was right to establish an international elected institution, which Bahá'u'lláh called the Universal House of Justice. In 1963, 100 years after Bahá'u'lláh's declaration of His mission, the first Universal House of Justice was elected. It is re-elected every five years by all the members of the National Spiritual Assemblies. The Universal House of Justice is housed on Mount Carmel, as part of the Bahá'í World Center.

The new world order of Bahá'u'lláh

The idea of a new world order is central to Bahá'í aspirations. In 1931 the great-grandson of Bahá'u'lláh, Shoghi Effendi, wrote an essay entitled "Towards the Goal of a New World Order," which was later published in a collection entitled "The World Order of Bahá'u'lláh."

The development of the Bahá'í World Center, on Mount Carmel in Israel, is an important part of

Through his worldwide travels, Abdu'l-Baha helped to establish the Bahá'í faith as a major force for social and religious reform

the move toward establishin[...] world order. Mount Car[...] steeply from the Mediterra[...] of Haifa, a town where th[...] population of Jews, C[...], Muslims, and Druze live in [...]. The site is special to Bahá'í[...] it was chosen as the spo[...] Shrine of the Báb by Bahá'u[...] ing a visit to the mountain[...] Bahá'u'lláh said of Mount[...] "Ere long will God sail His [...] thee." This is a refer[...] Bahá'u'lláh's own writings, [...] described as an Ark. As in th[...] Noah, the Ark represents th[...] he only refuge of humanity fro[...] or- ruption, greed, and materia[...]

[...] became Guardian of the [...] established the assemblies [...] the Bahá'í Faith

The magnificent Bahá'í Wor[...] Haifa is built on the site of th[...] remains of the Báb[...]

The basic principles that Bahá'ís believe will form the basis of the new world order include:

One God and one human race
Equality between men
and women
Universal education
Harmony between religion
and science
Non-confrontational consultation
in the political realm
Unity through a celebration of
the diversity of mankind.

The buildings of the World Center are classical in style and built in an arc representing, in spirit and form, the teachings of Bahá'u'lláh. The first to be completed, in 1957, was the International Archives. This was followed by the Seat of the Universal House of Justice. Three more buildings are being constructed, and Bahá'ís believe that world leaders will increasingly turn to the World Center for guidance.

BEING A BAHÁ'Í

The Bahá'í Faith is a global religion, which aims to create unity and harmony between the diverse peoples of the planet. Therefore, it must be possible for a person from any cultural background to be a Bahá'í, in any geographical setting. Being a Bahá'í means fulfilling certain obligations laid down in the writings of Bahá'u'lláh. Among these are requirements for prayer and fasting, and laws regarding marriage.

The most important Bahá'í prayers are those said privately. Bahá'ís are exhorted to pray and read their scriptures daily. In general Bahá'ís read the prayers revealed by Bahá'u'lláh and Abdu'l-Baha rather than make up their own. There are several volumes of revealed prayers covering many different themes.

The Bahá'í fast is from sunrise to sunset for 19 days during March. It ends on the eve of Bahá'í New Year, which falls on March 21, the beginning of spring. The Báb revealed a calendar of 19 months, each of 19 days; at the beginning of each month, Bahá'ís gather locally at the Nineteen Day Feast, so called because it falls at the end of each 19 day cycle. On this day, Bahá'ís take the opportnity to pray together, read the scriptures, consult with representatives of the local spiritual assembly, and socialize.

Bahá'ís believe very strongly in the sanctity of marriage, and that stable marriages and harmonious families are the bedrock of properly functioning societies. To help maintain family unity and harmony, the consent of all living parents is required before a marriage can take place.

As well as attending the Nineteen Day Feast, Bahá'ís attend periodic meetings for prayer, for study and for teaching others about their religion.

Bahá'í spiritual beliefs

Bahá'ís conceive of God as an unknowable essence, revealed through messengers such as Moses, Buddha, Jesus, and Muhammad. Bahá'ís believe there is only one God, and only one religion, which is being progressively revealed to one humankind.

Bahá'u'lláh did not change the basic spiritual concepts common to most religions. Bahá'ís pray , believe in life after death, and strive to be moral and caring. The Bahá'í concept of heaven and hell is that they are not separate places, but rather the states of nearness to, or distance from, God. Once we pass on to the next life, we continue to progress through all the "Worlds of God."

While in Baghdad, Bahá'u'lláh revealed a collection of short verses called "The Hidden Words," which starts with the exhortation to "possess a pure, kindly and radiant heart." Its verses convey many of the basic Bahá'í spiritual beliefs. These include detachment from worldly possessions, acceptance of the will of God, avoidance of bad influences and emotional behavior, exercising generosity, caring for others, valuing actions over words, and fulfilling spiritual potential. The heart is used as a metaphor for the place in each person where God resides if He is welcomed in. "Thy heart is My home," Bahá'u'lláh says. "Sanctify it for My descent. Thy spirit is My place of revelation; cleanse it for My manifestation." An important Bahá'í spiritual principle is that all human beings should know themselves and fulfill their spiritual potential. In "The Hidden Words" Bahá'u'lláh says "Ye are My treasury, for in you I have treasured the pearls of My mysteries and the gems of My knowledge."

THE BAHÁ'Í HOUSE OF WORSHIP

The Arabic name for the Bahá'í House of Worship is Mashriqu'l-Adhkar, literally meaning "the dawning place of the remembrance or mention of God." It was Bahá'u'lláh's intention that every community would have a place of worship where people of any faith could gather each morning for prayers and meditation.

The Mashriqu'l-Adhkar is a concept as much as a building, in that, as Bahá'u'lláh said, it is "Any House raised in towns or villages or for mention of Me." There are no pictures or statues in a Mashriqu'l-Adhkar. Copies of all the world's major scriptures are housed there, and prayers may be read, sung, or chanted, though there is no preaching. Abdu'l-Baha formalized the general design for a Mashriqu'l-

Adhkar, ordaining that it should have nine sides and be surmounted by a dome. This basic idea has been spectacularly interpreted in the seven "Mother Temples" that have so far been built, with at least one on each continent.

Attempts have been made in the architecture of each House of Worship to reflect something of the culture of its setting. For example, the New Delhi Temple, in India, is symbolically based on the lotus, and its design was only made possible through the marriage of state-of-the-art computer technology and ancient craft skills.

Abdu'l-Baha intended that each House of Worship should be surrounded by buildings that serve the sick, the

---

Rising serenely over central Haifa is the golden dome of the Shrine of the Báb, completed in 1953 to house the remains of the Báb

The Bahá'í temple in New D[...]
based on the fo[...]

elderly, disadvantaged chil[...]who
wish to study. He hoped tha[...]ple
of different faiths to pray a[...]jor
part in the building of wor[...]

Social and econo[...]

As The Bahá'í Faith has es[...]has
become increasingly invo[...]mic
projects on a global scale. P[...]vel-
opment programs that are [...]tion
to literacy, agriculture, he[...]t of
women, and conservation

The first Bahá'í schoo[...]ran
in 1899, followed by a gi[...]out
the first half of the 20th c[...]t up
clinics, promoted health [...]acy,
and encouraged the educa[...]ond

half of the 20th century Bahá'ís around the world have
continued this pattern. The essence of all Bahá'í social and
economic development is firmly rooted in grassroots
involvement, sustainability, and consultation.

In order to ensure sustainability, these projects are generally small scale and local. One example is the network of
tutorial schools. At these schools, trained adults offer
classes in literacy, husbandry, fish farming, reforestation,
crop care, or health care. In some countries, particularly
India, Pakistan, and Bangladesh, this has led to the setting
up of free health and dental care camps. In Africa there are
many modest but vital village healthcare centers set up for
the distribution of medicine.

Another example is the Bahá'í Vocational Institute for
Rural Women in Indore, India, which was recognized for
its work at the United Nations World Summit on the
Environment in Rio de Janeiro in 1992. The institute helps
village women to become literate and to gain practical skills,
such as sewing. They also develop confidence in consultation and decision making.

PERSECUTION OF BAHÁ'ÍS

Since the time of the Báb, followers of The Bahá'í Faith have been persecuted for their beliefs, particularly in Iran. After the deposition of the Shah of Iran in 1978, followers of the Ayat'u'lláh Khomeini seized power and began a systematic persecution of Bahá'ís. Between 1978 and 1992 tens of thousands of Bahá'ís were deprived of jobs, pensions, businesses, and educational opportunities. During this time, over two hundred were executed or killed by mobs.

The experiences of Bahá'ís in Shiraz, Southern Iran, were typical. From the outset of the Iranian revolution they witnessed the destruction of their homes and the confiscation of property, businesses, salaries, and pensions. The

The persecution which Bahá'ís have suffered can be traced from the garrison in Acre in which Bahá'u'lláh was imprisoned in 1868 (below) to the execution of Mona Mahmudnizhad (above) by the Iranian government in 1988

House of the Báb was destroyed and Bahá'ís were excluded from the rationing and education systems.

On one night in October 1982, 40 Bahá'ís were arrested in Shiraz by revolutionary guards. Imprisonment, interrogation, and trial were often followed by execution. The teaching of Bahá'í children was among the crimes of those who were hanged for their beliefs.

The nightwatchman

From the time of His exile in Baghdad in 1853 to his passing in Israel in 1892, Bahá'u'lláh revealed the fundamental laws and practices that underlie the Bahá'í faith through numerous volumes of letters, tablets, prayers, and books. His writings are distinguished by the poetry of his style, and for the beauty of his metaphors and illustrative stories. "The Seven Valleys" was one of Bahá'u'lláh's early writings. It is a profound essay written in response to questions put to Bahá'u'lláh by a Sufi judge. Written in the Sufi style, it delineates the stages of the ⸺ the object of its being. The seve⸺ wl- edge, unity, contentment, ⸺ true poverty and absolute n⸺ of Knowledge" Bahá'u'lláh re⸺ose making this spiritual journe⸺ed that a believer will ultim⸺ nd guidance from God.

"There was once a love⸺ad sighed for long years in se⸺nd wasted in the fire of remoten⸺er had all but lost hope of ever⸺as weary and his patience wand⸺nd day, but the pain of separati⸺nd nights sleepless. He was "wo⸺ve given anything for one brief ⸺y. His doctor could find no cur⸺is friends shunned his compan⸺

In hopeless desperation t⸺t life had no more meaning. As⸺ht drew in he set off for the mark⸺ht in some way end his life. Hi⸺e attracted the attention of a wa⸺d shops. Seized by panic and con⸺g why, began to run away. The su⸺. Hearing the footsteps other wa⸺e in the chase and soon the ar⸺f surrounded and all routes of ⸺l out in desperation and he ⸺ watchman must truly be his a⸺

Delirious with grief he s⸺ without care for his safety t⸺ enclosed garden. As he lay the⸺ fragrance of roses he notice⸺ lantern. Illuminated by this li⸺ his beloved who was out sear⸺ way the star-crossed lovers we⸺ called to God to give glory to⸺ saw, not as an angel of death,⸺ angel of mercy who was to gu⸺

Bahá'u'lláh, whose shrine is shown here, spent forty years as a prisoner and an exile

The lover realized that what he had perceived as tyranny proved to have a secret justice and he had failed to see the mercy in the watchman's actions. If the lover could have seen into the future, he would have blessed the watchman from the outset and showered him with praise.

From "The Seven Valleys," Bahá'u'lláh, Nightingale Books 1992, page 32.

RASTAFARIANISM

"Sit in the dust and head rest with Jah

The Rastafarian movement is a response to four interrelated processes that have profoundly influenced the history of the African continent: slavery, colonization, missionary Christianity, and economic migration to the West since the 1950s.

These processes have also influenced people of African descent from the Americas, the Caribbean and other parts of the world. The message of the Rastafarian movement is that these factors did much to destroy the self-esteem, self-understanding, and self-identity of black people in Jamaica and throughout the Caribbean and the Americas. The aim of Rastafarianism is to restore dignity and pride to the black race and to recreate the African way – described as the natural way – of being and living. The movement is millennial in that it believes that natural living in an African paradise will soon come about through divine intervention. Meanwhile, members are encouraged to live as best they can in accordance with African attitudes, customs and outlook and to shun white society, which is contemptuously referred to as "Babylon."

Rastafarians believe tha⬛⬛⬛⬛⬛⬛⬛⬛ nd doomed society, held ⬛⬛⬛⬛⬛⬛⬛⬛⬛ hat tyrannizes and discriminate⬛⬛⬛⬛⬛⬛⬛⬛⬛ it contrives to subjugate and st⬛⬛⬛⬛⬛⬛⬛⬛ en-tity. Rastas go to great leng⬛⬛⬛⬛⬛⬛⬛ of white society, and in most ⬛⬛⬛⬛⬛⬛⬛⬛ ke other people aware of this ⬛⬛⬛

They speak a language ⬛⬛⬛⬛⬛⬛⬛⬛ ks, have their own style of dre⬛⬛⬛⬛⬛⬛⬛⬛ wn domestic style, their own ⬛⬛⬛⬛⬛⬛⬛⬛ nd beliefs, their own saints a⬛⬛⬛⬛⬛⬛⬛⬛ are Marcus Garvey and Bob M⬛⬛⬛⬛⬛⬛⬛⬛ ile Selassie, and their own para⬛⬛⬛

Priests in Ethiopia, the spiritua⬛⬛⬛⬛⬛⬛⬛⬛ which emphasizes the culture⬛⬛⬛⬛⬛⬛⬛⬛

Marcus Garvey

Marcus Garvey organized and led the first genuine mass black movement in the United States, the Universal Negro Improvement Association (UNIA), founded in Jamaica in 1914. Its aims were the repatriation of Africans in the United States to Africa, the creation of independent African states, and the engendering of pride of race. Garvey was inspired by the richness of Africa's history and the achievements of African civilization, and had come to believe that the only place in the world where black people would be respected, as a race, was in Africa.

The Garvey movement was born out of the despair of never-ending injustice and discrimination in white society. Garvey was by no means the first to call for repatriation, or to try to focus the attention of black people and the world on the great cultural wealth and achievements of Africa. Nor was he the first to speak of a black God, the God of Ethiopia, to counter the image of God as white. For Garvey, it was not a question of rejecting the universal nature of God, but of seeing Him and interpreting His will from an African perspective.

Opposition

As he expressed it: "We Negroes believe in … the Everlasting God … that is the God in whom we believe, but we shall worship Him through the spectacles of Ethiopia." This endeavor to relate to God in an African way led to the founding, in 1921, of the African Orthodox Church, which set about destroying the conventional association of white with God and black with the Devil. Garvey was sentenced to five years in prison in Atlanta in 1925, ostensibly for fraud. The Garvey movement faced opposition from many quarters, including other black rights associations and African governments, and lost much of its influence and appeal. Garvey himself was deported to Jamaica in 1927; he moved to London in 1935 where he died in 1940. By this date the Rastafarian movement had already started, and was attributing to Garvey a millennial prophecy which exhorted black people to look to Africa, where a black king was to be crowned "for the day of deliverance is near."

THE BLACK MESSIAH: RAS TAFARI

The crowning of Ras Tafari, better known as Haile Selassie, as emperor of Ethiopia, in 1930, was regarded by many clergymen and political activists as a sign that the advent of a black Messiah, as foretold in several parts of the Bible, was close at hand. The Rastafarian movement began to develop in the 1930s as these clergymen took the message to the people of Kingston, Jamaica, that Ras Tafari was the god of Ethiopia whom Garvey had foretold would be crowned in Africa.

One of these clergymen, Howell, had a Rasta Bible composed, which spoke of the distortion of God's message by whites who turned all prophets into people of their own color. Howell also spoke of Haile Selassie as the clearest sign from God that the black race, as descendants of the people of the Torah, would return to Africa. In 1937, Haile Selassie had created the Ethiopian World Federation (EWF) which gave impetus to the Rastafarian movement in that its main aims were to unify black people throughout the world, to defend the integrity of Ethiopia, which by divine right belonged to all black people and which was being threatened by Italy, and to assist all African countries to regain their independence.

In 1941, Haile Selassie returned to his kingdom after driving out the occupying Italian forces. His followers interpreted this as the fulfillment of the Book of Revelation 19: 11–19 which speaks of the first battle of the End, in which the King of Kings and Lord of Lords inflicts mortal ruin on his enemies and destroys Babylon.

Two further developments occurred in 1955 which strengthened Rastafarian belief that the black race was about to be saved by the divine intervention of Haile Selassie. First of all, the New York branch of the EWF put out the message that the emperor was building a fleet to return Africans to Africa. Secondly, in the same year, the EWF reportedly told members in Jamaica that the emperor had

Prince Ras Tafari, crowned as Haile Selassie, emperor of Ethiopia, in 1930, is revered as a god by Rastafarians

After the Italian invasion of E▓▓▓▓▓▓▓▓▓▓▓
sailed to England, and was ▓▓▓▓▓▓▓▓▓▓

set aside land in Ethiopia for ▓▓▓▓▓▓▓▓▓▓▓▓
the late 1950s the movement ▓▓▓▓▓▓▓▓▓▓▓▓
to attract people of differen▓▓▓▓▓▓▓▓▓▓▓ t
also became increasingly comp▓▓▓▓▓▓▓▓▓▓ t
groups offering different int▓▓▓▓▓▓▓▓▓▓▓ .
Some claimed that this was ▓▓▓▓▓▓▓▓▓▓▓▓
psychological than in a physic▓▓▓▓▓▓

The high point of the first ▓▓▓▓▓▓▓▓▓▓ s
history in Jamaica came with ▓▓▓▓▓▓▓▓▓▓
1966, his aircraft bearing the ▓▓▓▓▓▓▓▓▓▓
revered by Rastas. Although the▓▓▓▓▓▓▓▓▓
status, this was thrust upon ▓▓▓▓▓▓▓▓▓▓▓
Rastafarian movement was the▓▓▓▓▓▓▓▓▓▓
the dethronement of the Emp▓▓▓▓▓▓▓▓▓
and even more so by his death i▓▓▓▓▓▓▓▓▓
he had died, believing him to ▓▓▓▓▓▓▓▓▓
their lyrics, immortal: "As Jah (▓▓▓▓▓▓▓▓
ning, Jah is now and ever mus'▓

*Believing Haile Selassie to be immortal, many Rastafarians were shocked
by his deposition in 1974 and his death the following year*

RASTA BELIEFS

Rastafarians believe that every individual must discover truth for him or herself. Rastafarianism has a theology and philosophy, but no agreed system of beliefs for all members. Truth may be found by "head resting with Jah" – meditating on personal experience – or by attending "reasoning sessions" or "groundings," where members reflect on the Bible and on the history and fortunes of the black race. In this way a person may experience "dread," that is the confrontation of a people with a primordial but historically denied racial selfhood.

Despite the lack of a systematic creed, there are several beliefs which are at the root of Rastafarianism: God, or Jah, is within each and every person; divinity is more recognizable and developed in some people than in others; divinity is most discernible and evolved in Jah Rastafari, or Haile Selassie, whose immortal spirit dwells within every living creature; black people are descendants of the early Israelites and were sent

Above: *The Rastafarian version of the Lord's Prayer, written in Amharic. Rastafarians accept the Bible but interpret it differently*
Left: *Christmas ceremonies in Ethiopia, where Jesus is seen as one in a line of black prophets stretching from Moses to Haile Selassie*

into exile (slavery) for their transgressions; Ethiopia is the promised land, while Babylon, or white society, is hell; Haile Selassie, the black Messiah, will return around the year 2000 and repatriate black people to Africa and take revenge on whites for enslaving them.

There is also the belief that death will only affect the unrighteous. A Rasta version of reincarnation states that the same person with the same identity persists from one birth to another; thus all those whom the movement claims are black prophets, from Moses to Jesus to Haile Selassie, are essentially the same person. The way these beliefs have been interpreted has undergone change, particularly in the case of repatriation: this is now often understood as not being about an actual return to Africa, but about the development

of a true understanding of ▓▓▓▓▓▓▓▓▓▓▓▓▓ and for Africa, as well as Africa ▓▓▓▓▓▓▓▓▓▓▓

Rastafarian ritual

The principal Rasta rituals ▓▓▓▓▓▓▓▓▓▓▓▓ to Haile Selassie and reasoning ▓▓▓▓▓▓▓▓▓ ell each other about what they ▓▓▓▓▓▓▓▓▓▓▓ di-tation and dreams. It is du▓▓▓▓▓▓▓▓ nja (marijuana), known as the '▓▓▓▓▓ or sacred ▓▓▓," is taken. Ganja is regarded a ▓▓▓▓▓▓▓▓▓ pi-ration, nutrition, relaxati▓▓▓▓▓▓▓▓▓ he atmosphere for the taking ▓▓▓▓▓▓▓▓ by the playing of drums, the cha▓▓▓▓▓▓▓▓ d-ings. While there is no obl▓▓▓▓▓▓▓▓ st members do so. The Bible is u▓▓▓▓▓▓▓▓ a, and it is believed that the sm▓▓▓▓▓▓▓▓ ie most natural way to worshi▓▓▓▓▓▓▓▓ d participants pray to the god w▓▓▓▓▓▓▓▓ a.

The cultivation of dreadl▓▓▓▓▓▓▓▓ i-cally based practice and as bei▓▓▓▓▓▓▓▓ s

of Nature. Dreadlocks symbolize strength and are a reminder of the power of Samson. By cultivating dreadlocks, Rastas identify not only with Old Testament warriors but also with African peoples.

Dreadlocks symbolize the stage of wandering through the wilderness to the promised land. The shape and style of dreadlocks is often inspired by the biblical description of the head and mane of the Lion of Judah, who stands for a new, vigorous life and the rebirth of the African race. Dreadlocks fulfill a biblical injunction and inspire Rastas with confidence and the hope of a new order. They also engage in a form of symbolic confrontation that aims to send a message to the wider society that people of African origin are no longer prepared to conform in order to be accepted. This was the mistake Africans made in the past and one which led to their enslavement.

Controversially, Rastafarians believe that there is biblical support for the use of marijuana in the worship of God

RASTA CULTURE

Rasta language is important in cultivating an awareness of individual and group identity. The most obvious example is the use of the personal pronoun "I." This forms either the prefix or suffix to a wide range of words, and continually recalls to the Rasta the idea of his own personhood, which slavery, colonialism, and economic migration undermined. Often a Rasta will substitute "I-n-I" for we, "I-ceive" for receive, "I-sire" for desire and "I-rate" for create, and place an "I" after the Messiah's name making it Haile Selassie-I. Natural food is "I-tal" food. This language sustains Rasta reality, gives greater cohesion to the group, and affirms its goals.

Rasta music was developed at reasoning sessions and is identified by its popular rhythms (*ridims*) and three drums painted in the movement's colors of red, green, gold and black. The music is normally called "reggae" music. The most popular and well-known reggae band is Bob Marley and the Wailers. Not all Rasta music is secular; some of it is of a religious, or, in the language of the group, "churchical" character. This difference notwithstanding, Rastas relive within both hymn and song the call to return to their African heritage and way of living naturally.

Living naturally

Weary of living unnaturally in exile in Babylon, the Rastafarians long to live in accordance with "Nature's Laws." An essential part of Rasta well-being is "sitting in the dust," that is, remaining close to the earth. In the West it has become almost impossible to "sit in the dust," for in the West the approach for too long has been to disrespect Nature's laws. In practice, living naturally means living off the land and producing only organic food, thus respecting the land's sacred character by refusing to treat it as a saleable commodity. Great hostility is expressed to the exaggerated stress on consumerism that characterizes much of contemporary society, where the products of Nature are bought and sold.

The role of women

A frequent criticism of Rastafarianism is its treatment of women, whose status is one of subordination and service. The Rasta position is that men are the head of the household and the spiritual leaders of the movement. Women take little part in reasoning sessions. They are considered unclean during menstruation, which is the basis for the restrictions placed on their religious role. The Buba Shanti, the most orthodox of Rasta groups, endorses these rules unquestioningly and even adopts a limited form of *purdah*, or female seclusion.

Not all Rasta women accept these rules, and some assert that their status as Rastafarians is, in fact, higher than that of Western women. They point out, among other things, that their dignity is recognized and their status enhanced by being given the title "queen." Critics say that women's subordinate status is clearly indicated by their being referred to as "daughter." Rasta men present a dignified image of women, and often take care of the children and of domestic matters. However, there is still the belief that women can only be saved through men. This is a belief found in the teachings of several religions.

Drumming and chanting, based on African rhythms, play an important part in Rastafarian social and religious life

...out Rastafarian, reached a mass audience
...d politics into the lyrics of his songs

LOVE AND RACE

The two great commandments of the Rastas are love of God and love of neighbor. There would appear to be a contradiction between the Rasta moral law expressed in these two commandments and its thinking on race, because African society is presented as qualitatively and spiritually superior to white society, symbolized by Babylon. This inconsistency is shown up in Rasta music, particularly in the so-called peace and love songs, one of which says: "Wid a hammer and rammer I will ram dem [Europeans] down" and another: "Peace and love is based on love and justice. Europeans shall find no peace."

There are Rasta sects which exclude whites from membership, and Rastas believe that Africans are the chosen race. Even so, there is no general Rasta view on race. Some members accept that the movement has a problem in this area and are striving to overcome it, stressing that it is a duty of all righteous Rastas to wrestle with racism and destroy it. Others emphasize that skin color is irrelevant, stating that Rastafarianism is "not about this but about how one feels" and that "I and I [we] no longer check for the skin any more, we check for the spirit." The sentiments on race expressed in certain Rasta hymns make the same non-racial and non-racist point. A verse of one reads: "Jah in the white, Jah in the black, Jah in the red. In any color you want to name, Jah in him."

Undoubtedly, there is a long tradition of black protest against white society and its attitudes to people of African origins. This has led to hatred in some Rasta quarters of white society, for its crucial part in the slave trade and for the evils of colonialism. But, in practice, this opposition and condemnation is not about hatred and revenge but more a program of Rasta self-discovery, and the creation of a culture in which that new-found sense of self can be expressed.

Rastafarian icons include the movement's colors of red, black, green, and gold, and portraits of Bob Marley

Rastas in Harare, capital ▨▨▨▨▨▨
growing movement with ▨▨▨▨▨▨

The Rasta movem▨▨▨▨

The Rastafarian movement▨▨▨▨▨▨▨▨▨▨▨▨▨▨▨▨ldi-
tion to those who criticize▨▨▨▨▨▨▨▨▨▨▨▨▨▨rds
women, there are black pe▨▨▨▨▨▨▨▨▨▨▨▨▨▨t it
presents a distorted and ▨▨▨▨▨▨▨▨▨▨▨▨▨▨ce,
presenting a picture of it▨▨▨▨▨▨▨▨▨▨▨▨▨▨inst
progress and change. Oth▨▨▨▨▨▨▨▨▨▨▨▨▨▨ion
for indulging in drugs and▨▨▨▨▨▨▨▨▨▨▨▨▨ no
reliable statistics available ▨▨▨▨▨▨▨▨▨▨▨▨ but
the movement's influence ▨▨▨▨▨▨▨▨▨▨▨▨s of
members alone. It is no ex▨▨▨▨▨▨▨▨▨▨▨flu-
ence of the movement, no▨▨▨▨▨▨▨▨▨▨▨ the
African diaspora, but ▨▨▨▨▨▨▨▨▨▨▨▨re,
has been incalculable. Rast▨▨▨▨▨▨▨▨▨▨on-
sible for this.

Today there are Rastas in almost every country in
the world, and Rastas of every race and color. For
example, across Europe and the United States there
are Rastas of African, Caucasian, Indian, and Latino origin;
in New Zealand there are Maori Rastas and Rastas
of European descent; in Brazil there are Rastas of African
and European descent.

Paradoxically, while created to provide the path to self-
awareness and self-esteem for Africans of the diaspora, the
Rastafarian movement contains many ideas that are found
to be appropriate and relevant to the modern condition
which is why Rasta ideals have been embraced by many non-
Africans. Rasta sympathizers are legion. Millions, whatever
their cultural and racial origins, have internalized and come
to empathize with Rasta values on natural living and internal
self-development. Rastafarianism was among the first of the
modern Self-Religions, those contemporary religions that
believe the inner self is divine and whose adherents devote
themselves to the pursuit of self-growth.

Created to foster the self-esteem of exiled Africans, Rastafarianism
contains many ideas relevant to the modern condition

Prayer, 21, 64–5
    The Bahá'í Faith, 228, 230
    Christianity, 136–7
    Islam, 153, 164, 164–6,
    169–71, 175–7
    Shinto, 182, 186, 187
    Sikhism, 200
Priests, 21, 23
    Hinduism, 37
    Rastafarianism, 235
    Shinto, 182–4
Primal religions, 14–23
Promised Land, 48, 49
Prophets, 21, 45, 154, 156–7, 175
Public service, 83, 84–5
Puja, 36
Puranas, 27
Pure Land Buddhism, 95
Purification, 185, 187, 188, 189
Purim, 67

Q

Qur'an, 151, 153–4, 157, 159–62,
    164–5, 169, 171–2, 176

R

Rabbis, 45–7, 50, 53, 56, 58, 61–2,
    64
Rabin, Y., 55
Race, 242–3
Rahit Maryada, 200
Raja yoga, 40–1
Rama, 30, 39
Ramadan, 164, 169
Ramanuja, 40
Ramayana, 27
Ranjit Singh, 194–5, 196

Ras Tafari, 236–7
Rastafarianism, 234–43
Rationalism, 124
al-Razi, 172
Rebirth, 32–3, 40, 92–3, 108, 113,
    115, 118–19
Reflection, 11
Reform Judaism, 53
Reformation, 146
Reincarnation, 15, 94
Reiyukai, 245
Religious Taoism, 207, 217, 218,
    220–1
Revelation, 7, 62
Rig Veda, 27
Rites of passage, 20–1, 138–9
Rituals, 7, 15, 25
    African religions, 20–1, 21
    Buddhism, 94
    Confucianism, 73
    Hinduism, 35, 37
    Islam, 164–5, 177
    Judaism, 46–7, 56
    Rastafarianism, 235, 239
    Shinto, 182, 185, 187, 188–9
    Sikhism, 204–5
    Taoism, 220–1
Rock paintings, 18
Roman Catholicism, 148
Rosh Hashanah, 67

S

Sacraments, 140–1
Sacrifice, 20–1, 145
Salvation, 113, 115, 120, 126
Samsara, 32, 89, 93
San people, 18–19

Satan, 58
Science, 11, 42, 125, 172–3
Scriptures, 25, 30
    The Bahá'í Faith, 228, 229, 230,
    232–3
    Buddhism, 92, 93, 94, 96–7,
    98, 108
    Jainism, 116–17
    Sikhism, 200, 204
    Taoism, 207
Sefardic Jews, 51
Sefer Yetzirah, 61
Seicho No Ie, 247
Self-control, 113
Seventh Day Adventists, 246
Shabbat, 66–7
al-Shahadah, 153, 164
Shakti, 28, 30
Shakyamuni Buddha, 87, 90, 95
Shamans, 15, 18, 19, 23, 180, 212–13
Shankara, 40
Shari'ah, 174, 177
Shavout, 67
Shaytan, 169, 171
Shi'ites, 246–7
Shinto, 178–89
Shiromini Gurdwara Parbandhak
    Committee, 196, 198
Shiva, 27, 28, 30, 32, 39
Shoghi Effendi, 226, 227
Shoguns, 181
Shrines, 22, 23, 101
    Hinduism, 36
    Shinto, 178–83, 185, 187
    Sikhism, 191
Shudras, 34
Shunyata, 89

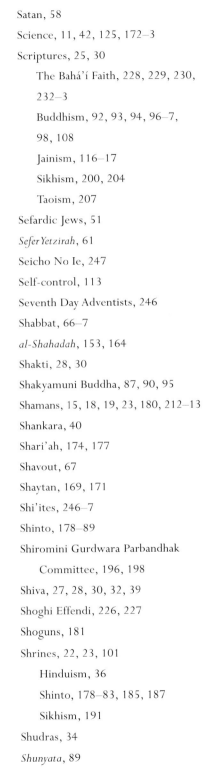

Sikhism, 12, 190–205

Six Day War, 55

Sky–being, 15, 16

Soka Gakkai, 245

Solomon, 49, 64

Soloveitchik, J., 53

Spiritual healing, 132

Spirituality, 102–3

Staal, F., 25

Storytelling, 17, 43, 68–

 The Bahá'í Faith, 233

 Buddhism, 97

 Christianity, 126

 Confucianism, 75

Succot, 67

Sufism, 162, 232, 247

Sunnah, 160

Sunnis, 246–7

Sustainability, 231

Sutras, 89, 93, 95, 96, 1

Swaminarayan moveme

Synagogues, 45, 57, 62

T

Tai Ch'i, 12, 214–15

Tai kwon do, 12

Takehiko, O., 85

Talmud, 45, 50–1, 56

Tang, 207

Tantras, 94

Tao Chia, 207

Tao Chiao, 207

Tao Te Ching, 207, 2(

 220

Tao Tsang, 207

Taoism, 71, 75, 181,

Tawaf, 171

lomon, 49, 64

196, 199, 230–1

dments, 45

28, 30, 125, 184, 190

rtents, 79

uddhism, 92–3, 95–6,

9

dhism, 94, 107, 109

on, 96

4

, 113

7, 50, 53, 56–7, 60,

6–7, 154, 236

religions, 14–23

, 41

ntal Meditation, 244

tion of souls, 27

ntiation, 141

myths, 19

4–5, 153

ng–shu, 79

reality, 30–1

2

Negro Improvement

iation, 235

ables, 34, 114

ds, 27, 30, 40

34

a Buddhism, 94

4

, 40

!5, 27, 40, 42, 43

Vishnu, 27–8, 30–2, 39–40, 42

Visualization, 94, 102

Voodoo, 244

W

Watchmaker argument, 7

Wawilak sisters, 16

Weizmann, C., 55

Wesak, 106

Western Buddhist Order, 111

Witchcraft, 22–3

Women *see* Gender issues

World order, 226–7

Worship

 Christianity, 136–7

 Hinduism, 36–7

 Islam, 151

 Jainism, 122–3

 Sikhism, 204–5

Y

Yang, 218–19, 220–1

Yin, 218–19, 220–1

Yoga, 12, 32, 40–1

Yom Kippur, 67

Yoruba people, 18, 19

Z

Zazen, 94

Zen Buddhism, 94–5, 97–8, 102–3,

 109

Zionism, 55

Zohar, 60, 62–3

Zoroastrianism, 143, 244–5

Zulus, 21

Contributors

GENERAL EDITOR

Chris Richards is currently General Inspector of Religious Education and Humanities and an Office for Standards in Education Registered Inspector in Northamptonshire, UK. He is a previous vice-chair of the Association of Religious Education Council for England and Wales.

PRIMAL RELIGIONS AND RASTAFARIANISM

Peter Clarke is Professor of the History and Sociology of Religion at King's College, University of London. He is director of the Centre for New Religions at the college, which he set up in 1982. He has written widely on the world's religions and is currently researching Japanese New Religions.

HINDUISM

Dilip Kadodwala came to Britain in 1968. He studied comparative religions at undergraduate level and went on to advise teachers on religious education. He has written a number of books for students and teachers on Hinduism and religious education in schools.

JUDAISM

Brian Lancaster is Senior Lecturer in Psychology at Liverpool John Moores University, where his research encompasses both brain science and the psychology of religion. His work on religion has focused on Judaism and he has lectured extensively on Jewish themes, both in the UK and Israel.

CONFUCIANISM AND TAOISM

Stewart McFarlane lectures in Religious Studies at Lancaster University, specializing in Chinese religions. From 1992 to 1993 he was Visiting Professor at the Chung Hwa Institute of Buddhist Studies in Taipei. He is writing a book on religion, power and identity in Chinese martial arts.

BUDDHISM

Denise Cush is Senior Lecturer in Religious Education and Study of Religions at Bath College of Higher Education in the UK. She has written widely on Buddhism and is Chair of the Religious Studies Section of the National Association of Teachers in Further and Higher Education in the UK.

JAINISM

Richard Fynes is a lecturer in South Asian Studies in the Department of Historical and International Studies at De Montfort University in the UK. His first degree was in Classics at the University of Leeds, and he went on to do his PhD in the Oriental Studies Department at the University of Oxford. He reads ten languages.

CHRISTIANITY

Ruth Holmwood studied theology at Oxford University. She is currently an Advisory Teacher for religious education in Northamptonshire and has prepared and led training courses on many of the world's religions. She has written books on both Buddhism and Christianity.

ISLAM

The Islam section has been written for the IQRA Trust by Dawud Noibi, formerly Professor of Islamic Studies at the University of Ibadan in Nigeria, with Harfiyah Haleem. IQRA is a charity based in London which aims to give clear, accurate and reliable information on Islam and the Muslim way of life.

SHINTO

Brian Bocking is Professor and Head of Study of the Religions at Bath College of Higher Education, UK. He is currently researching Sino-Japanese Buddhism, Japanese religions, contemporary East Asian religions and contemporary religiosity. He is President of the British Association for the Study of Religions.

SIKHISM

Gurharpal Singh is a Senior Lecturer at De Montfort University and course leader of Contemporary Asian Studies. He has regularly broadcast on Indian affairs on BBC World Central Television and BBC radio stations. He is Director of the Association of Punjab Studies in the UK. He was educated at the University of Warwick, UK, and London School of Economics.

THE BAHÁ'Í FAITH

Kevin Beint teaches in Northamptonshire and is a member of the Bahá'i community. He has represented his faith on national and international conferences and has helped to produce educational materials for schools on The Bahá'i Faith.

Picture Acknowledgements

Ancient Art & Architecture Collection: p58

Bahá'i Publishing Trust: p222B, 223T, 224, 225, 226, 227T, 228, 232.

Kevin Beint: p223B

Bridgeman Art Library: pp26: Private Collection; 27: Victoria & Albert Museum, London; 30: National Museum of India, New Delhi; 31, 38T: V&A; 59: British Library, London; 71: Bibliothèque Nationale, Paris; 90: British Museum, London; 91: Oriental Museum, Durham University; 97: Chester Beatty Library & Gallery of Oriental Art, Dublin; 101B: V&A; 109: Musée Guimet, Paris; 113, 116: National Museum India; 131TL: Hotel Dieu, Beaune; 131TR: British Museum; 133: Michaelis Collection, Cape Town; 144B: Tretyakov Gallery, Moscow; 145B: Prado, Madrid; 151: British Library; 155: Chester Beatty Library; 157: Louvre, Paris; 158: Bibliothèque Nationale; 161: British Library; 171: Musée D'Orsay, Paris; 173: British Library; 198B: V&A; 203: British Library; 210: V&A, 216: Oriental Museum, Durham; 217: National Palace Museum, Taipei, Taiwan.

Brian Bocking: pp182, 186BL

Denise Cush: pp86T, 87, 110

E. T. Archive: pp1, 33, 42B, 51, 67, 74, 77, 79, 89, 96, 124T, 129, 134, 135, 136T, 142B, 152, 154, 156, 180, 207, 208-9, 219.

Fine Art Photographs: pp8, 124, 128, 130, 143.

Ruth Holmwood: p141.

Hulton-Getty: pp28T, 52, 53T, 194B, 195, 234, 236, 237.

Hutchison Library: pp6, 14B, 18, 19, 20T, 22, 23, 32, 35TR, 36, 37, 39, 42T, 53B, 63, 68-9, 70L, 72-3, 75, 85, 94, 95, 98B, 101T, 108, 111, 112L, 114B, 115, 118, 119, 122T, 123, 127, 138, 139, 142T, 160, 164, 177B, 190R, 193B, 197B, 199, 200, 201, 204, 205, 213T, 231, 233, 234B, 238T, 242T, 243T.

Image Bank: p169

Malcolm Ness: pp9, 146B, 147, 163T, 177T, 179, 185, 187, 196

Retna Pictures: p241

Rex Features: p55

Robert Harding Library: pp46-7, 48B, 83, 102T, 117, 146M, 174

Science Photo Library: pp132, 172

Still Pictures: pp14T, 16, 34, 98T, 99B, 120, 122B, 126, 137, 164TR, 175, 197T, 239, 240.

Werner Forman Archive: pp112, 212, 213B, 220, 221B.

Zefa Pictures: pp2, 3, 7, 10, 11, 12-13, 15, 17, 21, 24, 25, 28, 29, 35TL, 35BR, 38B, 40, 41, 44, 45, 49, 54, 56, 57, 60, 61, 64, 65, 66, 81, 86R, 88, 92, 93, 99T, 100, 102B, 103, 104, 105, 106B, 107, 121, 125, 136B, 140, 144T, 145R, 146T, 148, 149, 150L, 159, 162-3, 165, 166, 167, 168, 170, 176, 178, 183, 184, 186, 188, 189, 191, 192, 193T, 202, 211, 214, 222T, 227B, 230, 235, 238B, 243B.